About the Author

HARRY STEIN is the author of eight previous books. *The New York Times Book Review* called his recent memoir, *How I Accidentally Joined the Vast Right-Wing Conspiracy (and Found Inner Peace)*, "a wickedly funny and moral book." He has also written for numerous publications, including the *Wall Street Journal*, *The New York Times Sunday Magazine*, *Playboy*, *GQ*, and *Esquire*, for which he created the "Ethics" column. He lives in Hastings-on-Hudson, New York.

THE
GIRL WATCHERS
CLUB

ALSO BY HARRY STEIN

Ethics (and Other Liabilities)

Hoopla

One of the Guys

Eichmann in My Hands (with Peter Malkin)

The Magic Bullet

*How I Accidentally Joined the Vast Right-Wing Conspiracy
(and Found Inner Peace)*

THE
GIRL WATCHERS CLUB

Lessons from the Battlefields
of Life

HARRY STEIN

Perennial

An Imprint of HarperCollinsPublishers

FIRST PERENNIAL EDITION PUBLISHED IN 2005.

Designed by Nicola Ferguson

The Library of Congress has catalogued the hardcover edition as follows:

Stein, Harry.
   The girl watchers club: lessons from the battlefields of life/
Harry Stein.—1st ed.
   p.   cm.
ISBN 0-06-621172-7
   1. World War, 1939–1945—Veterans—California—Monterey—Biography. 2. Monterey (Calif.)—Biography. I. Title.

D736.S784   2004
920.0794'76'09045—dc21
[B]   2003050940

ISBN 0-06-093640-1 (pbk.)

05   06   07   08   09   ❖/RRD   10   9   8   7   6   5   4   3   2   1

For JONATHAN,

WITH GRATITUDE AND
DEEP AFFECTION

INTRODUCTION

Taking Life Seriously (but Never Themselves)

"I guess we'll have to cancel today's lunch," I tell my father-in-law. "We'd better call the guys."

My father-in-law, Moe Turner, looks at me, incredulous. "Why in hell would we do that?" he demands, his west Arkansas accent even sharper than usual.

Why in hell would we do that? It is, after all, the morning of September 11, 2001, and as I stand there in my in-laws' sunny living room in Monterey, California, the TV across the room is once again showing the slow-motion collapse of the World Trade Center.

"Listen, Moe, I really don't think anyone will feel like coming over."

"Sure, they will," he snaps. "We gotta talk about it, don't we?"

It's not that I can't see Moe's point. He and the others due here today are part of a luncheon club, informally known as the Girl Watchers, that has been meeting for nearly four decades. Ranging in age from the late seventies to mid-eighties, these men have literally grown old together, and around one another, nothing is off limits. If—make that *when*—they say things that would leave today's politically correct aghast, no one even seems to notice. The talk ranges free and uncensored, from their thoroughly enjoyable (if frequently misspent) boyhoods to the war—no one has to ask which one—to the annoying particulars of aging and their own impending demise. They banter about religion and politics; about personal triumphs and persistent regrets; about love and family, about jackasses they have known and individuals they've greatly admired; about what, finally, it all adds up to and the definition of a well-lived life. And all the while they'll be having a helluva good time.

In the six months I've been attending these gatherings as a sort of fly on the wall—albeit a fly with an occasional big mouth—*this* is what I've found most striking about these men: how much they find to laugh about even when the subject is painful or grim.

For the lives they've lived have given them something so many of us who've had it easier conspicuously lack, a fully operational sense of per- spective. All veterans of the war that spared the world the barbarism of Hitler and imperial Japan, they have long been keenly aware of the human capacity for unspeakable evil; and in their private lives they have experienced their fair share of tragedy and pain. But what they've learned along the way is that hand-wringing does no good and pes- simism is absolutely deadly; and if you can't always make your own luck, good or bad, you sure as hell decide how to deal with it.

Nothing seems to throw them; their very manner conveys reassurance.

Yet if ever there was a moment to test their unflagging confidence in the future, this is it. Even the newscasters and reporters on the tube barely seem to be holding it together. Some are already saying what's happened today signals the end of our entire way of life.

"C'mon, Moe," I add now, "why don't we just reschedule for next week? We were only going to have a partial turnout anyway."

"Oh, what a bunch of nonsense! We got all that food ready; let's go!"

As we shall see, Moe is a complicated case; and like so many men of this generation, he will go to almost any length to avoid open expressions of emotion. Indeed, it would take some yet-to-be devised form of torture to get Moe to express a fraction of his love for his friends. On those rare occa- sions he reveals anything at all, it is usually via a kind of code in which the words he speaks tend to have only the barest relation to what he means.

Translation: At this most horrific and precarious instant in our nation's history, he needs the Girl Watchers to help make sense of it.

Still, when my father-in-law is as adamant about something as he is now, there's generally no stopping him.

"Okay, Moe," I give in, turning back to the horror on the TV screen, "have it your way."

"You just watch; they'll want to come!"

He was right, and I was wrong.

The first to show up, Harry Handler, an old colleague of Moe's from the Naval Postgraduate School, is among those not even expected, since he called a couple of days ago to say he was committed to lunch with some ex-colleagues from the physics department. "But I just went over to the Navy School, and the whole place is closed down," he tells me at the front door. "So here I am—I figured there wasn't much chance Moe would be shutting this down."

"Quite a day, isn't it?" I say, as we head into my in-laws' living room. "Just terrible."

"How are you doing?"

Harry is an exceedingly gentle man, whose puckish humor, lively eyes, and neatly trimmed white beard call to mind an overgrown elf, and I am expecting the standard-issue expression of shock and pain. Instead, he thinks about it a moment and says evenly, "Well, you know, personally I don't get teary."

This is so dramatically at odds with what already is the tenor of the awful day's public conversation that, product as I am of this touchy-feely age, I must show some surprise.

"Of course, it's probably a kind of protection," he quickly adds, almost apologetically. "I've been that way ever since I got back from the war. What I am is *angry*—I want to hit these people back, very fast and very, very hard." Then, shooting me a quick half-smile: "I do cry at opera. Catch me at *La Boheme*, and, I guarantee, you'll see the tears flowing."

"Hey, Harry!" Moe enters the living room, appearing from his bedroom in back. "Didn't expect to see you."

"They closed down the Navy School," replies his friend mildly. "So I chose the least objectionable available alternative."

Moe shakes his head in disgust. "What nonsense! Only idiots think you're *ever* going to be totally safe. You can't live in that kind of fear."

"That's right," agrees Handler. "Because this is going to go on a long time."

At this point a third Girl Watcher, Boyd Huff, strides into the room, having availed himself of the open front door.

He's not supposed to be here either!

"Hello, gentlemen," booms Huff, the retired head of the Navy School's history department. An eighty-six-year-old bantam rooster, barrel-chested and ruddy-faced, with keen blue eyes and thick white hair, he bears more than a passing resemblance to the older Spencer Tracy, if you can imagine Tracy in a red fleece San Francisco 49ers vest; and as with Tracy, his manner is direct and his language salty.

"What happened to Nevada?" demands Moe, for Huff was supposed to be off on his annual visit to a close childhood chum in Reno.

"Christ, we never got off the ground! They had us sitting on the goddamn tarmac for over an hour without telling anyone what was up!"

"I hear they've grounded all air traffic in the whole country," I say.

"They finally let us off, so I hustled over here."

"Well," says Harry, "I thought you'd have reenlisted by now."

Boyd laughs. "I'm still haggling over my commission."

"The commission you'll get is ten cents." Harry rises to shake his friend's hand. "Quite a thing, isn't it?"

"Over ten thousand dead, they're saying. Those pictures of New Yorkers running in the streets—Christ, I've never seen anything like it."

"I'll tell you one thing," says Harry—for at this point everything is still uncertain—"those definitely weren't American pilots. Even if you put a gun to an American pilot's head, you'd never get him to fly into a building."

"And that last plane," says Moe, "the one that crashed in Pennsylvania, I'll bet you anything some of the passengers found out what happened in New York, and they made damn sure it wasn't gonna happen again. You can bet your life on it! You see evil, you gotta at least try to stop it."

"I'm sure that's right," agrees Harry, the mild, unflappable retired physics professor. "That's what I would've done, wouldn't you?"

✦ ✦ ✦

It was my wife, Priscilla, who first suggested I write this book. She grew up around the Girl Watchers and recalls how even as a child, listening to these men talk about the war, she was struck by their matter-of-factness and inexhaustible humor. She said you could tell it wasn't just courage or luck that got them through; it was also an attitude—a whole set of attitudes. It had to do with being deadly serious about what mattered yet never taking themselves too seriously.

For all the differences in their backgrounds, these men were shaped by common experience, both in the war and afterward, and by the values of an era in many ways dramatically at odds with those of our own. If, indeed, no small group can ever be wholly representative of their generation in its breadth and diversity, the Girl Watchers, irreverent, addicted to thinking for themselves and to saying precisely what they think, surely come pretty close.

For me, being around them has been not just a pleasure but an extended character booster shot, forcing me to think hard about all sorts of things I'd otherwise relegate to the second tier of consciousness. That though conformity is a safe harbor, only independence of mind and spirit generates real contentment. That envy is a disease. That loving one woman beats all hell out of what those young guys with the babes seem to have in the beer commercials. That "honor" is less an abstraction than a life plan.

I realize that for many of my contemporaries all this sounds pretty cornball. Believe me, for a long time I would have sneered at it myself. Like most in our circle, my wife and I were student radicals (in her case at Berkeley, the very epicenter of the abortive rebellion), and when we met in our late twenties, we remained as sure as ever of our rectitude and of our selves.

After all, hadn't we, as a generation, been proven right about Vietnam? Weren't we right about feminism? Aren't we even now on the right side of the new arguments about multiculturalism and gay rights?

And hadn't those of the previous generation, that of our parents, revealed themselves to be hopelessly out of date on these counts and a thousand others?

In that sense, for me, this book is by now almost as much about our generation as theirs. For though no one talks much anymore about the generation gap that in the sixties made battlefields of innumerable American homes, the conflict has remained as sharp as it was then, only with the volume muted. That may sound odd, since in one sense over the past decade or so the World War II generation has been on the receiving end of more adulation than any in the nation's history this side of the founding fathers. They have been the subject of a rash of best-sellers and numberless documentaries and high-budget films, been lauded from countless podiums and even featured in commercials seeking to equate life insurance and prescription drugs with heroism and honor.

And yet, what has gone almost universally unremarked upon in the groundswell of "Greatest Generation" nostalgia is that for all the tributes paid such men, the attitudes and values with which they came of age have been everywhere in retreat. Indeed, through the eighties and nineties the very qualities most readily associated with the World War II generation—love of country, a sense of duty, a strong commitment to family—were precisely the ones for which they were often dismissed as dinosaurs or (talk about a misnomer!) as "angry white men."

Raised in an era of greater affluence, but one in which *judgmental* has become a pejorative, many of us even a couple of decades younger can barely conceive of what they went through to reach so advanced a state of backwardness—or, even now, what they are thinking. It has been this way at least since the sixties when, under their very noses, we sat listening to Bob Dylan in our rooms, deeply stirred by his admonition to our clueless elders not to "criticize what you can't understand." These days, the TV and movie dads of our formative years are much derided as tradition-bound patriarchs, though the truth is most were generally loving and supportive, and came down hard only when a kid told a bald-faced lie or otherwise violated a clear familial rule. It was only a decade or so later—which is to say, around the time our generation began writing and directing them—that movies in particular began giving us a succession of harsh and unapologetic authority figures, incapable of understanding their more sensitive and liberated offspring and all too ready to crush their tender spirits.

While the previous generation's work ethic and expectations had been forged by the Great Depression, we came of age taking much for granted, not least our right to happiness. And some of us, when we don't find it, even now in our forties and fifties, casting about for excuses and others to blame, continue to fixate on our parents. Several hundred thousand times a day the nation's vast population of therapists, psychologists, and psychiatrists hear about the ways our mothers and fathers failed us; how they didn't grasp our loneliness or our self-doubt or our pain; how they were cruel or distant or overly demanding.

Never mind the pervasive terror among us baby boomers about growing old, far too many of us have scarcely started to grow up. Not that for a long time I wasn't more or less with the generational program. Years ago, in my thirties, writing about fathers and sons, I listened with keen understanding as men my age and older spoke of having been left permanently wounded by the inattention of their fathers. "I remember once when I was three or four," noted one, "I made a deal with my father that I'd take a nap if, while I was asleep, he would build a castle out of my favorite blocks. I'll never forget it: when I woke up, there was nothing there but two rows stacked haphazardly on top of one another. It must have taken him all of fifteen seconds."

Yet somewhere along the way I lost all patience with this sort of thing. Partly it's having had children of my own and so learning some humility. But it's also having lost a lot of my former enthusiasm in general for the undemanding values of the sixties. I've seen too many of my contemporaries continue to think of themselves as good and moral for opposing war or sending money to environmental groups even as they screw around on their spouses; seen far too many messed-up kids whose parents split for no better reason than that in someone's eyes the grass momentarily looked greener; seen too much narcissism and selfishness and hypocrisy and too little willingness to call it what it is for fear of being called intolerant.

Now, in my fifties, I listen to the Girl Watchers and find myself invigorated by their moral clarity. In a frenzied age in which the young and even the middle-aged endlessly seek contentment in the next new thing, they continue to subscribe to older verities, perhaps most emphatically to those once unembarrassedly known as "the manly virutes"; self-reliance, honest effort, commitment to ideals larger than themselves. Having learned "personal responsibility" long before it was a catch phrase, during a time of unprecedented poverty, most of the guys I am following here became the first in their families to go to college. All went on to distinguish themselves in a newly technological age where brains, know-how, and perseverance trumped family connections. Even now they take nothing for granted, understanding that personal contentment, like success, is earned incrementally; and that as there are principles worth dying for, so there are others without which life will always be empty.

It is no coincidence, nor really a matter of partisan politics, that during Bill Clinton's travails over Monicagate, Clinton pollster Dick Morris was able to anticipate the outcome with uncanny accuracy simply by dividing the population into thirds. The baby boomers, said Morris, would by and large have little trouble with the president's misbehavior because, having come of age in the sixties, they recoiled at the idea of moral judgment and "many of them had probably done the same thing." Younger voters, the so-called gen-Xers, may have widely disapproved of Clinton's conduct and thought him a poor model for their own children, but generally liked his policies enough to overlook his personal transgressions. Only the oldest group, as a rule possessed of less relative standards of morality, would want to hold him to account.

Needless to say, for my peers—at least those who think of themselves as progressive and, yes, open-minded—this is merely further confirmation of the previous generation's terminal provincialism. Irony and cynicism have long been our style; we are the generation that gave the world *Saturday Night Live* and *Seinfeld* and made even the comics page hip. In fact, this very week of September 11 in *Doonesbury,* which Moe reads every morning in the *Monterey Herald,* Mike Doonesbury's World War II vet father is mocked as a foolish blowhard, spouting off to his deeply bored son about supposed long-ago battlefield heroics.

In contrast, the previous generation's iconic comic strip was Bill Mauldin's *Willie and Joe,* a pair of bedraggled but dogged foot soldiers, which began in *Stars and Stripes* during the war. Mauldin, only eighteen when he began the strip as a GI himself, is soon to die from Alzheimer's. It is no surprise that after one veteran learned of the cartoonist's condition, and called on others for a show of support, literally hundreds of letters started showing up daily at the facility where he was being treated.

"I really can't stay long," announces Stuart Walzer, the next Girl Watcher to arrive at Moe's this late morning. "My wife's pretty shaken by this, and I don't want her to be alone."

Easygoing and open, with a bemused, philosophical take on life and its travails, Walzer is the very antithesis of the public's image of what he once was—a hotshot Los Angeles divorce lawyer. In the group's lively back-and-forth he will often go for the heart to make a point, but never for the jugular.

Boyd Huff nods his understanding. "This is going to be hard on a lot of women."

"Men, too," I say, belaboring what strikes me as the obvious.

"Maybe," Huff allows. "But women, God bless 'em, are more peaceable beings. I fear they may have a harder time adjusting to what's coming."

"Which will not be pretty," agrees Walzer. He takes off the well-worn peaked cap he's never without—it covers his bald pate during the hours he spends every day working his garden—and takes a seat in the deepest chair in the room. "You know, watching those planes slamming into the World Trade Center, it struck me those SOBs must've read Tom Clancy along with their Koran—except they didn't understand the

parts about decency and honor. These are going to be adversaries oper-
ating in ways that defy our entire conception of morality and logic."

"You die if you have to," agrees Harry, "but you don't go out of your
way to do it."

"On the other hand," adds Walzer with a sudden smile, "if you promised me seventy-two virgins the instant I die . . ."

Moe bursts out laughing. "You'd take it, would you?"

"I'd at least have to think about it."

There is a knock at the front door, and I leave the room to open it.
A very grim Earl Godfrey extends a hand. "Sorry I'm late."

"No problem."

"I hope I haven't kept everyone waiting."

The politeness is not pro forma. A career navy man, onetime skipper
of the massive carrier *Kitty Hawk*, the strapping Godfrey is the very model
of what used to be known, admiringly (that is, before the term got
decreed so old-fashioned it was just as likely to be employed mockingly),
as a thorough gentleman. Indeed, in his decades in the navy, that pre-
sumptive far-flung, floating den of inequity, his nickname became the
oath that sprang to his lips on those rare occasions he got really, really,
really angry: Judas Priest; and he remains so aggressively modest that it
would be months before I'd learn, secondhand, that as a young, movie-
star-handsome fighter pilot, he was the star of a *Life* magazine photo
essay. Yet for all his solicitous manner, Earl is one seriously tough cus-
tomer, unshakable in his convictions and never less than entirely
straightforward about what is on his mind. I have never seen him in uniform, but even in a cardigan and loafers he retains an aura of command.

"Don't worry about it," I tell him now, "we're still waiting for Gene
Cooper."

As I speak, Cooper's white Lexus comes into view over his shoulder.

"Okay, the gang's all here."

"They handling it all right?" he asks, as we linger waiting for Cooper.

"These guys? Are you kidding?"

"Good." He allows himself a small smile, as Cooper, a tall, eighty-five-year-old Texan in a string tie moves purposefully across the gravel. "Sounds about right."

"So," Harry greets the new arrivals as we join them in the living room, "you fellows reenlisting? That's my question of the day."

"I'm waiting to be called," says Godfrey.

"And they'll surely call Earl before they get to me," adds Cooper.

"Gene, we've been discussing what steps we ought to take," says Walzer, "and we need you to resolve it."

Facetious as the remark is, it reflects Cooper's unofficial standing as the sage of the group. An exceptionally gifted engineer, the unflappable Cooper was long ago dubbed His Omniscience by Boyd Huff. Over the years he has been a particular guru to my father-in-law, who seeks his advice on almost every subject. Cooper is always a quick phone call away when Moe runs across an especially tough electronics or engineering problem, needs financial advice, or is pondering which starter musical instrument would be best for his grandchildren. My wife tells me he even called Cooper before the veterinarian when a family dog was hit by a car—and as usual his advice was right on target.

For all that, Cooper tends to be so undemonstrative that the wisdom of much that he says can slip by unnoticed; more than once, in fact, I won't realize how keen a Cooperian insight was till reflecting on it later.

But now, respecting the enormity of the crisis at hand, Cooper more or less avoids the question. "I expect there are some reasonably bright people in Washington already working on that," he says, "coming up with ways to make damn sure those who did it will rue this day forever. Let's just hope there are enough left over to start dealing with the social and economic repercussions of this thing, because those are going to be massive."

"The impact on the insurance industry and on the airlines alone," ticks off Walzer, "and the whole business of airport security."

"And of course it'll play havoc with our relationships with all kinds of countries in that region," says Godfrey, "and maybe even some of our allies."

"We're obviously going to have to rethink immigration policy," notes Harry. "And I sure wouldn't want to be an Arab-American just about now."

"Don't forget oil," adds Moe. "We're going to have to focus on conservation, Could be this'll end up really helping electric car research."

All in all, it is an uncannily accurate summary of the chief elements of the coming national conversation, except it's happening with most of America still reeling in disbelief and in emotional turmoil; a product of the roughly 490 years of collective experience and solid thinking of the old men in this room.

I'm by no means saying men of this generation are without their characteristic shortcomings, or that these cannot be serious and debilitating. Many of us have indeed been hurt and frustrated by our fathers' emotional inaccessibility.

Yet it can also be argued that we Americans have in recent decades taken this business of psychological exploration several steps too far; that it has become a kind of indulgence that erodes rigor. A whole raft of terms unknown a generation ago—*dysfunctional family, sex addiction, in recovery*—are today the stuff of everyday conversation. Snap on the TV, and you risk encountering yet another excuse-making, self-pitying celebrity or some commentator peddling another mixed message about right and wrong, or a pitch for pills to ease stress, anxiety, or depression. Victimhood often seems to get more respect these days than the very qualities of strength, persistence, and character essential to rise above it.

Shouldn't the real bottom line be how one acts, not what he feels or why?

True enough, precious few of our fathers were what Oprah or Dr. Phil would describe as "in touch with their feelings." But they also sure as hell weren't whiners.

My time with the Girl Watchers has proven a vacation from the all-but-inescapable culture of complaint. Through the decades, these guys have remained unapologetically who they are. Though the uninitiated might find their willingness to kid around in the face of today's horror strange, perhaps even unseemly, over their long lives they have proven, time and again, that when put to the test they will be fully accounted for.

But there is something else I have started to notice. Even in the brief time I've been with them, the Girl Watchers are slowing down. The changes are not yet dramatic—a bit more trouble than before rising from a deep chair, maybe, or getting more winded by a short walk—but they don't really have to be. As the oft-repeated statistic has it, we are losing 1,300–1,400 World War II vets every day. JFK's "new generation of Americans, born in this century, tempered by war, disciplined by a hard and bitter peace," will shortly be gone entirely.

The men themselves regard this with characteristic equanimity. The question, as they and the millions like them depart, is whether we really know how extraordinarily much we will miss their example.

"Let's not forget the whole intelligence area," adds Huff, the retired diplomatic historian, meaningfully. "I've been saying for a long time we've been responding to crises on an ad hoc basis, especially in the Middle East, instead of training agents to get them in there."

"Amen, to that," concurs Godfrey.

"There's only one trouble," says Walzer, laughing, "you've been saying it to *us*."

"Think those bastards'll take advantage of the fact we Americans forget fast?" Boyd throws out the key question. "We don't exactly have the perseverance our ancestors did in seventeen seventy-six."

"It would sure help if the enemy would dress their troops in red coats and those big bear hats," observes Harry mildly.

Moe laughs. "Still, any way you look at it, those guys were the real greatest generation."

"Well, you know," replies Godfrey, "maybe, starting today, this is a different America. Our trouble is, we move so quickly, maybe it takes something like this to see what we've lost."

THE GIRL WATCHERS

JOHN TURNER, JR.

NICKNAMES: The Count (to his kids' friends), Moe (to everyone else)

BORN: Ft. Smith, Arkansas, 1918

MILITARY SERVICE: Navy ensign, 1943–46; during war served in Pacific and worked on early jet engine and rocket research; participated in atomic bomb tests at Bikini as radiological safety officer, 1946.

CAREER: With Edward Teller's team at Livermore, worked on H-bomb and fusion, 1953–55; professor of electronics, Naval Postgraduate School, 1955–76.

FAMILY: Married Ruth Mary Benedict, 1946, five children.

NOTABLE EARLY FACT: Moe is ambidextrous; during his youth his father tried to turn him into a left-handed pitcher and instead gave him a lifelong hatred of sports.

INFLUENTIAL FIGURE: "To be honest, I don't think there's anyone that influenced me very much; I just sort of flowed downstream. Maybe Herbert Hoover, since he was the first engineer I ever knew of, and put the idea in my mind of being one. But in other ways I couldn't stand the guy."

OBSERVATION: "It used to be that if you were lucky you'd get a kiss from a girl on the first date. Now lots of guys jump into the sack with girls in the first ten minutes. They don't realize there's twenty-four hours in a day, and sex takes very little time."

THE GIRL WATCHERS

HARRY HANDLER

NICKNAME: Hatchet Harry (conferred by his students)

BORN: Butte, Montana, 1925

MILITARY SERVICE: First lieutenant, 96th Division, 382 Infantry, 1944–46; Battle of Okinawa.

CAREER: Researcher at GE's Hanford facility in Richland, Washington, conducting experiments on critical mass, 1955–58; professor of physics, Naval Postgraduate School, 1958–85.

FAMILY: Married Pat Boynton, 1980; four stepchildren.

NOTABLE EARLY FACT: Grew up believing his paternal grandparents had been killed in a pogrom in Poland, until a cousin doing family research discovered they actually made it to Cleveland. "It really ruined a great story."

INFLUENTIAL FIGURE: High school physics teacher Alfred Scheer. "He was of German extraction, so World War I kept him from getting a decent job in engineering or science. Even though I wasn't born yet, that turned out to be my good luck."

QUOTATION: "If you can justify cheating in school, you'll cheat at cards, and chances are good you'll cheat in your marriage. All these things are interrelated. If you cut corners in one area of your life, it very easily becomes a habit."

The Girl Watchers

BOYD HUFF

NICKNAME: Cigar, Huffer

BORN: Independence, Oregon, 1915

MILITARY SERVICE: Lieutenant, 106th Infantry, 1942–45; Battle of the Bulge; German POW.

CAREER: Professor of history (and chairman of history department), Naval Postgraduate School, 1956–88; wrote classified reports for naval intelligence.

FAMILY: Married to Martha Louise Wislander, 1941–93; one surviving child (of three); married Beverly Moss, 1999, two stepgrandchildren.

NOTABLE EARLY FACT: While interned in a Nazi POW camp, taught American history in "university" set up by captured men.

INFLUENTIAL FIGURES: His parents. "They were just wonderful people—very kind, with remarkable minds, and interested in just about everything. And, Christ, the two of them loved each other more than I can tell you."

OBSERVATION: "There was perfectly good reason to dislike the [Vietnam] war. What I could never understand was ... how so many young people could doubt the fundamental goodness of the country?"

THE GIRL WATCHERS

STUART WALZER

NICKNAME: Stuey ("Mainly used by girls. Oh, in the army I was sometimes called Shithead.")

BORN: Chicago, Illinois, 1924

MILITARY SERVICE: PFC, 106th Infantry, 1943–45; Battle of the Bulge.

CAREER: Divorce attorney in Los Angeles; leading figure in divorce reform movement; teacher and writer.

FAMILY: Married Paula Silverston, 1951; four children.

NOTABLE EARLY FACT: Flunked out of University of Wisconsin before fighting in the war; afterward, graduated with honors from UCLA and Harvard Law.

INFLUENTIAL FIGURE: High school friend Burton Zolo. "A good part of my interest in music and literature goes back to my friendship with Burt."

OBSERVATION: "Deep down inside, we're all about fourteen years old and in the first year of high school. Everybody else is bigger and smarter and knows more than we do. And we spend our lives looking for someone who has the answers. But here's the big secret: Nobody has them. Every human being, even the most successful, is basically flying by the seat of his pants."

THE GIRL WATCHERS

EARL GODFREY

NICKNAMES: Judas Priest (in the Navy); Goof ("But I'm really not too proud of it")

BORN: Cozad, Nebraska, 1924

MILITARY SERVICE: Joined navy in 1943 as an aviation cadet; retired in 1974 as captain.

CAREER: Flew in World War II and Korean War; test pilot for carrier aircraft, 1958–61; served in Pentagon on secretary of the navy's staff, 1966–67; skipper of aircraft carrier *Kitty Hawk*, 1969–71.

FAMILY: Married Geraldine Stimfig, 1946; four children.

NOTABLE EARLY FACT: Was all-state Nebraska guard in high school.

INFLUENTIAL FIGURE: Jim Ferris, his former commanding officer in a fighter squadron in 1957–58. "There wasn't one guy in that command who wouldn't walk off the flight deck if he told them to do so."

QUOTATION: "Leadership isn't so much a matter of charisma, which can be abused, as of character. Only someone who, when he says he's going to do something, you *know* he's going to do it, is worth following."

The Girl Watchers

GENE COOPER

NICKNAME: His Omniscience (conferred by Huff)

BORN: Galveston, Texas, 1916

MILITARY SERVICE: Navy lieutenant, 1942–46; worked on radar technology at MIT and Annapolis.

CAREER: Naval Postgraduate School, professor of electrical engineering, 1949–85; worked on very early TV technology, including first-ever operational cable system; consultant on numerous military and civilian projects.

FAMILY: Married Josephine Badalment, 1939; two children.

NOTABLE EARLY FACT: As a teenager, played baseball and tennis with the legendary Babe Didrikson Zaharias.

INFLUENTIAL FIGURE: Patrick Underwood, who taught him mathematics in high school. "He'd been teaching since the eighteen-eighties . . . [and used] old texts from the English public schools. He really made us sweat blood—but, boy, did you learn your stuff!"

OBSERVATION: "We weren't visionaries, just damn hard workers. . . . the fact there's a program of an entire human being in a single cell . . . make[s] everything we humans have achieved look like child's play. Man, a boll weevil walking around has more going on in its brain than any computer ever built."

THE
GIRL WATCHERS
CLUB

✦ CHAPTER 1 ✦

THE COUNT OF MONTEREY

MOE TURNER AT THE NAVAL POSTGRADUATE
SCHOOL, MONTEREY.

First things first: there probably would be no Girl Watchers Club, at least not in its current form, were it not for my father-in-law. Though Moe wasn't among the handful of original members in the midsixties, for the past couple of decades he has been the one who has arranged the meetings, deciding which of the area restaurants they'll congregate at this week—the Del Monte Golf Club coffee shop, the Thunderbird over in Carmel, the Sea Harvest near Cannery Row, or Chef Lee's on Freemont—and more to the point, he is the one who keeps in closest touch with the other members in between.

Moe's devotion to his friends is a wondrous thing to behold. Generally given to a certain gruffness, in their presence he is perpetually on the verge of laughter; bored to distraction by most of what passes for popular entertainment, with them he'll sit for hours telling stories, sharing views, and generally figuring out how to cure the world's ills. They are everything to him.

This is why, the first time I called my father-in-law from New York with the idea for this book, his reaction was so guarded.

"I don't know," he said, with characteristic imprecision, "sounds pretty goofy to me."

"Goofy?"

"I really don't know if the fellows will be interested."

"Well, would you be willing to sound them out?" Over the years I had come to know some of his friends reasonably well, but others were virtual strangers.

"Why should I?"

I don't know—maybe because his son-in-law was asking him.

"Maybe because they'll *want* to," I said. "Maybe because what they have to say might be of interest beyond the group."

Silence.

"Never mind, Moe. I'll call them myself. Will you at least give me their numbers?"

"Oh, hell, I'll do it!"

But Moe is nothing if not an open book, and it took just a few minutes for the real reason behind his ambivalence to come out. I had told him that my hope was to focus on six men, sitting in when they got together as a group and coming to know them as individuals. But all told, between regulars and part-timers, as many as fifteen guys are liable to turn up at the Girl Watchers' regular Friday luncheons. He was worried about those who would *not* be prominently featured.

"What about Smitty?" he demanded now. "And Len? And how about Alex Grba? They're all neat guys."

"Look, I know, but there's no way to keep track of that many people in a book. A half dozen will be hard enough."

"That's the dumbest thing I ever heard; that makes no sense at all." He paused a few seconds, then did what men of his age and disposition often do when faced with emotionally fraught situations: he changed the subject. "So tell me," he said suddenly, "what's that granddaughter of mine up to?"

Moe's friends, for their part, return the feeling in kind—though when they talk about him, even in his presence, it is often as one might discuss a naughty but very precocious child. Moe is not an easy man to understand and, as the other Girl Watchers know, an extremely easy one to *mis*understand if certain allowances are not made for his distinctive quirks. As Gene Cooper, who has been closely observing my father-in-law for nearly half a century, at work and at play, said when I finally did approach him about this project. "All I can say is you've got your work cut out for you—no one'll believe Moe is for real."

But that's the thing. Moe is *entirely* for real; a full-blown eccentric who (for this is the trait that fully confirms the fact) genuinely doesn't give a whit what others think of him. Sure, he knows he has some wires crossed—or, at any rate, fully appreciates that a lot of other people think so. But when he bothers to reflect on it at all, it is only to wonder how so many of *them* manage to get so many things so consistently wrong.

To start where most people will, there is the matter of my father-in-law's appearance. His sartorial taste runs primarily to mismatched, thrift shop clothes, brilliantly colored socks (a nickel at the Navy School thrift store) and sneakers, though you can never tell when he'll throw in something odd even by his own standards—including, once, a pair of pleated women's pants. (His explanation: "What does it matter?")

More than twenty years ago, nervous when I was about to meet my fiancée's father for the first time, Priscilla gave me a crash course in Moe. Studying his photograph, struck by the craggy figure staring back imperiously through deep-set eyes, his face topped by a mass of unkempt white hair, I thought I would please her by remarking on her father's resemblance to Andrew Jackson. For an instant she looked startled, then cracked up. "Jackson never had *that* bad a hair day." She laughed again. "And I don't want to think of what my father would do if he was even close to that kind of power. Because, believe me, he'd use it."

To put it simply, Moe, wholly unbound by traditional constraints on thought or behavior, has extremely strong opinions on almost every subject and has never been shy about expressing them, even if he is the one buried by the falling chips. One of the early stories Priscilla told me about her father was set just before the start of the June 1967 Six Day War between Israel and its Arab neighbors. Growing up in Arkansas, Moe did not knowingly meet a Jew for the first twenty years of his life; but when he moved into the serious sciences, in graduate school and later working in various labs, he found himself with a number of Jewish friends and a shared intense sympathy for the new Jewish state. That late spring, with Israel under threat of imminent annihilation, Moe decided he had to get involved. Abruptly setting aside the book he'd been reading, he strode into the kitchen and announced to his startled family, "I'm gonna give Israel the bomb!" His wife and children stared at him dumbstruck; this was not necessarily an idle threat. As a nuclear engineer, Moe not only had been part of the team under Edward Teller that developed the H-bomb but, so it was said, had once worked up an atom bomb with a bunch of pals for kicks. The story goes that my sweet and gentle-spirited future mother-in-law, who over the years had learned to react to such pronouncements with saintly resignation, this time leaped from her chair and plastered herself against the front door. "Don't do it, Moe," she implored. "You'll lose your job."

This was certainly a possibility, since Moe's job was to teach engineering at Monterey's Naval Postgraduate School, a government facility presumably unaccustomed to employees with private foreign policies. Hating, as always, to be crossed, for a few tense minutes Moe persisted in his intention. But he is also possessed of a mercifully brief attention span, as well as a notorious lack of follow-through; which is to say, the family was soon able to lure him back to his reading chair and his biography of Berlioz.

Yet, given the mix of Moe's impulsiveness and passion, occasionally such an episode ends less benignly—like the one that eventually did bring his quarter century at the Navy School to a close. Suffering severe abdominal pains, Moe, who has always had a consuming suspicion of doctors—also lawyers, but that's a whole other category of stories—left them untreated. It was not until he became delirious, a bony, wild-haired figure wandering around the house spouting quadratic equations, that the family finally dragged him to a hospital. The diagnosis was an infected gall bladder, and by now the prognosis was grave. At this crucial juncture, all but dead and knowing it, Moe instructed his wife to fetch pen and paper, and he proceeded to dictate letters to a number of colleagues with whom he had had problems, including his immediate superior, telling them he was *glad* to be dying, because he had always thought them fools and now he would never have to see them again.

Then he recovered. His career at the Navy School didn't. Assigned to teach courses he had never taught before, some not even in his discipline, staying one chapter ahead of his students in the text, he soon accepted voluntary retirement.

His friends embrace Moe's forays to the fringe along with all the rest. What matters is not that he has such strong opinions but that he is so interesting and provocative, always intensely interested in what *they* have to say. Wholly secure in his own view of the world, he relishes being challenged and prodded, even mocked. The more unusual an idea, the better he likes it. My wife describes a childhood home of barely controlled mayhem, with Moe liable at any moment to whip the place into a frenzy with one of his schemes. There was the time he suddenly decided to build a cupola on top of the garage, featuring a revolv-

ing weather vane that would bang out the hour; and the traumatic day
he announced he was going to change all the kids' names to do honor
to their colonial forebears (my wife was slated to go from Priscilla Ann
to Meigs McKinney); and the time he had a ton of sand dumped in a
corner of the backyard for use in some soon-to-be abandoned project—
then decided he wanted it moved to another corner of the backyard.
Among the images Priscilla will never shake is the sight of her then-two-
year-old brother Whitney wearing only a diaper, tears streaming down
his face, toddling back and forth across the yard trying to get the job
done a teaspoon at a time.

Yet it was also a home perpetually bristling with good conversation,
against a soundtrack of Beethoven or Bach, with books stacked high in
almost every corner. During the sixties, when the homes of many of her
friends became perpetual battlegrounds, Priscilla's was the neighborhood refuge. "With my father, people could always talk about things
they couldn't with their own parents—politics, music, books they were
reading, even sex. He didn't care what age anyone was; he just loved
batting around ideas." In fact, she adds, for a few years there Moe was
actually ahead of the curve sartorially. "Other parents used to be aghast
at how their kids were dressing, but he was delighted to suddenly have
all this company on his runs to the thrift shops."

There is a consistency to the more serious of the Moe stories:
beyond mere independence of mind, they express a determination to
identify the right in every situation and then act on it. His friends are
keenly aware of this; and though they long ago learned that there was
no point in trying to anticipate what would come out of the man's
mouth next, it is the glue that bonds them so tightly to him. No one has
any doubt, for instance, that had he lived in occupied France under the
Nazis, Moe would have hastened to join the Resistance; the only question is how soon one of his indiscretions would have gotten everyone
else killed.

Intensely social, Moe will strike up a conversation with just about
anyone, just about anywhere—from an elderly woman he spots water-

ing her garden during his daily walk to a Hispanic kid working the supermarket checkout line—and inevitably, somewhat more than occasionally, something he says will rub someone the wrong way. It might be a joke deemed "sexist," or a good-natured reference to "this neat Jap gal I used to know," or even something he finds amusingly shocking in a book he has just read.

I have seen this happen a number of times, and the experience is always both surprising for him and painful. For all his brashness, at heart he is an exceptionally kind and generous man. The possibility that speaking one's mind might strike someone else as hurtful never seems to cross his mind until it is too late.

For the record, Moe doesn't discriminate—he's as allergic to careful, euphemistic speech with his friends and family as he is around strangers, maybe even more so. More than once, I have observed him searching for exactly the right phrase to express precisely what he wants, then inventing offensive phrases on the spur of the moment. "Great," I recall him reacting when my wife informed him his other daughter was pregnant. "You know if she's planning to have the cretin test?"

His friends, having seen how easily he is wounded, can be touchingly protective. "Beneath that hard shell," as Harry Handler will tell me, "Moe is all custard. Once you get past the bluster, in many ways he's still the innocent, small-town boy who left Arkansas to go to war."

While Moe's softer side rarely gets expressed in words, it shows itself all the time in his amazing impulsive generosity. Whenever he is with someone he likes, or even with someone he thinks he might get to like, Moe will start pushing things on them, the value of which is limited only by a Depression-era mentality that keeps him from buying almost anything new. If you happen to mention you're shopping for shoes, he'll dash to his closet and return with a thrift shop pair (dismissing your plaint that they're a half size small, and not at all what you're looking for, as niggling quibbles); if you observe that something he is eating looks good, it will instantly be speared from his plate and thrust your way. There are friends he hasn't visited in years without bringing along a book he thinks they'll enjoy—and who cares that he paid only ten cents for it at a library sale?

Moe has five children, and, as these things go, they grew up regarding their father's distinctive perspective on the world as normal. But to an outsider, it is anything but. That long-ago evening when I was about to get the once-over from my wife's famously unsparing father, I prepared myself for an ordeal by fire. Even the imperial nickname bestowed on him by my wife's closest childhood friend was intimidating: the Count.

And, sure enough, that first evening Priscilla and I were basically summoned into his presence.

We had known for some time Moe would be coming from Monterey to New York; we just didn't know exactly when. Then, again, neither did he. Constitutionally opposed to paying airline rates, back then he flew only on military aircraft, standby, which usually meant it took him several days of hopscotching from one far-flung base to the next to reach his destination. In this case, he had last been sighted leaving the house in Monterey early on a Monday morning, on foot, toting a World War II vintage duffel bag.

When he hadn't been heard from by Friday night, Priscilla and I cautiously accepted an invitation to play poker at a friend's that evening. So that's where we were, in the middle of a hand, when the phone rang. Moe had just arrived at Priscilla's sister's across town, and, as he put it to Priscilla, "If you're not here in fifteen minutes, I'm leaving!"

Yet when I was finally face-to-face with him, the impression he made was less of power than of fragility. He was rail thin and spent from his journey—his last plane had deposited him at an air force base far upstate in Rome, New York, and he had hitchhiked the final long leg—even his voice sounded dog tired.

Nonetheless, within just a couple minutes, the real Moe began to emerge. He peppered me with questions about my past, my family, my work, my plans; the sort of fatherly examination of a suitor far more likely found these days in vintage movies than in real life.

"Well," he announced finally, out of the blue, "I brought you something."

"Really?" I said, surprised.

He made no reply but simply stood and dumped the contents of his duffel bag on the table. Rooting through the dirty underwear and socks, he found a vintage solid-gold pocket watch.

"Here," he said, placing it in my hand.

"Is that what I think it is?" I looked more closely. "And it's inscribed!"

I silently read the inscription:

To F. W. Leeper, in recognition of having met the annual sales quota in the month of October.
—The Pepsi-Cola Co., 1941

"Wow" was all I could think of to say. "Thanks."

"Got a good deal on it at a yard sale. You better treat my daughter right, or I'll take it back."

Then, unexpectedly, he smiled; letting me know the watch was just a token, or at least a precursor, of a gift he considered of infinitely greater value: his friendship. I didn't quite have it yet—with his child's well-being at risk, there would be many, many tests to come. But at least he would give me a chance.

"So," he put it to me one early Saturday morning all these years later, the day after my arrival at my in-laws' home in Monterey to start work on this book, "you coming out with me and Huff or not?"

CHAPTER 2

We had just a splendid view of all the young women . . .

—BOYD HUFF

BATHING BEAUTIES, CIRCA 1945, IN <u>LIFE</u> MAGAZINE.

Fifteen minutes later, a spiffy little Daewoo turns into the Turners' driveway.

"Hello there!" booms Boyd Huff, emerging from the driver's side.

"Hey, Boyd," I return the greeting. I've had a passing acquaintance with him for a good ten years, but the idea today is to begin seriously delving into his background. I want to come to know the guys individually before getting together as a group.

"All right, enough of this talk," says Moe. "Time to hit the road."

They'll be spending this morning, as they have just about every Saturday morning for almost as long as either can remember, roaming the Monterey Peninsula, hitting garage sales in search of items of interest; in the case of Huff, former chairman of the history department at Monterey's Naval Post-graduate School, almost exclusively books on history and world affairs to add to his extensive collection; in Moe's, just about anything that happens to strike his ever-evolving fancy. In fact, Moe's yard sale fixation has left the Turner home and yard a virtual museum of useless stuff.

Of all Girl Watchers, Huff is the one my father-in-law has known the longest and with whom he still spends the most time. They met in the immediate aftermath of the war when both were newly married gradu-ate students at Berkeley and the Turners lived in a building where Boyd was picking up extra cash as manager. Several years after that, when Boyd, with his freshly minted history Ph.D., was looking for work, he learned that the Navy School's history department had no openings but the engineering department did, and passed the information on to Moe. Moe returned the favor several years later when in its wisdom the Navy decided it might make sense for its top officers to have some grounding in history and international relations in addition to techni-cal matters, and so was expanding its liberal arts faculty.

Five or six years after that, it was Boyd who introduced Moe to the recently organized (to the extent they have ever been organized) Girl Watchers. Over the roughly four decades since, the group has gained and lost members, but Boyd and Moe have been among those most unwavering in their devotion.

Now, as the three of us shoot down Highway 1, Huff begins filling me in on the group's earliest days.

"Looking back on it, I guess you'd have to call Morton Buck the founding father, wouldn't you say so, Turner?"

Beside him in the passenger seat, Moe looks up from the *Monterey Herald* he has been scrutinizing, folded back to the ads for garage sales.

"Say, Boyd," Moe misreplies, "tell him about that old guy you killed in the Battle of the Bulge."

"Christ, weren't you listening? I don't even know why I ask you . . . !" Huff turns slightly to shoot me a quick glance in the backseat. "Turner's always trying to get me to tell about killing somebody over there—that's cause his own service in the war was so antiseptic."

"That's true," agrees Moe, amiably. Though he turned down a draft-exempt job at RCA to join the navy, after brief and uneventful service on a seaplane tender in the Pacific, he ended up back in the States working on engine design at the Bureau of Aeronautics. "I didn't hardly see anything at all. The only dead body I laid eyes on the whole time was that time we went swimming when our ship was anchored in a lagoon and this squall came up. After, when we looked down—it was so clear, you could see sixty feet under—there was this sailor lying at the bottom."

"Well, I was talking about the origins of the Girl Watchers." Huff pauses. "You see, Buck was one of the original members of the group, as well as the one that named it. Back then we used to go for lunch to a restaurant called Las Laurales over in Carmel Valley. It was adjacent to a swimming pool, and we had just a splendid view of all the young women. This was back in the early sixties—Buck's been dead quite a while now."

Huff pauses, peering out the windshield at the approaching exit off the two-lane highway. "Well, what about it, Turner? That where we get off?"

Moe picks up a Monterey County street map. "Just hold on . . ."

"Christ, what the hell have you been doing? What's that street we're looking for?"

"Mesa." Moe motions vaguely to the right. "It's somewhere off over there."

Too late, we're already speeding past the exit and, with it, a highly promising garage sale. "Goddamn it, Turner, it's just lucky you weren't in the infantry—*none* of us would've made it."

"You can say that again. I've got no sense of direction at all."

"Well, dammit, go ahead and figure out where we go next—what about Carmel Valley?"

"There's nothing good in Carmel Valley."

"Like hell there's not; I read those ads this morning. That's another characteristic of yours—you just lie deliberately to make a point. Just make up facts."

Moe turns back to the paper—the most likely ads are circled and starred. "How about that church sale in Pacific Grove?"

"They have books there?"

"Of course. You always find good books at church sales."

"All right, then."

"Especially the Jewish ones. Jews always have the best books."

"They're called synagogues, Turner," observes Huff dryly.

Moe nods at me, his Jewish son-in-law. "He doesn't mind; why should you?"

"Just calling the thing what it is, Turner."

The *Odd Couple* quality to this back-and-forth is no accident. For all the years they have been friends, in the obvious ways they could hardly be more different: Boyd, highly focused and detail oriented, elegant in speech and manner; Moe, with his heavy Arkansas accent, his unending stream of observations, quips, opinions often only vaguely related to the subject at hand.

But of course what they have in common dwarfs the superficial distinctions. More than just great good humor and keen intelligence, more even than all the years of common experiences, they share a set of fundamental attitudes about life and how it is rightly lived. If the Girl Watchers' defining trait is an inextinguishable sense of optimism and purpose, it is Huff who perhaps most fully embodies such an outlook on life.

Never have I known anyone who has suffered such a litany of personal loss. A decorated survivor of some of Europe's worst fighting and a harsh spell in a German POW camp, he returned home to start a family and became a devoted and loving father. But one of his three children died as an infant, and a second in adolescence, in a horrific gun accident; then he lost the third to schizophrenia. Soon afterward, their mother, his companion and best friend through it all, fell ill and died.

Yet much as these hurts remain with him, evident in an occasional random remark or observation, through it all he has pressed on with unerring dignity and good humor. Even among his friends, his relentless focus on the future is a source of wonder. In fact, having remarried just a year ago, at eighty-five, he now finds himself with a brand-new family, including, for the first time, to his unbounded delight, grandchildren.

In a time when so many wear victimhood as a badge of honor, such astonishing wellsprings of resilience and optimism will register to some as nearly unfathomable. But when I ask him to explain it, as I will in various ways over the coming months, Boyd himself always seems mystified by the question: it's inconceivable to him that there could be any other way to be.

Then, again, he provides at least the beginnings of an answer whenever he starts talking about his early years growing up in the Pacific Northwest, an idyllic, old-fashioned, rough-and-tumble boyhood that seems equal parts Mark Twain and Andy Hardy. His father, a highly principled individualist and self-taught intellectual, was the Northwest regional branch manager for Winchester Arms, as well as the Washington state skeet-shooting champion; his mother, equally independent and driven to succeed, was as indulgently loving as she was adamant that in all things he never be anything but his best. From an early age, Boyd knew his way around both the outdoors and his parents' history library; and as, in their fierce devotion to learning, it was always assumed he would not only go on to college but excel, it was also presumed that as an adult he would be possessed of what were then known, without irony, as the manly virtues: honesty, strength of character, self-reliance.

"Huff was a hunter," says Moe now, in the car. "Loved to kill things."

"Only when necessary," counters his friend amiably, "only when necessary." He glances at me. "We lived on the edge of Spokane, just a block from the woods, and when I was twelve, my father gave me a Winchester twenty-two."

"Huff was an only child, spoiled rotten."

"Thank God. Loved every minute of it."

"The only thing I ever shot was a bird," says Moe. "It nearly killed me to see it lying there."

Boyd nods. "I shot some birds at first, but my father thought it was terrible. And of course I came to agree with him." He pauses. "Marvelous man, my father. My parents were two people who really wanted to go to college but weren't able to due to family circumstances. But they saw to it I got a splendid education. The University of Washington, then Brown and Berkeley—my God, but it was marvelous. Did I ever tell you, Turner—when I was an undergraduate my Grandmother Boyd moved to Seattle, and I'll be damned if she didn't sometimes come along with me to the lectures."

"Quite different from me. My daddy didn't try to talk me into going to college; he tried to talk me out of it. Wanted me to go to work."

"Really?" I say. "I never knew that before." For all his willingness to hold forth on any subject that flits through his brain, Moe has always been strangely guarded about his early life. "In fact, I hardly know anything about your father at all."

"Well, see, I didn't have it easy like Huff."

"Another sob story from Turner." His friend chuckles.

"Boyd," I ask, "you think there's the same reverence for old people today as there was back then?" He looks surprised by the question. "I'm thinking about what you said about your grandmother . . ."

"I don't know. I haven't had much to do with elderly people. Except Moe. I can't say I have any reverence for him."

For Moe, this instantly calls something to mind. "A guy told me a good joke yesterday over at the Navy School thrift store. There's this elderly couple in a rest home. The first night he holds her hand, and she smiles. The second night he holds her hand, and she smiles. The third night he reaches for her hand, and she says, 'Not tonight, I have a headache.'" Moe cackles. "Pretty good, don't you think?"

"I've heard a lot better."

"Boyd also had a good Jesuit education for high school," notes Moe.

"That's true. At Gonzaga Prep. Christ, four years of Latin required, regular lessons in elocution. . . . I can probably still recite Lincoln's Letter to Mrs. Bixby—that poor woman who lost all those sons in the war."

"You also had a pretty great social life in high school. Tell him about that."

"Turner, there's nothing to tell."

"How about that gal who wanted to stop all the boys from joining up with the Jesuits?"

Huff laughs. "Oh, hell, there was this one girl, Pat, who just hated the Catholic Church! So we all used to go over there and tell her we were thinking of becoming Jesuits. Boy, would she ever put out trying to convince us not to." He laughs again. "Not all the way, but three-quarters."

"I gather it was really frowned upon back then for a girl to go all the way," I observe.

"Oh, not entirely, not at all. Actually, my first time was with a neighbor girl back in high school I was teaching to fence. I was quite a fencer in high school and college. Did you know that, Turner?"

"You've mentioned it."

"Christ, I was over there all the time banging her and teaching her fencing. And then we had lots of sex in college"—he laughs—"though too much of it in the backseats of cars."

"So there wasn't all that much of a stigma attached to girls who went all the way? I always heard there was."

"Oh, no—it was just usually expected that you'd go steady with them. Of course, there were some determined to remain virgins, and that had to be respected. You could get 'em awfully excited, but you had to know when to stop and be a gentleman."

"The curse of ethical standards," says Moe evenly.

"I'll never forget this one girl I was going with, a Kappa, Kappa Gamma," continues Boyd. "I took her home one night, and we were flirting tenderly in the doorway, and we could hear the girls talking in the room right above. And one girl said, 'Jesus Christ, he had me so hot he could have screwed me with a red hot poker.' " He laughs. "I looked at my girl and said, 'That's my exit line; good night.' "

"God," says Moe, "I was afraid to look at a girl back then. I was pathetic!" He glances out the window. We're approaching Pacific Grove, and a young woman in a fire engine red Camaro convertible zooms by on our right, her red-streaked hair flying in the wind.

"Say, Boyd," he pipes up again, "you hear about this show they got on this week on the History Channel? They got women talking about prostitution and stuff."

"You plan to watch it?"

"Of course." He pauses, watching the red Camaro dart between lanes up ahead, and head into Livingston Tunnel beneath old Monterey. "I'll tell you, you can really tell a lot about a woman by the way she drives. When I was working up at the lab in Livermore we had this gal that drove like hell. We used to call her Fire in the Sack."

"Of course, in your case, it was purely speculation."

"Oh, too true." Moe chortles. "I'll tell you what gets me," he picks up as we enter the tunnel ourselves, "all these gals who work all week long at some menial job, then on the weekend they go out with some guy and give it away for free. Just seems like a wacky distribution of resources."

"Turner, you have a goddamn theory for everything." He pauses. "That'll be Cannery Row a little up ahead."

"Weren't you buddies with Doc Ricketts, Boyd?" says Moe, referring to the local legend, the renowned sidekick of John Steinbeck.

"Yes, I was. Right after I was drafted, just starting my training, we were in the same company over here at the Presidio. Ricketts was about forty at the time, and here he'd gone and joined the army, so they let him continue living at his residence up here on Cannery Row. Lovable guy, very well read. We had some wonderful discussions about books." We emerge from the tunnel and he points. "Right across the street over there were all the whorehouses. Ricketts was the impromptu psychiatrist for all the girls after they had their breakdowns."

"A lot of 'em broke down, did they? Why's that?"

"Oh, who the hell knows? Overuse probably."

"You ever run into Steinbeck?" I ask.

"Never met the guy. Actually, I was in army intelligence there, and, Christ"—he gives a hearty laugh—"he was considered subversive for having written *The Grapes of Wrath.*"

"My God, what nonsense!" exclaims Moe.

"Lucky they weren't poking around your thoughts, Turner." He points again. "And here's the Presidio on the left. And there's Cannery Row right up ahead. Used to be all sardine canneries and whorehouses. It's all been transformed, of course." He points one more time. "Sly McFly's—that one they kept the name."

"All for the tourists now," observes Moe, though many of the old facades remain, and it's clear much effort has been made to preserve the area's old-time feel.

"Nothing wrong with that, lifeblood of the community. You oughta try some of these restaurants sometime, Turner, excellent seafood."

"All of 'em overpriced, too."

"I guess that's true if you're a goddamn cheapskate." He slows as we approach a plain weather-beaten clapboard building just up from the entrance to Monterey's renowned aquarium. "Here's Doc's—Eight Hundred Cannery Row. I think they made it into some kind of men's club or some damn thing."

A couple of minutes later we enter the residential area of Pacific Grove, back in garage sale mode.

"Is this the street we're looking for?" asks Huff.

"Can't you read?"

Huff shoots him a dark look. "My glasses are in the shop, goddamn it. Should I turn or not?"

"Just look for a bunch of cars out front. You can see that, can't you?"

"Yes, Turner, I can see that."

"Right there." Moe points. "St. Mary's-by-the-Sea."

The instant we pull to the curb, Moe throws open the passenger door and hurries toward the church. Emerging from the driver's side, Huff watches the scrawny form hurrying ahead, dressed as usual in not quite well-fitting thrift store jacket and khakis. "He does that every time. A complete lack of breeding."

By the time we reach the church, Moe is already in spirited conversation with the elderly woman seated at a table in front. "Look at this," he indignantly calls our way, "they're charging four bucks to get in!"

"It's not a regular sale," explains the woman. "There are antiques in there."

"Well, I'm an antique; I should get in for nothing."

The woman laughs. "So am I—and it's still four dollars."

"Well," Moe says, starting back to the car, "it sure doesn't sound very Christian to me."

Back in the passenger seat, Moe suddenly picks up, "What do you mean your glasses are in the shop?"

"Getting the frames repaired. I have frames I like very much, but they always want to sell you new ones at excessive rates."

"You should let me get you glasses over at the Navy School; it's a lot cheaper."

"That's not the point, goddammit." In fact, having long ago made some canny investments in local real estate, Huff has plenty of money; and among other good works, he subsidizes the educations of several students at Monterey Peninsula College. "It's a matter of principle."

"Well," presses Moe, "you can see now, can't you?"

"Oh, I can make out all right." He pats his breast pocket. "If I have to, I have an old pair of smoked glasses I can use."

"What you oughta do is get your eyes fixed up with that danged operation."

"Hardly worth the bother. I'm in that stage known as predecomposition."

"You have macular degeneration, is it?"

His friend nods. "I'm told it's from malnutrition during my POW experience."

"I thought you wore glasses ever since you were a kid."

"True, but that seems to have greatly accelerated the process." He falls silent a moment, then softly chuckles. "I'll never forget the first day I showed up at school with my glasses on—I must've been thirteen— and finding myself greeted with"—he lets out an amiable bellow— " 'Hello, Four-eyes!' "

Moe laughs. "That's how it was, all right. We had a boy in my crowd with one eye; we used to call him Good Eye. Another guy was crippled; we called him Crip."

What, I ask, was the origin of his own nickname?

"Oh, you know, a circus came to town, and there was this sideshow guy called Moe-Joe the Dog-Faced Boy."

"Your friends noticed the resemblance . . ."

"Right. That's just how it was; no one's feelings got hurt." He pauses thoughtfully. "I'll tell you what I'm grateful for, that women aren't like men that way—they don't immediately size you up based on looks. If they did, I'd've been sunk."

At the next sale, also in Pacific Grove, there's all manner of stuff to be had, since the house has just been sold and the family is relocating to Arizona. Almost immediately, Moe spots an old, banged-up, gas-driven pump. A sticker indicates it is priced at seven dollars.

"I'll give you two bucks for it," he tells the woman in charge.

She seems momentarily stunned by the offer, but it's getting late in the morning and you can be pretty sure this is an item that hasn't aroused much interest.

"Make it three," she counters.

"How 'bout two?"

"How 'bout two-fifty?"

"Boy," he says, reaching into his pocket, "you are a hard woman." He pauses, pointing to a second pump. "You gonna give me both of them?"

Within a few minutes, Huff is back in the car, with an oversized children's book he's bought about the American Revolution. "I have a little grandson now," he says, "and I've started reading to him about history. Eight years old—still in the pictorial stage."

He starts flipping through the book, pausing at an illustration of revolutionary soldiers freezing at Valley Forge. "Look at that," he says softly, "sonsovbitches had rags for shoes." He glances up. "Turner's probably struck up a conversation with some poor soul. That, or he's trying to skin somebody—I know all the characteristics." He laughs. "I swear, it's so damn embarrassing; I've caught him haggling for twenty minutes over a dollar purchase. When he goes, it's going to be the garage sale to end all garage sales."

I remark that my mother-in-law seems to feel overwhelmed by all the stuff in and around their house. Over the years, Moe's purchases at sales like these have run from the valuable and semi-valuable (china, porcelain and crystal, silver sets, antique clocks, Civil War swords, and oriental prints) to the sort of thing most people would set on the curb to be hauled away (crummy broken clocks, cheap prints, kitschy brass "artwork," an array of plaster busts and gargoyles). But it is the Turner backyard that truly reveals Moe in all his loony, obsessional glory. Walk out there into the bright California sunshine, and you're confronted with a mini-slum, consisting of structures of various sizes and materials—from the two-story wooden A-frame to an array of ramshackle, Plexiglas-topped sheds—as well as a trailer (with four flat tires) and an old sailboat sitting permanently on blocks. All of them, even the sailboat, are packed nearly to bursting. From time to time, the objects of his desire have shifted. The old toaster ovens stacked in piles and the barrels of electric shavers are no longer nearly so prized as the bread makers, gelato machines, and microwave ovens of more recent vintage.

The rest of the family tends to regard Moe's monomania with affectionate despair. On her last visit home to Monterey, my wife's younger sister presented her father with a sixteen-by-sixteen-inch tote bag on which she'd written in bold Magic Marker:

MOE'S OFFICIAL TAG SALE BAG

IF IT FITS IN HERE: OK

IF NOT: FORGET IT!

NO MORE:

Toaster ovens

Cuisinarts

Dehydraters

Electric griddles

Boats

Pots & pans

"Clever" gadgets you plug in

Weird things you don't know what they do

Out-of-date travel guides

Outdated computer software

And we haven't even gotten to the books. A compulsive reader, interested in absolutely everything, from the latest developments in math and physics to the lives of politicians and musicians to the collected wisdom of Dear Abby, on an average day Moe reads, or at least closely skims, six or eight volumes. Better known at the Monterey Public Library than some of the people who work there, he also has an immense private collection, randomly housed everywhere from the aforementioned trailer to cardboard boxes in the corner of the dining room.

True enough, once in a great while, Moe actually strikes pay dirt. Whenever someone starts giving him too much guff about his purchases, he will raise his most spectacular triumph: the time he shelled out one dollar for an oil painting that turned out to be by the California impressionist Benjamin Brown and worth more than twenty thousand dollars!

Still, observes Huff, even including that, "after all these years of judicious purchases, he'll still leave a net loss." Huff shakes his head in mock despair. "Good old Benny"—my mother-in-law's nickname, short for Ruth Mary Benedict—"she says her first call will be to the Goodwill, her next to the undertaker. Except she'll probably find she'll have to pay people to haul most of it away." He chuckles. "What a grand fellow."

For all his gruffness and reticence, indeed, because of it, at moments like this the tenderness Huff feels for my in-laws is striking. Neither Boyd nor Moe ever mentions the fact, but during the couple of years Huff's first wife, Martha, was institutionalized with Alzheimer's at a Catholic facility close to my in-laws, he came by their home for lunch after visiting her almost every day. Boyd's new wife, Beverly, tells me Huff believes it was only through the grace of the Turners that he survived that trying time well fed and healthy.

"Oh, Jesus," exclaims Huff now, as Moe appears from around the corner of the house, arms full, "is that a goddamn sandwich maker he's got? And—what's that—a goddamn crab net?!" He rolls down his window. "Stick that stuff in the trunk, Turner. I don't want it in the backseat."

A moment later, Moe climbs inside. "I got some pretty useful stuff there."

"We were just talking about Benny," reports his friend, "and wondering how in hell she manages to put up with you. Saint Benny—that's what Beverly calls her."

"It's true," agrees Moe. "If there's a heaven, no question that's where she's going. Unfortunately for her, there's not."

"You don't know everything, Turner," observes Boyd mildly. Though hardly dogmatic in spiritual matters, Huff, raised a Catholic and educated by Jesuits, remains loyal to the Church and its tenets.

"I sure as heck know that," counters Moe, the scientist and cynic. "When you die, that's all there is to it—it's just like a dead leaf falling off a tree. You really think this guy sat around up there for fifteen billion years waiting for us bunch of idiots to start running around on this little speck in the universe called earth?"

"This *guy*? You mean God?"

Moe nods decisively. "Lemme ask you this: We have DNA that's ninety-nine percent the same as chimpanzees—you think chimpanzees have a soul?"

"The question is, 'Do you?' " He pauses. "I trust you don't talk this way to your bride."

"I never talk down the Church—if it makes her feel good, then okay. I'm live and let live."

Boyd turns my way. "He ever tell you he used to teach Sunday school when he was in college?" He laughs. "Is that what turned you off to religion, Turner, your Sunday school experience?

"I can't believe I ever did that—I was only trying to make an impression on a girl who was in the Presbyterian Church."

"You didn't get her, obviously."

"That's beside the point." Moe pauses a moment; he has something more important on his mind. "You know that house back there?" he says, nodding vaguely in the direction of the one we just left. "Can you believe they sold it for eight hundred fifty thousand dollars?!"

"When it comes to real estate around here, I can believe anything."

Moe shakes his head. "I paid fifteen for my house. I bet it's worth five hundred now."

"Remember that superb lot I got you," asks Huff, "that half-acre lot with a view up the valley? What'd you sell that for?"

"Twice what I paid for it."

"Oh, yes . . . ?" his friend presses.

"I bought it for twenty-five hundred and sold it for five thousand."

Huff laughs. "Got any idea what that'd be worth now?" Over the past twenty years real estate on the Monterey Peninsula has soared in value as dizzyingly as anywhere on the planet.

"I don't want to talk about it."

"Maybe half a million." He pauses for effect, then taunts. "We're heading over that way—I'll point it out."

Moe's former lot, now part of a wealthy residential district, is only one of local points of interest they show me over the next couple of hours, in what continues to double as an impromptu guided tour of this most breathtakingly beautiful corner of the world.

"See there?" notes Moe at one point as we cruise down Asilomar Boulevard, the cypresses hauntingly bent against the wind on one side of the road, the wild, boulder-strewn Pacific on the other. "That's Point Lobos, we go walking around there sometimes, don't we, Boyd?"

"Goddamn lovely, don't you think? From across the bay, it looks like a big crocodile."

Moe snorts. "Guys go out here in wet suits—they're always hauling out some idiot. Dimwits have no understanding of the power of nature." He nods vaguely toward the kite flyers on the nearby beach. "Tell you what I'd like to do—hang gliding."

Huff shoots him a skeptical look. "Excellent plan, Turner. I'll help pick up the pieces."

"Well, I used to drive a motorcycle, didn't I?"

"Christ, that was in the nineteen forties. But go right ahead."

"Maybe I will."

Ignoring this, Huff points. "All these homes over there on the other side of the road are new. Vacation homes, owned by people from San Francisco and San Jose. You should've seen it around here in the early fifties."

Though very much a capitalist, Huff is distressed by the seeming inability of so many to grasp what has been lost in the mania for expansion.

"And now," he adds, "they're going after the farmland. That's one of the great charms of this area, how the farmland comes right up to the town. If the heirs of enough of the present owners start selling off, pretty soon it'll be just like Santa Barbara."

In short order we turn onto hilly Seventeen Mile Drive, heading through fragrant woods of thick pine.

"Now we're going up toward Carmel," says Huff. "That's where my boys grew up. I used to be very active in the schools over there."

"That so?" says Moe.

"Carmel High was a wonderful place then—that was before all these doctors of education got in there to try out all their theories. They had a classical program, lots of mathematics, lots of English, a wonderful history department. Jerry got just a magnificent education."

Huff talks fairly often about Jerry, his now fifty-five-year-old son, living in a halfway house for schizophrenics in San Jose; far less about Andy, Jerry's younger brother, who died at fifteen in a shooting accident in their Carmel Valley home.

"Jerry was quite an athlete," says Moe.

"Yes, he was. He put together a superb record as a pitcher. We had a regular pitcher's mound and plate out in the backyard. When I got home from work, it used to be my chore to go out there and catch him for about an hour."

"Didn't he also pitch in college? For Arizona?"

"For the freshman team. Before he got sick." Huff smiles. "You know, back when Jerry was in high school, I'd occasionally have a student in one of my classes at the Navy School who'd played baseball at Annapolis. I'd always make a point of having them over for dinner."

"In other words, you'd bribe 'em into goin' out there to coach Jerry."

"Didn't have to bribe 'em; they enjoyed it. Jerry had real talent. Excellent fastball, good curve. He had all sorts of possibilities." He smiles. "Remember the time he tried to kiss Priscilla, Turner?"

"Did he?" The reference is to my wife.

"Christ, yes! In the woods; he must've been about fifteen. Boy, did she ever get mad!" He laughs. "But, hell, you gotta stick your neck out, gotta take some risks. If you're passive, they'll have no respect for you."

"That's true."

Boyd is silent for a long moment. "Why don't we head over to Carmel Valley, show him where the group got started?"

Moe nods. "We can stop at Cooper's. I got a couple of books here for him."

"God, no! Don't you think the Coopers are on to you? You always come right at lunchtime!"

"I won't eat anything; I just want to give him these books."

"You know they'll invite us in."

"Well, then," says Moe, not missing a beat, "you're gonna have to pull over to that food store up over the hill so I can pick up something to cook up at home." Catching Huff's glance, he chuckles. "Boy, oh boy, if looks could kill, I'd be dead as a doornail."

A few minutes later we pull into the parking lot of the small food market, and Moe heads inside.

"You ever meet Jerry?" asks Huff after a moment.

I tell him I haven't.

"Jesus, he was so goddamn promising before that schizophrenia hit. They just thought the world of him in Arizona. I try to make it up to San Jose every couple of weeks." Glancing out the window, he sees Moe heading back to the car with a shopping bag. "You might want to go up there sometime; he'd enjoy that."

"Go where?" asks Moe, getting back in the car.

"To see Jerry."

"He still comes down here sometimes, doesn't he?"

"They've limited it to twice a year, July and Christmas. Which is just as well. Beverly's wonderful with Jerry, but I recognize it can be a strain."

Moe nods. "She's a great gal, that wife of yours—the life of the party."

"That she is," agrees his friend, chuckling. He pulls the car back onto Seventeen Mile Drive. "What's that you got?"

Reaching into his shopping bag, Moe pulls out a shrink-wrapped tray of chicken legs. "You gonna come by my place for lunch?"

"Fine. After Carmel Valley."

"Boy, oh boy," says Moe, shaking his head, "you're just lucky I don't tote up all the lunches I give you at my house."

"If you did, I might have to present you with the bill for hauling you around all these years."

"God, just the way you go through my homemade plum jam!"

"Turner, I won't insult you by mentioning all the dinners I've treated you to over at the Yacht Club."

"You got me there. It sure is neat over at the Yacht Club."

Ten minutes later, as we turn onto Carmel Valley Road, Huff at last resumes the story of the origins of the Girl Watchers. "Like I was saying, it was the brainchild of Morton Buck. Mort was in public relations in New York, retired out here, and started buying real estate in the valley, which you could get for a song. I met him down at the Little League." He laughs. "Mort had no children of his own—he was there as an observer—so we elected him league president. After a while, Buck and I and this other fellow, Ed Hogan, started to go to lunch once a week at Las Laurales, just the three of us. I mentioned it around the Navy School, and after a while, some of the other fellows started coming. Not much of a story, really. But it's been a helluva good time."

"Buck had a wonderful wife," says Moe, "but he dumped her for someone else's wife."

"She was a pill, that second wife," mutters Huff. He suddenly makes a sharp right, heading down a drive. "That's Buck's place right there."

We stop at a gate flanked by a pair of imposing stone pillars. A hundred or so yards beyond it is a sprawling, single-story white home shaded by oaks, the surrounding yard meticulously landscaped. Huff cuts the motor and surveys the scene.

"Still a beautiful place," he observes.

"Can you believe it? No children! Two people in a house like that!"

"Okay, time to be heading back."

"Ole Mort," muses Moe, still gazing at the house, "we saw him the day before he died, didn't we, Boyd?"

"We did," he says softly.

"An' Huff here tells him, 'Be sure to say hello to my son Andy when you get there.' Buck just looked at you and answered, 'You don't believe that nonsense, do you?' "

" 'Don't give me that nonsense,' that's what he said." Huff gives a quiet laugh and starts the motor. "Let's get moving. It'll take you some time to cook up that chicken, Turner."

CHAPTER 3

I wanted to be a real American kid—not a frightened

outsider, an American manqué, like my father was.

—STUART WALZER

RED CROSS STATION DURING THE BATTLE OF THE BULGE. WALZER IS
AT CENTER, BETWEEN THE SOLDIER IN THE RED CROSS HELMET
AND THE WOMAN.

Stuart Walzer, the most recent member of the group, is also in some
ways the most unlikely. Six years ago, having recently retired to Carmel,
he was strolling on the beach minding his own business when he found
himself waylaid by a skinny old guy with wild hair and an Arkansas
accent.

Moe had spotted Walzer's T-shirt: "So Many Books, So Little Time."

"For Moe, that T-shirt was like a red flag," recalls Walzer, laughing. "When he learned I really was an avid reader, he saw me as a potential buddy. When he found out I was Jewish, that pretty much sealed the deal. He's totally fascinated with Jews."

The intensity of the connection Walzer soon made with the Girl Watchers surprised even him. On the face of it, his is a classic American success story—an insecure kid from Chicago pulls himself together, goes to top colleges, marries the love of his life, and enjoys a long and lucrative career—but Walzer admits it never quite felt that way. To the contrary, like so many successful, assimilated children of immigrants, he never fully ceased seeing himself as an outsider; the attitudes and ideas with which he came of age, even more than the distinctive customs and cuisine, having left him permanently estranged from the larger culture.

One afternoon, early on in my research, I decide to get Walzer together with Boyd for lunch, with Moe tagging along for color commentary. The idea is to talk about their war experiences, and specifically the Battle of the Bulge, a pivotal moment in both their lives.

"It's funny," Walzer is saying instead, moments after we sit down in a Chinese restaurant called the Happy Dragon, "but only now, in my seventies, with this group, do I feel accepted as a real American."

"As a 'real American,' you say?" asks Huff, genuinely baffled.

Then, again, why wouldn't he be? For Boyd, highly practical and utterly without prejudice, what he is hearing lacks all sense and logic. After all, the man before him is as American as anyone.

"I'm just saying most of you guys have led classic American lives," explains Stuart, "some of your families go back before the Revolution. Our backgrounds couldn't be more disparate; we have different political and social views." He turns to Boyd. "I remember the first time I asked what you thought of gun control."

"Let's not even start with that—my father was a gun dealer."

Walzer smiles. "Same thing you said the last time."

I get it, even if the others at the table probably never quite will. Even as the *grand*child of immigrants, raised in the overwhelmingly Jewish suburbs of New York in the fifties and sixties, I grew up with that sense of being distinctly apart from the larger culture, the feelings of pride and superiority all jumbled up with resentment and envy; this despite the fact I suffered zero actual discrimination and a mere handful of modest slights.

Those lingering feelings of exclusion, common as they are to Jews and other assimilated and largely privileged ethnic and religious groups, may seem hardly worth noting in a culture still grappling with the volatile issue of race, but they also play a role in undermining Americans' view of themselves as a coherent whole. I grew up believing, for instance, that Republicans were not only wrong but evil and that any white with a southern accent was undoubtably a moron and on some level to be feared. A lot of people I know still feel that way; all the while, thinking themselves open-minded and tolerant.

In my case—and, I'm getting the impression, in Stuart's also—the change in attitude was very much helped along by Moe, a man capable of obliterating all preconceptions about WASPs and southerners and, for that matter, scientists, every time he opens his mouth.

"But what I've found with this group," Stuart adds now, "is that what we share transcends all the rest."

He is talking mainly about the values they have in common, but to a great extent those are grounded in a wealth of shared experiences. The war comes up almost every time any of the Girl Watchers get together, the universal touchstone, and it doesn't take us long to get there today; specifically, back to the Ardennes Forest on that December nearly sixty years ago when both Stuart and Boyd were with the 106th Infantry, virtually within shouting distance.

For me, as for many kids of the postwar generation, this World War II battlefield stuff is an endless source of fascination—probably a lot more than men like this can understand. We grew up playing at *being* them; dressing in makeshift GI fatigues and carrying cowboy rifles as we dove into mud puddle foxholes and fearlessly took the hills behind our suburban homes. Like Winston Churchill, who sharpened his strategic skills on his nursery floor by moving to the attack brigades of superbly crafted Queen's Grenadiers and Highland Fusiliers, we maneuvered vast armies of green men of molded plastic, deftly placing the guys with flame throwers up front and the guys with bazookas behind, spaced just so. We watched Vic Morrow in *Combat* on Tuesdays (passing up *Laramie* and Marshal Dillon) and (at least us true aficionados) *The Gallant Men* on Saturdays; knowing that while the good guys would take a few hits, in the end it was always the Nazis who bit the dust.

Even during the sixties, when so many of us were in the streets protesting Vietnam, the lessons we absorbed a decade earlier in our backyards and bedrooms and dens remained very much with us. Indeed, in our incredible self-regard, we liked to say we were incensed precisely because America—and our elders!—had so cavalierly deserted the very principles of decency and fair play (the concept of fighting for the little guy and the moral right) we had been duped into so completely taking to heart!

This sounds silly in retrospect, but it is also the truth; and it is how human beings come to be who they are. Without question, World War II had everything to do with turning me into both an idealist and a history buff; both of which, to a greater or lesser extent, I remain.

And of all the episodes of that war, none is so stirring as the Battle of the Bulge. It is a great and noble tale. There were the Americans, following the Herculean effort of D-Day and the breakout from the beaches, seemingly invincible, moving inexorably on Germany. But— also typically American—we are a bit arrogant, convinced the longed-for victory has basically already been won. So we are caught short when the enemy launches his surprise attack, ripping through our thin lines in the forest, murderously ruthless and brutal, sending his best English speakers into our ranks in American uniforms to mislead and sow confusion, and we are sent reeling. Then the heart of the story: the recovery. The Americans rally. Against all odds, they hold. When the Germans surround the key town of Bastogne and demand the Americans' surrender, Brigadier General Anthony McAuliffe's one-word answer shows all the respect they would have gotten from the Little Rascals: "Nuts!" And this is followed by the message to McAuliffe from General Patton—"Xmas Eve present coming up"—as he relentlessly drives his Third Army at breakneck speed, arriving to break the siege like the cavalry in a John Ford movie (and, ultimately, the one scripted by Francis Ford Coppola about Patton himself). Now, finally, the last Christmas miracle—and the final nail in the Nazi coffin—as the skies clear, allowing Allied aircraft to once again assert their dominance in the skies.

With the Girl Watchers I play it cool, but this is incredible stuff! The idea that these guys were there still gives me a thrill. It's like getting to sit down with veterans of the Battle of Bunker Hill in 1830 or the Battle of Gettysburg in 1915. My kids, and certainly theirs, will surely wonder why more of us didn't seize the chance.

Moe—reacting to Stuart's "outsider" ruminations—lurches us toward the subject of the battle now.

"Were you afraid of being captured? As a Jew, I mean."

Walzer gives what I will come to think of as his Moe smile, at once startled and, given his own affection for candor, appreciative. "Well, Moe, it wasn't the most pleasant possibility I could think of. We were already hearing rumors about the camps—nothing solid, but what we heard wasn't encouraging. So the question became, should you throw away your dog tags? 'Cause they had a big *H* on them, for *Hebrew*."

"What would you have done?" I ask, having wondered the same thing myself.

"I don't know; I never had to make that choice. But I had a Jewish roommate after the war who got captured. He kept his dog tags and was treated okay."

"How about in the hundred and sixth?" asks Huff, who was a captain in the division where Walzer was a lowly PFC. "You run into much anti-Semitism there?"

"Oh, sure. There was even some pro-German sentiment among our guys."

"You're kidding!" exclaims Moe.

Walzer smiles. "Well, maybe that's overstating it—let's just say they *understood* the German position. I mean, no one was going to shoot you in the back because you were a Jew—"

"Actually," I cut in, "a friend of mine's father was threatened *exactly* that way."

"Really?" exclaims Moe, surprised and delighted.

"Someone I knew when I was a kid. His dad was part of the first wave at Normandy, and the son, Jimmy, used to tell about how, a couple of days before the invasion, his father overheard one of his men boast, 'When we hit the beach, I'm gonna shoot that Jew lieutenant in the back.' He said his dad got out of his tent, took off his officer's insignia, and beat the crap out of the guy. Then later, on the beach, he saved the same guy's life."

"The father told him this, did he?" inquires Boyd, dubious.

"Actually, no, his uncle. His father never talked about the war."

In fact, that was an intriguing angle all its own. Jimmy probably had the most difficult relationship with his father of any kid I knew. Even I, a fellow self-absorbed kid, couldn't help but notice how awkward Mr. Fisher was at communication and, a couple of times, how scarily quick to anger; a stunning contrast with my own father who, ten years older, had remained on the home front during the war, working with damaged families as a psychiatric social worker. But those questions—the enduring emotional impact of the war, its effect on their performance as fathers—are best left for another conversation.

"I, for one, absolutely believe it," says Walzer. "Because there was definitely real hostility."

"Did that surprise you?"

"At the time? Not a bit." He stops, takes a bite of moo-shu pork. "Of course, my parents were horrified I was in a combat division to start with. My father couldn't believe I would volunteer for the infantry. 'Why the infantry?' he kept asking. 'Why you of all people?' "

"Was he in the First War?" asks Huff.

"In the navy. He worked in the cafeteria at the Great Lakes Training School, and he thought I should try and get a cafeteria job also."

Huff cracks up. "Helluva dangerous place to be! Lighting off steaks!"

"Let's just say he wasn't the most assertive guy around—he allowed everyone to walk over him, starting with his wife. And there were so many things about this country and its people he didn't get. He looked down on physical labor; he couldn't even begin to conceive why anyone would be interested in sports. In general, he was afraid to ever put himself on the line in any meaningful way. I consciously rejected all that. From a very early age I knew I didn't want to be like my father." He pauses. "He never knew how terribly embarrassed I'd always been by him and the cafeteria."

"You seem to still feel pretty strongly about it," I say. While I'm used to hearing younger men go on about their fathers—my own self-absorbed peers have turned the complex and often troubled father-son bond into a whole new field of academic study, coining phrases like *father hunger* and discovering a tribe in New Guinea where the word for *father* translates as "stranger"—I don't think I've ever heard anyone of his generation talk this way.

"Well, you know, it's a funny thing," says Walzer, "but just because you get older, it doesn't mean you become impervious to those feelings. I think our relationships with our fathers, or lack thereof, shape almost all our lives. We either seek to emulate them or in important ways react against them."

"So that's how come you joined the infantry?" says Moe, impatient to get back to the meat of the story.

He nods. "Because I wanted to be a real American kid—not a frightened outsider, an American manqué, like my father was."

"Well, I'm sure you found the infantry far more congenial," says Huff.

"Actually, friendship was hard for me," says Stuart. "I was a bookish kind of guy. I was also very dyslexic, which didn't help matters."

"And you were a Jew," points out Moe.

"Yes, Moe, that's true, too."

"Did some of the other men used to give you a hard time?" asks Huff.

"A few. There was one guy in my company named Calvin Pigg, a big lanky farm boy from West Virginia, must've been about six-two. That was his real name, not a nickname. He really had it in for me. He'd stomp on the back of my feet and say things about New York. Well I wasn't from New York—I kept saying I'm from Chicago—but I knew what he meant: You New York Jew. Well, finally he stomped on my heels one day—this was when we were still training in England— and I just womped him as hard as I could. The sergeant quickly separated us with, 'Okay, you guys are going into the ring.' I guess they didn't want me to get killed right then, 'cause"—he laughs—"they were saving me for later, when we went into combat. Anyway, Calvin and I went round and round; we really slugged it out for about three-quarters of an hour. And even though he was much bigger than me, I did all right; I really got in some good licks. I ended up with a big shiner, but Calvin didn't look so good either. It was the first time I really saw how wiry and tough I'd become in training. And from then on he never bothered me.

"Of course, pretty soon after that we went into combat. The next time I saw Calvin Pigg close up, we were standing about three or four feet apart in the woods—somehow we'd come across one another in the confusion of the battle—and there was a tree burst, shrapnel every-where. See, when you're in a woods and the shells come down in the trees, they send a tremendous scattering of shrapnel. I didn't get touched, not a scratch, but Calvin's face came out bloody all over. God's will, you see. And he looked at me with the greatest surprise—as if *I'd* done it."

Everyone laughs.

"I was chasing girls in Washington at the time—that was my war," notes Moe matter-of-factly. "And a losing war, at that."

"I can't tell you how much it hurts when you say that," says Walzer. "God, it was cold out in the Ardennes—the coldest winter in something like fifty years."

In fact, the extreme cold and overcast skies were key elements in the extraordinary German successes early on, not only rendering useless the massive Allied air superiority but providing cover for the sneak attack. And it lasted day after day after day—so long that Patton at last ordered the Third Army chief chaplain to compose his famous prayer requesting divine intercession for relief from the elements.

Almighty and most merciful Father, we humbly beseech Thee, of Thy great goodness, to restrain these immoderate rains with which we have had to contend. Grant us fair weather for Battle. Graciously hearken to us as soldiers who call upon Thee that, armed with Thy power, we may advance from victory to victory, and crush the oppression and wickedness of our enemies and establish Thy justice among men and nations."

"Wet and cold," moans Huff, wincing at the memory, "wet and cold. Jesus Christ, we had wet feet for months. One of the most glorious moments of the war was the day they delivered a load of galoshes."

"Man, I wouldn't've lasted five minutes over there," says Moe. "I saw something on TV where they said over in Europe they had fifty thousand cases of trench foot. I mean, these guys' feet were just rotting away."

"That's right," says Boyd, "I saw it all around. Of course, when it got cold, the advantage was the bodies didn't rot, which kept the smell tolerable."

"Exactly," agrees Walzer, "they'd freeze. You'd come to a crossroads and see a German corpse set up to direct traffic, one arm pointing this way, one pointing the other."

"Of course, for the week or so before the attack, my unit was living pretty well. We were a reconnaissance unit, so we were right up front, occupying what had formerly been German dugouts." He smiles Walzer's way. "It was marvelous, all warm and toasty in this wonderful, concrete German dugout."

"Didn't you see some German tanks before the attack?"

"Christ, don't get me started. See, my unit was involved in what they called 'deep range patrolling,' slipping behind German lines to find out where their deployments were. So there we are, sneaking around the woods, and suddenly, I'll never forget, maybe a hundred yards away, dead ahead in the trees, is a goddamn tank park! About twenty Tiger tanks, great big bastards with eighty-eight-millimeter guns! Christ, they were sitting ducks, a perfect setup for artillery fire. So we made our way back, and I told Craig, our commanding officer—wonderful fellow, ROTC product from Maine—and he called in the report to headquarters. And—can you believe this?—they wouldn't give our artillery permission to fire! Said they'd used up their ration for that day. Christ almighty! I can still hear Craig screaming. 'You dumb sonsovbitches! What the hell are you thinking?!'" Huff gives a grim laugh. "The very next day they hit us with those same tanks."

"December sixteenth," says Walzer. He pauses. "Even now it's hard to describe the psychological impact of that offensive. Everybody thought the Germans were done for, including us."

"They were smart cookies," says Moe, "you have to give them that."

"And we weren't," says Huff, still miffed a half century later. "Hell, we could've wiped out those tanks so damn easily."

"How far apart you guys figure you were?" I ask.

"A mile, if that," says Huff.

"God, what a morning that was. We woke up with the ground shaking like the world was coming to an end," recalls Walzer. "Our guys were in dugouts in the ground—we'd chopped down trees and put logs over them—and it took a while before it occurred to us: Jesus, we could be entombed down here! So I grabbed my rifle and boots and scampered out. It was maybe six A.M., still dark out, and I didn't have my boots laced, and they were jingling—you know, those little wire snaps they had on them all up and down?"

"Oh, Christ . . ."

"You got it—all the guys start screaming, 'Your goddamn boots are gonna bring down fire on us!' So I lace them up, and I'm running around, trying to figure out what to do, and almost immediately we see the Germans coming at us out of the mists, these ghostly figures . . ."

"Wearing those white uniforms," says Huff softly, "those snowsuits of theirs . . ."

"I mean, the fog hanging over everything. It was so tremendously eerie."

"Were you scared?" I ask.

"You bet your life I was scared! But you're *always* scared. You've been scared from the moment the artillery started. As soon as you get anywhere near the front, you have a physical reaction—you hear those guns going off, and there's a knot in your solar plexus that never goes away. Ever. It was there throughout the battle.

"But, you know, I try to reconstruct the battle and I can't, not with any real precision. I mean, sure, I've read a lot about it since; I can give you the historical facts: it started on the sixteenth, and those of our company who got out reached St.-Vith on the twentieth. But being in the middle of it, most of what happened in between was just wandering through the woods, trying to stay alive. Since I had no maps, most of the time I had no idea where I was. And sometimes even now I'll ask myself, 'What did we eat? Where did we get our rations?' Basically, I had a worm's-eye view of the battle, constantly diving and hitting the ground. One thing I can do is summon up the texture of grass poking through the snow. And of course I vividly remember isolated episodes. But even with those, it's almost like I dreamed them or read about them in a book, like they happened to someone else."

"What kind of episodes?"

"I mean, at one point I went off with a lieutenant to reconnoiter, and we got cut off from our unit. That night, he and I found a barn and grabbed a couple of hours' sleep in the loft. And when I woke up, there's the lieutenant at this little window, firing. Looking over his shoulder, I see a whole German column going by, with horses pulling their artillery! So I start screaming at the guy, 'For God's sake, what are you doing? We've gotta get out of here!' And just as their artillery zeroes in on the barn, we escape out the front door."

"That lieutenant sounds like a fairly dim bulb," observes Moe.

"Well, you know, you don't always act rationally in battle. I remember at one point they were pouring shells down on us—'screaming meanies,' those early rockets they'd developed—and I heard these terrible screams, like a wild animal screaming in agony—and then I realized it was me."

"Part of that is to equalize the pressure on your ears," says Huff.

"That's true; they say it's partly involuntary. Anyway, I liked the lieutenant; he was a good guy. He was in his thirties, which to us was ancient—anyone over twenty-five immediately got called Pops."

"You were older than that, weren't you, Boyd?" teases Moe. "Anybody ever call you that?"

"Not to my certain knowledge. They wouldn't dare."

The bill has arrived, and the four of us settle up. The plan is that we'll head back to Moe's for dessert.

"There's one other night that really stuck with me," adds Walzer, "probably the worst night of my life." He pauses as the waiter scoops up the cash from the table and heads for the register. "It's raining and sleeting like crazy, and I'm stuck in my foxhole, and I can't come up because there are Germans all over the place. And suddenly these huge Tiger tanks start rumbling by. It was just this awful combination of bone-chilling cold and pure dread. Believe me, there really *are* no atheists in foxholes: I'd learned the Twenty-third Psalm in Sunday school and never paid much attention to it, but now I just kept repeating it over and over. There was no question in my mind I was going to die that night. My parents weren't going to have a son; I wasn't going to have a wife or kids; it was all about to stop right there. I was just waiting to get ground down and become part of the clay in that hole." He stops. "But, I have to tell you, at the same time, I also think of it as a great moment in my life. I mean that. Because it gave me a tremendous sense of perspective. Everything since then, every moment I've lived, everything I've experienced, has been pure gravy."

✦ CHAPTER 4 ✦

Huff was . . . a real crack shot, from all the hunting he
used to do. One time, up in Alaska, he got a bear with one
shot, which really paid off in the war.

—MOE TURNER

HUFF PREPARES FOR WAR, ALASKA, 1938.

"I got some ice cream from Alaska," says Moe, as we emerge from
Huff's Daewoo before my in-laws' home, "I think you're gonna really
like it!"

"Alaskan ice cream?" says Huff. "Christ, Turner, where in hell did
you come up with that?"

"Cooper told me about it."

Cooper. No further explanation required.

"I'll be damned," Huff exclaims five minutes later, as the four of us sit at my in-laws' dining room table, "this stuff *is* good."

"Oh, ye of little faith!" proclaims Moe.

"I never doubted, Moe," says Stuart. "Alaska, ice cream—it all makes sense." He turns to Huff. "So how, exactly, did you get captured, anyway? Because I'm still sort of amazed I wasn't."

"Oh, hell, there was almost no way around it. Those goddamn tanks of theirs cut off our guys in enveloping thrusts—they got between us and the retreating American lines. So, Christ, here we were, sitting ducks."

"They started mortaring you, did they?" asks Moe.

"A creeping barrage, forcing us forward over a hill. We'd learned about this back in England when we studied their tactics, so we knew precisely what they were doing. It was what they called 'a reverse slope situation.' They force you forward, then open up with heavy machine guns. Damn effective. The whole damn outfit was pinned down, maybe three hundred of us, Jesus Christ, I'll never forget as long as I live— they'd been reforesting the side of this hill with all these little fir trees, maybe four feet high, and the bullets were shearing off the tops of these things, with all these branches and twigs raining down on you."

Walzer nods. "Right, you're lying there, and it becomes so surreal and disjointed that your mind can't grasp it. You don't even know if you've been hit."

"There was one guy in our unit who, whenever we came under fire, he'd just start crying and bawling," says Huff, "and needless to say he started up now. I remember Craig snapping at him to shut up."

Craig—just Craig, never a first name. Boyd will mention him a number of times over the coming months, always with deep appreciation, for the guy embodied the quality he still most admires all these years later: a no-bullshit, full-speed-ahead approach to completing the task at hand.

"I myself was very fast at digging holes," continues Boyd, "so now this guy creeps over and tries to take my hole from me. Hell, I kicked him out. It wasn't that good a hole, but it was the only one I had!"

"We also had guys that cracked," says Walzer. "To me that was the one thing scarier than dying. I remember in St.-Vith, there was a fierce tank battle going on, all hell breaking loose, and in the middle of it there were some of our guys being led out with these blank expressions, just absolutely stony-eyed, and other guys were sneering at them, saying, "they're Section Eights." We just felt absolute contempt; we were sure they were faking it. But of course now we know it was real."

"Well, that's fine," says Huff, "but I'd had problems with this hole-stealing sonovabitch long before this. Earlier, back in France, we were attacking some village, and he was supposed to provide covering fire. Instead, he crawled into a goddamn ditch, which really put us in a spot! Afterward I beat the hell out of him."

"You did?" exclaims Moe, impressed. "You get in trouble?"

"Oh, hell, he reported me for abusive actions by an officer. When I heard about it, I beat him up again. Sonovabitch could've got us *all* killed!"

"You were pretty tough, I'll give you that," says Moe appreciatively. He turns to me. "Huff was also a real crack shot, from all the hunting he used to do. One time up in Alaska he got a bear with one shot, which really paid off in the war."

"Oh, Christ, it's no big deal. I was working up there as a surveyor, and this black bear came out of hibernation, half starved and just mean as hell. I got him in the eye from about twenty feet."

"It only took you one shot, too, to get that German major in the staff car."

"Enough, Turner. I'm telling about the Germans who were hunting *us*. So, anyway, there we are stuck on this hill—and in case we get any ideas about getting away, they start dropping in mortars right behind to encourage us to stay. And, dammit, that first volley killed Craig."

"How close was he to you?" asks Moe.

"Maybe ten feet away. Goddamn pity."

Given my own baby-boomer fixation with psychology, pop and otherwise, my tendency is to look for the emotions lurking beneath the surface, the hidden suggestions of hurt or desperation or sorrow (which, truth be told, most of the people my age don't really try all that hard to hide). Yet now, and not for the first time, I'm struck by how much, with Boyd, what you see is what you get. Sure, he cared about Craig, and always goes out of the way to give him his due, but there's no point dwelling on it.

If, indeed, in most such conversations among the Girl Watchers, moments that seem emotionally fraught get stepped on, or hurried past, or played for laughs, that merely reflects an unspoken consensus, alien to the contemporary mind, that the deepest feelings are and should be a very private thing; and, more, that the best way to make sure you never get anything done is to waste your time dwelling on them.

Huff turns to Walzer. "Didn't you find the German use of machine guns highly effective? Really, it was just marvelous."

For Huff, mechanical excellence is beyond ideology, "Christ, you really had to hand it to the bastards. They had the MG-forty-two, the most wonderful machine gun then in existence. They only had to screw the barrel in, and she was ready to go, so much more efficient than our air-cooled machine guns. They used an eight-man squad: one guy to carry the gun; three guys, usually great big ones, who all they did was carry ammunition; and the rest carried extra barrels, so if you burned out the gun, you just screwed in another barrel. And these things created a concentration of fire that was just incredible."

Stuart looks momentarily startled, unused to giving the Nazis credit for anything. "They'd had enough experience by then," he concedes dryly.

"But you got your guys out . . . ," prompts Moe.

"In a manner of speaking." Boyd laughs. "See, I still had my twenty men behind me, including Porter, the no-good, crying sonovabitch.

And while the rest of the regiment's being herded from behind by these mortars and some of 'em are starting to surrender, we get up real fast and head down the far side. We hit this little road and start moving down it, and we figure we're okay. But after maybe just half a mile, we run smack into a German unit. Christ, they saw us coming, covered us all, and started shouting, 'Hands up!' In English." He gives his heartiest laugh yet. " 'Hanzzup,' that's how they pronounced it. Just like they'd seen it in the movies. Christ, they were so young! It was like being taken prisoner by a bunch of high school kids."

Huff pauses for a long sip of coffee. "They started us marching back toward Germany. They marched us through villages and a number of larger towns. Christ, the Germans thought they were winning the war again; the elation was tremendous."

"For a while there, we weren't so sure they were wrong," observes Walzer.

"And as we're marching back, we see the German replacements coming up to the front in these big old European buses—incidentally, each with a big red cross painted on top."

"Those dirty bums," laughs Moe. "How were you holding up?"

"Damn fatigued and hungry as hell. The Germans took all our K rations—they adored our K rations—so I hadn't eaten for a day and a half. We went through one town, and here was this German girl standing on her doorstep eating an enormous cookie. So the guy next to me says, in his bastard high school German, *'Ich habe Hunger'*—I have hunger. She looked at him and said, *'Das ist gut.'* " He bursts out laughing at the memory. "Then, just to rub it in, right in our faces she took another enormous bite."

"They were not fond of us," says Walzer.

"Oh, we had our uses. If nothing else, we made for good protection. See, the first place they marched us was a POW dispersal camp, where we were to be split up for shipment elsewhere. Well, I'll never forget, that first night I look through the wire, and I see hundreds of German civilians pulling up in their cars around the camp for the night. Turns out it was the only place they were sure they wouldn't be bombed."

From there, Huff goes on, the men were separated by rank and loaded into trains. As an officer, he got to ride third class for the rest of the journey to his POW camp at Goerlitz, in eastern Germany just inside the old Polish border. "The camp had been around a while, but it turned out we were the first Americans—there were already English officers, Australians, New Zealanders, French, even a few Poles. Well, since by then we hadn't really been fed in about a week, I figured, Christ, we'll live it up in this POW camp. Only there was a problem: it seemed there'd just been a breakout attempt at the camp, and the whole place was on punishment rations."

"Tunneling?"

He nods. "It was the English; they were tunnel mad! Only they'd gotten caught because they couldn't get rid of the dirt. They tried putting it in their pockets and sprinkling it here and there during the exercise period, but there was snow on the ground, and they sprinkled too goddamn much of it and the commandant spotted it."

The visage of Colonel Klink, the buffoon camp commandant on the old sitcom *Hogan's Heroes*, springs to mind, and the many ways the show trivialized what must have been a fairly gruesome reality. Searching the Internet prior to today's meeting, knowing something of Huff's experience, I've found all manner of accounts of camp life by former Allied prisoners. Most stress the cold, the hunger, the relentless boredom, and several remark on their fierce dislike of their captors.

"The commandant must have been a committed Nazi to get that job," I surmise.

"Not at all. He was a very fine officer, a World War I veteran who'd been called back to service. He thought he was just doing his job. Well, because I spoke a little German, I was elected to represent the newly arrived Americans on the matter, and I went in there and started spouting off about the Geneva Convention, arguing that those of us who hadn't been there ought to be fed." He laughs. "He told me, very politely, 'Oh, but that would make treatment in the camp unequal.' All in all, he saw that the camp was meticulously administered."

"Boredom must have been a terrible problem," I say. "I read a lot of guys got depressed."

"Well, being that we were fairly close to Switzerland, the Swiss had sent in a lot of books to the camp. So they had a university going."

"I thought you were the one that set it up," protests Moe.

"No, Turner, goddammit, it was already going when we got there."

"That isn't how I remember you telling it last time."

"It had been going for a *long time* before I got there!" Huff looks momentarily exasperated. "It was quite a nice little operation," he says, turning to me. "We had classes in mathematics, in several languages, literature, just about everything but the lab sciences. I'll never forget, there was one French officer who'd worked at the Louvre, and he gave absolutely wonderful lectures on art. Only, instead of using slides, he'd very quickly sketch out whatever work he was discussing on a blackboard—everything from medieval art to the impressionists.

"Well, I wasn't there a week before they had me teaching U.S. history. I decided on a basic survey course, starting with the English colonies and going all the way to the present. I always played to a big house, two or three hundred—including some of the German officers and guards. I must say, all things considered, our relationship with them was rather congenial."

"I wonder if it would have been as pleasant for Jewish guys," I say.

"As a matter of fact, there were some Jews at this camp. We had some guys who were sick, and three of them were Jewish. And the commandant knew they were Jewish—in fact, I spoke to him about it, 'cause I was worried about him shipping these guys off. He told me, 'Don't worry about it; they're going to a military hospital; they'll be treated as American soldiers.' And by then I knew this man well enough to know he wasn't bs-ing me. I heard from all three of these fellows afterward, and they all went to good hospitals and were well taken care of, God bless 'em." He pauses. "These people were German, but they weren't

Nazis. That distinction was more meaningful than you'd think from a lot of the movies and TV shows they have today."

"I also think it's fair to say that by this late in the war, with the Germans struggling to hang on, the brutal efficiency of the regime wasn't quite what it had been," notes Walzer.

"It's true, things were starting to go to hell. After I'd been there three months we heard the Russians had broken through and we had to move. So now they started marching us back west, and, Christ, it seemed like all of eastern Germany was going with us. The roads were just inundated with refugees fleeing the Russians. They were in Volkswagens, farm wagons, any goddamn thing that moved.

"We were basically in the hands of broken-down old Wermachters, most of whom were in worse shape than we were. One day on the road one of these old guys got so tired he took off his gun and gave it to an American soldier to carry. The officer in charge of the column, the *hauptmann,* looked at this and just shook his head."

"And they weren't giving you much to eat," calls Moe, heading out of the room for the tub of ice cream.

"Well, see, they used that to their advantage. One of their officers told me straight out, 'We rule the Americans through their stomachs,' and goddamn it if it wasn't true. In the morning they'd tell us: 'We've got a long march today, sixteen or eighteen kilometers, but at the end of it, there'll be pea soup.' Sometimes there would be and sometimes there wouldn't be, but the mere possibility was enough to keep us going.

"We also found out pretty quickly we couldn't drink the well water in these little villages; there was too much seepage from animal waste. I'm pretty sure that's where I got my dysentery from."

"Spare us the details on that," says Walzer, "we'll use our imagination."

"How about that ice cream, Turner?" calls Huff, laughing. "We're hungry here!" He pauses. "Anyway, between the hunger and the dysentery, one day we were walking up a hill, and I'll be damned if I didn't just keel over and fall into a ditch! The goddamn column just kept marching without me. Probably figured I was as good as gone anyway. Weighed something like eighty-eight pounds."

Moe returns and scoops some ice cream into his dish. "Want some chocolate sauce with that, Boyd?"

"Sure I do!"

"Eighty-eight pounds?" I ask. The account has been so relentlessly upbeat, the actuality of the misery he and the others suffered has scarcely registered. "So you collapsed from malnutrition?"

"Oh, I suppose that was part of it. I only lay there maybe fifteen or twenty minutes. All I know is that when I woke up, there was some minor German functionary from a nearby village just beating holy hell out of me, trying to get me to march and catch up with the others." He smiles at Walzer. "That's the brutal German efficiency you were talking about. I just covered my face, and after a while the sonovabitch got tired of it and went away. I didn't realize till later how lucky I was; he just as easily could've shot me."

Stuart smiles. "Funny what used to pass for luck back then, isn't it?"

"That was just the start of mine. 'Cause after just a while, three French slaves—captured French soldiers who'd been put to work on a German farm—found me and dragged me out of the ditch. They said, 'Stay here; a dung cart will come by driven by a Belgian. He'll take you to a POW hospital.' And that's exactly what happened! This guy came by, loaded me onto this pile of shit, and dumped me off at this German hospital full of English prisoners. You can only imagine what I smelled like."

"Even before the dung."

"Well, anyway, soon as I got there, two English corpsmen took off my clothes and set to scrubbing the hell out of me with these long-handled brushes. I was in such a sorry state, I hardly noticed. But when they threw a bucket of ice-cold water over me, that woke me up fast, and I started screaming bloody murder: 'You sonsovbitches, what the hell are you doing?!' They just stood there laughing, and one of them said,

'Well, here's one that's gonna live.' Anyway, pretty soon after this a captured English doctor came in and looked me over and told me they'd be giving me sulfur. That's really what got me through. This guy knew what he was doing; right away the sulfur began to take care of the dysentery."

"Surprising they'd give sulfur to a prisoner," says Walzer. "That stuff was in pretty short supply."

"You're telling me," agrees Moe, rejoining us. "A friend of mine was in a tank that got hit and got captured by the Germans with a pretty bad head wound. They had no anesthesia, so know what they did before they operated? Hit him on the head with a rubber hammer and knocked him out!"

"Sounds like that one may be a little apocryphal, Turner."

"I don't think so; that's what he says."

"Well, I'm telling you, I can't say I have any complaints about my treatment at all. The commander of this camp was a fine old German doctor, and we got on famously. He took one look at me and started calling me Fatty. But, Jesus Christ, after just a week, one of Patton's columns blew through town and liberated our hospital. By then I was already up and walking around, so they took about twenty of us back to Patton's corps headquarters and threw us a little party. They had a black swing band there, all kinds of food, hot dogs—quite a switch from what we'd been through.

"Well, maybe you ran across some okay Germans," declares Moe, "but what they did back then was so unbelievable, you can't even call them human."

"I'm with you," agrees Stuart. "Even today, when I see a German tourist around my age, my first thought is always: Where were you then?"

"I met an old German guy once in Greece, going up to the Acropolis," recalls Moe. "When I asked him if he was in the war, he said he'd been in an American prison camp. So I said, 'Let me shake your hand!'

'What for?' I told him, 'You're the first German I ever met who wasn't fighting the Russians.' "

The others laugh.

"I'll tell you what worries me, though," adds Moe. "What would I have done if I'd been born in Germany? Because I'd've probably been like the rest of the damn Germans, and that scares me."

"I hate to tell you," points out Huff, "I hope it doesn't make you feel too bad, but you're not exactly the sort of raw material they prized."

"That's true," concurs Moe, reassured. "It's not like I did so well even in the American navy."

"I'll tell you why you wouldn't have just gone along," says Walzer. "I'll tell you what makes you different. The fact you're even asking yourself that question."

CHAPTER 5

We were supposed to go in at a very heavily fortified piece of the Japanese coastline. I'm telling you, looking at that map was like reading your death warrant.

—HARRY HANDLER

THE BATTLE FOR OKINAWA, MAY 1945.

Ten minutes later Harry Handler shows up.

The other infantryman in the group, having served half a world away in Okinawa, he had been unable to make the lunch.

"Sorry," he says. "I was under the direction of She Who Must Be Obeyed."

"Well, we got some Alaskan ice cream for you, anyway," says Moe, seizing the oversized tub. "Cooper turned me on to it."

"Moe, you know I'm not supposed to." Harry turns to me. "Diabetes. Nothing serious—I just take a couple of pills, watch my diet, and cry when I see my friends eating cookies and ice cream."

"I don't know why you do this to yourself, Harry," observes Moe, half meaning it, "seems to me you've lived plenty long enough already."

"Oh, what the heck—just a little." Handler surveys the scene and makes a guess. "Talking about the war?"

"I've been discussing some of my POW experiences."

Harry leans toward me and drops his voice. "Funny thing. Every time I hear their stories, they get more brave."

The line is vintage Handler, whose philosophy, as he later puts it, is "almost anything can be funny if you try hard enough." At the regular luncheons with the full group of Girl Watchers, Harry is a kind of one-man Greek chorus, quietly offering wry commentary on the ongoing conversation.

Still, for all his natural glibness, Handler is one of those men who will tell you that the war years were his making; that had he not served where and when he did, he'd likely never have acquired the fundamental seriousness of purpose that has shaped his life ever since.

Drafted at nineteen out of the University of Washington (as Boyd Huff had been several years earlier), the son of a Russian-born Orthodox Jewish father and an Irish Catholic mother—"she came down with a flu bug and was terribly disappointed when it turned out to be me," as he blithely puts it—Harry in his early years gave little indication of his potential for leadership. Just five years old when his father had a fatal heart attack while motoring from Salt Lake City to the family home in Butte, Montana, he spent his formative years as a bookish, uncertain kid under the sway of a "very, very strict disciplinarian" of a stepfather. But emerging from Officer Candidate School as a second lieutenant and shipped out to the Pacific, he abruptly found himself placed in charge of battle-hardened veterans. "I'll tell you, it was scary as hell. Not only had these guys already seen fighting; some were twice my age, they were married with families. I wasn't shaving yet, and I had this helmet that was way too big for me—like Dukakis in the tank. I figured the only way I'd survive the war was I'd stand up, and the Japs would laugh themselves to death."

The image is easy to summon—the slight, skinny Harry, wearing a bemused look beneath the ridiculous helmet—and I have no doubt he has used the line before. But, he immediately adds, without a trace of self-consciousness, "When put to the test, I performed. I did what I had to do, and that won their respect."

Over the years, I had read less about the Pacific war than about the events of the European theater, but of course I knew about Okinawa. The last link in the long chain of enemy-controlled islands that had to be conquered before the planned final push to the Japanese homeland itself, it was defended with a literally suicidal fanaticism; by the time this bloodiest battle of the Pacific war ended in late June 1945, nearly three months after it began, 110,000 Japanese were dead—more than ten times the number taken prisoner.

American casualties, 7,600 dead and roughly 32,000 wounded, sound modest only by comparison. Faced with a pitiless foe deeply entrenched in well-fortified hills and a moonscape of jagged cliffs and deep caves, our troops also had to contend with torrential monsoon rains that turned everything that wasn't rock into thigh-deep mud. "Sugar Loaf Hill . . . Chocolate Drop . . . Strawberry Hill," said a radio propagandist from Tokyo, of the names the Americans had given to various island objectives. "You can just see the candy houses with the white picket fences around them and the candy canes hanging from the trees, their red and white stripes glistening in the sun. But the only thing red about those places is the blood of the Americans."

That Harry not only served with personal distinction in that hellish place, but led men in battle, it is astonishing to contemplate how young he was. Nineteen!

Of course, such a thing is hardly uncommon in war; many men of my own generation did the same in Vietnam. Still, almost all the guys *I* knew back then around that age, certainly those with a shot at becoming academics or scientists, like Handler, were in school; indeed, just *starting* college, with years of graduate school to follow, hothouse flowers whose safe passage into the ranks of the intellectual elite was for some reason deemed more important than democratically spreading the hardships and risks of military service.

Many of us who were the beneficiaries of this system simply accepted the free pass as our birthright. Even if Vietnam had not been a war we regarded as unjust, it never would have occurred to us that we might have actually benefited from service; we had no conception that our own characters needed any building.

Sometime around the midseventies, hip magazines like *Esquire* and *GQ* published a spate of pieces by men my age who had contrived to avoid fighting in Vietnam but who now said they regretted missing out on the pivotal formative experience of military service. At the time I readily dismissed this as yet another round of self-reverential posturing, the ultimate in having-your-cake-and-eating-itism; they'd done what they'd done (and hardly for reasons that were entirely wrong), so they should live with it and shut the hell up. I remember talking to one actual Vietnam vet who told me that this sort of romantic twaddle made him want to throw up.

But I'm no longer so dismissive of those who feel such regrets, not after another quarter century of watching so many less reflective men of my generation—from high-powered business executives with gutter ethics to married guys I know who still regard casual sex as their birthright—behaving with such naked self-absorption and indifference to others. Frankly, I've occasionally come to wonder myself how I would have fared in what is, like it or not, a signal test of manhood.

The contrast with the guys in this room could hardly be more striking. I don't mean to come off as naive. I realize full well, there were enough jerks and screwups and self-interested SOBs in uniform during

World War II to make up several battalions. Still, looking at this generation of men, many of us know that in vital ways they were more grown up at nineteen than we will ever be.

"Bad as the fighting was," Harry muses now, "it was usually so quick and brutal, I wouldn't have time to get scared. My knees would only start shaking afterward. What really got to you was the physical grind—slogging through mud day after day hauling ammunition, sleeping in foxholes with water up to your neck, that awful, miserable cold food . . ."

"I'd have been willing to trade your mud for our cold for a few days," offers Walzer, "if only for a change of pace."

"I would've made that trade."

"Me too," agrees Huff. "Especially if I could've thrown in that foxhole-stealing bastard Porter for good measure."

"You also had a coward in your unit, didn't you, Harry?" asks Moe.

"Well, I wouldn't use that word. But, yes, there was one guy we knew we couldn't count on. He was useless. I remember one time we were going up to the line, and I'm counting, and I realize we're one short. So I go back, and I find this guy cringing in a shell-hole, and he starts pleading with me, 'I can't go up there; I can't go up; I've got two children.' Well, of course, some of the other guys had kids, too. So I asked him, 'How're you gonna like it when I write your wife about this?' But he didn't care, he just wouldn't come, so finally I sent him on back." He pauses. "The irony is that later he was cleaning out his foxhole and a grenade went off, and he blew off his thumb. I had no casualties after that, so if he'd stayed with us he probably wouldn't even have had a scratch."

"Well, he got what he wanted—he went home to those kids." Walzer pauses. "Though how much you want to bet they never heard the full story of their father's war?"

"Did you have a lot of guys killed?" I ask.

"We were lucky, only two," replies Harry. "In one case, the guy was right next to me when he was hit—we were out by a quarry, and a machine gun opened up on us, and he got it in the chest."

"But you had a damn close call yourself," points out Moe.

"Oh, Moe, it really wasn't that much," he pooh-poohs it. "A mortar shell landed almost directly between my legs, but it plowed into some deep mud before it went off, which saved my little fanny. Made a helluva racket, but the only thing you could see was a scar on one of my fingers—I didn't even report it to get my Purple Heart."

"And I'll bet you'd been *complaining* about all that rain and mud," says Stuart.

"Good point. It did come back to haunt me a few years later, when I was in college. One day I fell asleep in a chair and woke up with a siren going off in my ear. From that time on I've had high-frequency deafness. If I'm at a concert, the top three notes on the piano are just dull thuds, and I can't hear the violin's high notes at all. I'll also often speak in non sequiturs, which can be a little embarrassing. When my wife and I were first dating, we were driving one day in the winter, and I was sure I heard her say, 'My tits are cold.' So I'm sitting there thinking, 'Wow, I've got a hot date here!' I told her, 'Well, there's a sweater on the backseat.' She gave me this funny look and asked, 'What do you think I said?' So, I said, 'Well, what *did* you say?' She said, 'My sister called tonight.' Harry cracks up. "My wife says I should get a hearing aid, but I prefer to think of it as selective hearing."

"Well," responds Moe, "if I were you, I'd've gotten that Purple Heart."

Harry nods, but his mind is elsewhere. "I have to say, writing the letters to the families of those two men was the hardest thing I ever had to do in my life."

Nineteen. At that age my biggest worry was how to write papers for my required sociology course with as little effort as possible, then get my girlfriend to type them. "Were you close to those guys?" I ask.

"I was *friendly* with them. I tried not to get too close to people."

"A very wise policy," agrees Walzer.

"I foolishly made a couple of exceptions to that rule," says Harry. "I became close friends with two officers I met on the ship heading overseas. Later, on Okinawa, I ran across one of their bodies." He pauses. "I don't know how you guys feel, but one of the things the war did was change my thinking about religion. I saw some pretty nice guys killed, and I saw some bastards survive, and it didn't make a whole lot of sense to me."

"Well," says Boyd, "that's a whole other subject. I know plenty of people who became more religious as a result of the war. Including Earl Godfrey. He had some harrowing experiences flying planes out in the Pacific; he feels divine guidance had a helluva lot to do with his making it."

There is a momentary pause.

"I've got another tragic war story," says Harry. "One day my platoon sergeant and I were in a foxhole, and suddenly the whole side collapsed. It couldn't have happened at a worse possible time."

"During a firefight?"

He shakes his head no—then smiles. "Worse—it buried a bunch of cinnamon rolls the bakers had sent up as a surprise treat for the men."

"Oh, Christ!" says Huff, laughing. "That is a calamity!"

"I had to swear the sergeant to secrecy; we might have had a rebellion on our hands. The sergeant and I were so selfless, we hadn't even eaten ours."

I have no doubt that this last, while part of the riff, is also true; a tiny indication of the depth of concern Handler felt for his men. Years later students in his physics classes would dub him, with grudging appreciation, Hatchet Harry, for his demanding ways and refusal to tolerate their bs; but, undoubtedly, his rigor and vigilance helped his unit survive the hell of Okinawa.

"One problem I had was with souvenir hunting, which was a big deal for a lot of the guys in the Pacific—and some would actually risk their lives," he picks up a moment later, still obviously aghast at the sheer stupidity of it. "It wasn't just pistols and insignia; they weren't beneath going after gold teeth. One time we were going through an area where there were some Japanese bodies lying around, and suddenly I look around and realize one of my guys, a Hispanic from Texas, isn't with us—he's lingered behind to strip these bodies. Except one of them wasn't a body. The guy was only playing dead! The rest of us were helpless, too far away to help. I could see the Japanese guy had the business end of his gun and was going for the trigger. Thank God my guy managed to wrestle it away from him and club him to death. But it was that close."

"You think dead Japs smelled different from dead Americans, Harry?" wonders Moe, with clinical interest. "From what I saw, they did, but you smelled a lot more of 'em than me."

Harry allows himself a smile; Moe's observations from left field tend to have this effect. "Now that you mention it, that's probably right—based on diet."

"The Japs had sort of a fishy smell. Americans smelled worse, from all the meat we eat—don't you think?"

"Probably so, Moe."

Moe nods, the only other Girl Watcher who spent any time in the Pacific theater. "I remember when our ship stopped at Saipan, there was still lots of Japs out there in the woods. They had a sign up: 'No unauthorized Jap hunting.' "

"Well, in our case the hunting was fully authorized. And enthusiastically pursued."

"I remember," agrees Moe. "They'd put food down at night to lure the Japs out of the jungle, and then pop 'em. I saw one guy with a whole jar full of ears!"

"Well, that was definitely part of it, too," says Handler. "It was a democratic army; you'd run into every conceivable type of the species—including sadists and born killers. We had one guy, when he got a task to shoot somebody, you could just see his eyes light up."

"We had people like that over in Europe also," says Stuart. "The highest compliment you could pay someone in our company was 'He's a cold killer.' "

"Same with us," says Huff. "Christ, I had this cracker sergeant from

South Carolina who was a true hunter of men. He had a thirty-point-six with a scope on it, and by the end had dozens of notches on that thing. I've never seen anything like it. He'd go out where they had a head or something and just lay there for hours, studying the krauts. Just waiting till someone got careless. Listening to the click of utensils while they ate, waiting for them to finish. Then he'd pick someone off and come back with another notch on that thing."

Harry nods meaningfully. "I used to shudder thinking of my guy returning to society. To tell you the truth, when he was killed, it didn't hurt me a bit. Back in the sixties when that guy climbed up the bell tower at the University of Texas and started shooting people down below—that's what I envisioned."

This business of the suspension of normal standards of civilized behavior in wartime is of course about as morally complex as it gets, and the Girl Watchers are not about to come up with answers when the big-time philosophers are stumped. But they will also never pontificate or delude themselves about their own very human reactions to what they experienced and felt.

"I don't think that impulse is quite as rare as we like to pretend," as Walzer observes now. "I'd never describe myself as a born killer, but it's funny how it can grow on you, living down and dirty, not knowing if you're gonna live from one moment to the next." Despite himself, he starts laughing. "Really, I was getting so I kind of liked it myself."

Immediately, in recognition, the others join him.

"That's true," agrees Harry. "You're certainly not bored."

"I remember when I killed a man, I felt I should have felt haunted by it. But I didn't at all. Quite the contrary."

It's a good couple of hours since we started, and more than once I'd wanted to ask, but hadn't (it had seemed somehow . . . impolite), "How many guys did you kill, Stuart?"

"I'm pretty sure just the one. It was when I was wandering in the woods with that lieutenant, having no idea where we were. We spotted these two Germans down right below us in a field. I whispered, 'I'll take that guy, you take the other,' and we both leveled off. My hand was shaking so much from the fear and the cold, I could hardly pull the trigger. But I fired and my guy dropped.

"My first instinct was to go up and see who I'd shot. So I stumbled down the descent, and there, lying facedown in the snow, was this young kid, crumpled up in this terribly muddy greatcoat. He was carrying this antitank weapon that looked like a plumber's helper. I remember thinking, 'Jesus, I've killed the sad sack of the German army!' I was about to turn him over, hoping to get a pistol or something off him, when a machine gun opened up and I got the hell out of there. I don't even know where he was hit." He stops. "I've been asked what I felt, and it's a good question. I think my strongest sensation was relief. Because I'd finally earned my pay. I mean, for two years they had been paying me seventy-five dollars a month, and until that moment it didn't really seem like they'd gotten their money's worth."

"My experience was similar," says Harry. "I also know for certain I got one. Which actually was fairly unusual, since most of the fighting on Okinawa was long distance, so generally you didn't know if you hit something or not. I was out on patrol, just turning a corner around a stone wall, and I literally almost bumped into a Japanese officer. He was as startled as I was. We were no more than twenty feet apart, and I was frozen solid. It felt almost like slow motion: I watched him reach for his pistol, but he couldn't get his holster open, and finally I reacted and started shooting. I emptied the whole magazine—you could see the bullets hitting the ground moving toward him—and I'm pretty sure I only hit him once, but he went down. I got his pistol; I still have it." He looks at Stuart. "I'm with you; I can't really say I have any feelings about it at all. It's what I was supposed to do, and thank God I did it."

"Tell about that guy you killed in the command car," Moe instructs Boyd. The truth is, my father-in-law takes enough pride in his friend's wartime exploits for the two of them.

"Christ, Turner, what is it with you? It was nothing special."

"Go on, then."

He sighs. "It was a few days before the battle, and we were up in the woods, snooping around. And I see this guy standing up in his car, so I shot him. Then, just to be sure, I picked up my bazooka and let 'em have it in the side of the car."

"How about that kraut you killed with your rifle butt?" Moe presses again.

For an instant, Huff actually looks pained; a look I've never seen before. But after an instant he continues. "Remember what I was saying before, that we got pinned down on the reverse slope of that hill? Well, as we were going down, I ran right into this guy coming up. Goddammit, the two of us locked, and, very clumsily, he tried to use his rifle as a club. Well, we'd been taught to reverse the thrust and hit the guy in the face with the butt of your gun. So that's what I did: I popped him in the face with the butt of my rifle and smashed in his skull. Every time I . . . " He hesitates. "You know those wooden crates that fruit comes in, how they sound when you step on them? It sounded like that. And I looked down, and Christ, I'd killed an old man. He was in his sixties." He stops again. "I didn't like that. I was taught to venerate the aged."

"I figure it would be worse to kill a young man than an old one," Stuart reassures him. "At least he'd lived his life."

"You do what you have to," agrees Harry.

"You still have nightmares, don't you, Boyd?" says Moe evenly. "Your wife tells me you do."

"Sometimes," replies Huff. "They're not that bad." He turns to Harry and says, "Christ, it was just awful out there in the Pacific where you were. You hear lots of people complaining about our dropping the A-bomb on the Japs, but not many of them are ex-GIs!"

It is a seemingly casual observation, but it says everything about the difference between today's world and the one from which these men emerged. I have a friend, an ex-priest, who is so adamant on the subject of Hiroshima that the matter simply can't be discussed. For him, as for so many others in America and around the world, dropping the bomb was a war crime, pure and simple. He has statistics at the ready about the terrible toll in lives and the genetic defects that continue to plague survivors' families two and three generations hence; as well as what he claims is definitive proof that the bombing was strategically unnecessary, that the Japanese were on the verge of surrender anyway, that it was no more than an unconscionable display of fireworks for the benefit of Stalin's Russia, and on and on. There is of course a lot of this sort of thinking these days; in some circles, the presumption of Americans' moral backwardness, past and present, is the starting point for almost every discussion.

I also have not the slightest doubt that all the Girl Watchers' casual "Jap" and "kraut" talk will also offend more than a few contemporary ears. Yet such usage bespeaks more than just habit. Like the assumptions these men bring to their thinking about the bomb, it harkens back to a time when no one hesitated to call the terrible evil abroad in the world precisely what it was. Revisionist historians in today's academy, producing as evidence everything from major Hollywood productions to comic books, relish showing the lengths to which our side went to demonize the enemy, denying the Japanese and Germans their very humanity so as to destroy them without pity or remorse. True enough. But what is lacking in such an analysis is the reality that our adversaries truly *were* monsters, committing hitherto unimaginable atrocities as a matter of state policy. They had forfeited their own claim to humanity long before we entered the war; the Japanese in Manchuria and Nanking every bit as much as the Germans in Dachau and Bergen-Belsen. In fact, by that summer of 1945, the Japanese had considerable stores of biological weapons, including plague, which they had tested extensively on Chinese civilians, ready to spring on America's civilian population; and even as we closed in on the Japanese homeland, they were working feverishly to perfect a delivery system.

"When we got the news they'd dropped the bomb, we were aboard a ship for the Philippines to prepare for the invasion," says Harry. "We officers had been given battle maps, laying out what each of our units

was expected to do—we were supposed to go in at a very heavily fortified piece of the Japanese coastline. I'm telling you, looking at that map
was like reading your death warrant."

"We were scheduled to join you out there," understates Stuart, "and
it was not a pleasing prospect. I served two years, nine months, twenty-
eight days, and roughly six hours, which was just right."

"Boy, oh boy, if we'd actually had to go through that!" exclaims Moe.

"Christ, Turner, they might actually have gotten all the way down to
you."

Moe laughs as hard as the others.

"Well," says Harry, checking his watch, "I should probably be
pushing off."

The guys rise from the table and shake hands.

"I'll tell you one thing," says Moe, "any way you look at it, those days
in the service, they were the most important days of your life."

Harry nods. "Before I went overseas, I was such a kid, no self-
confidence at all. Afterward, I knew nothing would rattle me ever. And
nothing ever really has."

"What I still can't get over sometimes is how young we were," says
Walzer. "I mean, before I went in the army, I'd flunked out of college
and was just a mess. I got back, and I was a student like nobody's business. Because I'd damn well learned what it took to succeed." He looks
meaningfully at his friends. "I gotta tell you guys about something that
happened the other day. I got a call from my forty-two-year-old son,
who's a university professor, and he says, 'Congratulations, Dad.' I say,
'What for?' He says, 'For having survived the Battle of the Bulge.'
Apparently, he'd just been watching a thing on PBS showing how devastating it was and how many men died, and it really hit him. He's a very
cool person, my son, very structured and a little remote. This was his
way of saying, 'I love you, Dad; I'm glad you're still here.' "

Moe guffaws. "More like saying he's glad he's here."

Walzer smiles. "Maybe that too."

"If that kraut you got had shot a little sooner and a little straighter, you wouldn't be."

"Also true."

"Well," says Huff, with a booming laugh. "I guess we agree, then. Getting shot at and half starved to death was the best thing that ever happened to us. Even brought us closer to our families."

✦ CHAPTER 6 ✦

Turn a couple of fairly bright kids loose with a couple of diagrams, and there's nothing you can't build.

—GENE COOPER

GENE COOPER, AGE FIVE.

Gene Cooper fought a very different kind of war, never even leaving the continental United States. But that's not to say it didn't also have moments of high drama.

Indeed, the one time he did find himself face-to-face with hostile soldiers, the soldiers were American.

"It was in nineteen forty," he tells me, when I stop by his home in Carmel Valley for a preliminary chat, "more than a year before Pearl Harbor. I'd graduated from the University of Texas in electrical engineering and was teaching over at Southwest Louisiana State University in Lafayette, in Cajun country. I've always been pretty curious and enjoyed tinkering with things. So I put together a little device for tracking aircraft, based on an article I found in a technical journal down at the local library. Well, I got to playing with it, just for fun—set up a fairly simple system with a couple of antennas up on my roof and started tracking planes." He pauses; bemused understatement is Cooper's style. "It wasn't hard. There was a pretty big army airfield close by."

"So," I ask, "you'd describe this as—what?—an early radar device?"

"Not exactly. The basic idea was to take a high-frequency oscillator and change the frequency linearly," he breezily explains, as if only a simpleton could fail to grasp what he's talking about. "So as you're changing the frequency, if you get an echo back, the frequency you're transmitting will be different than the frequency of the echo. Using earphones and a sensitive detector, you could gauge the delay and figure out how far away the object was."

I nod, pretending to understand. "So what happened then?"

"Well, one day, out of the blue, three very heavily armed intelligence officers show up, acting very serious and pretty menacing. For a while they wouldn't say what they were worried about, but finally it came out they'd been picking up some kind of mysterious interference. So I took them up there and showed them this setup. Man, that got them *really* upset. They started going on and on about how this was highly classified stuff, and no one was allowed to have this technology, and generally letting me know I was really in trouble." Cooper smiles. "So, of course, I had to take them all over to the Lafayette Library and show them this material in a manual."

Moe, no slouch himself on technical matters, describes Cooper as the closest he's ever encountered to an electronics genius. Appearing on the scene when the field was just starting to explode, he made significant contributions to everything from early television to advanced weapons systems—and would have done even more had he been even mildly ambitious.

How, I ask Gene, would he size up his own talents?

"Oh, I guess I know what I'm doing. I've always had a pretty good feel for that sort of thing."

"Moe says you're about the best he's ever seen."

"Oh, you know how Moe is, he's really a character," he slides off the subject. "At the Navy School, the standing joke used to be that Moe would stand at the blackboard, write one thing, say another, and be thinking a third, with no relation between the three. But mixed in with that, there's usually some very clever stuff."

It's not that Cooper is shy about his achievements. But he is walking proof that utter self-certainty need not have anything to do with cockiness or braggadocio.

When it comes to the war years, Cooper is as proud of his contribution to the eventual victory as any of the other Girl Watchers, realizing full well that the scientists and technicians in labs and classrooms provided our side with a crucial edge. Their counterparts in Germany and Japan were obviously highly capable, and sometimes brilliant, but ultimately they were limited by the rigidity and brutality of the regimes they served.

"Imagination," as Cooper himself puts it now, "tends not to do quite so well under totalitarianism."

Cooper built his Carmel Valley home in 1951, when the Naval Postgraduate School, where he taught, relocated from Annapolis to Monterey. The small office where we're now sitting is very much his sanctuary. Here is his photographic equipment—he used to win a blue ribbon at the Monterey County Fair for photography almost every summer—and his books, and in a corner, alongside the computer he built himself, sits his cherished ham radio set.

Not that he uses it nearly as much as he used to. "Just a little bit, from time to time, to keep a hand in," he says. "I'm slowing down a little bit in general; my mind's not as quick as it was." He taps his head. "It's all still in there; it just takes a bit longer to come out."

"It's probably still a cut above mine."

He chuckles—but doesn't deny it.

"And, of course, I've also had a couple of health problems lately."

Another understatement. In recent years he's had a bout with the neuromuscular malady myasthenia gravis, as well as skin cancer and a heart attack that resulted in a five-way bypass.

"Basically," he says of this last, "I woke up one morning with some fairly bad chest pains—bad enough to know it wasn't indigestion. By the next morning they had me in surgery. Apparently, they decided that at my age this was the one shot at serious surgery they'd have."

"You look pretty good now."

"Well, all things considered." He smiles. "I think the genes are pretty good. My grandfather lived to be about ninety-two, and I can still see him sitting down at breakfast with three eggs and a big hunk of ham. And my brother's still going strong at ninety-three. Like most doctors, he did everything wrong—three-pack-a-day smoker, lots of stress—but he's managed to make it through throat cancer, vein transplants in his legs, all kinds of stuff. He and his wife are still in the same house in Austin where I roomed with him back in the thirties."

The Cooper boys were born about two hundred miles from Austin, on Galveston Island, sons of an accountant who later became the business manager for the local Ford dealership. Like other Girl Watchers, Cooper remembers a childhood so idyllic, so impossibly innocent, that it seems out of a sepia-tinged photograph. In his case, Galveston being a barrier island off the Texas coast, the photo would feature a beach scene peopled by young men and women in vintage bathing suits.

"We practically lived on the beach, playing, socializing, competing in this and that," recalls Cooper. "I can't remember when I couldn't swim."

By fifteen, he was part of an organization called the Tri-Five Club, whose members participated in a sort of early form of the Ironman competition: they had to stay in water over their heads for five hours, swim five miles, then run five more. He also played a lot of softball at the beach—with, among others, the legendary Babe Didrikson, the Olympic track-and-field star and champion golfer, who is still widely considered the greatest American female athlete ever. "Babe would show up from Port Arthur, and whatever we were doing, she'd take it as a challenge to do it better." One afternoon, his bunch was challenged to a game of softball by Guy Lombardo's band, who were performing at the nearby Hollywood Dinner Club. "They were pretty cocky—especially after we told them we'd use a girl pitcher. So when they got up to bat, I trotted out to left field—and we pulled that old stunt where all us fielders sat down. 'Cause, oh, man, could she ever pitch! Windmill style. Faster than any hardball pitcher I ever saw. Those poor guys didn't know what hit 'em." He laughs. "Of course, we wouldn't let her pitch very often—not against us."

Though Cooper loved sports and would go on to swim competitively at the University of Texas, his real passion has always been figuring out how things worked—and how to make them work better.

In an age when many parents seek to plot their kids' every waking moment, from infancy through the longed-for acceptance to a top college—along the way supervising play dates and music lessons, after-school sports and SAT prep—Cooper's childhood, like the childhoods of the other Girl Watchers, stands as a powerful object lesson. For they succeeded, in some cases brilliantly, without any guidance from their parents at all. Once out of sight, to their parents' enormous relief, kids of that generation pretty much were out of mind; their parents had almost no idea what they were up to. It's not that they didn't love them, simply that in those days children and grown-ups inhabited parallel universes and stayed out of each other's territory. It's all there in *Penrod,* the great best-seller during Cooper's early boyhood, and in *The Little Rascals* a decade later: that wondrous world of boys on their own, endlessly pursuing wild schemes, building surefire, guaranteed-to-be-fun contraptions and in a hundred other ways figuring out life for themselves.

Shortly before his death, as it happens, I interviewed the creator of *The Little Rascals,* Hal Roach, then close to one hundred, and asked about his inspiration for the series. He told me about the day he was auditioning an overly precocious child when he happened to glance out his office window at an adjacent construction site. Forgetting about the would-be child star, his attention fixed on a group of boys arguing heatedly over ownership of a discarded plank of wood. "That," he recalled, "is what I wanted to put on the screen—how real children act when no one's watching."

We have largely forgotten how much good can come of an unstructured childhood—the kind of intense creativity and drive and independence that can never be conferred by hovering adults or even the best after-school tutoring. With the right raw material and a little luck, such a childhood will produce an adult ready to help remake the larger world with the same assurance with which he once created a world populated only by kids.

Even as a small child, Cooper was building most of his own toys on the cheap. "The streets in Galveston were paved with oyster shell," he recalls, "which meant that after it was pulverized by enough automobiles, it became powdered calcium. Well, a couple of buddies and I figured out if you run the material through a fine sieve and mix it with water, it produced what amounted to concrete. We made all kinds of great stuff out of that: forts, castles, miniature racetracks. Then we'd build little cars to run on the tracks, cutting the ends off spools of thread for wheels; if you balanced 'em j-u-u-u-st right, man, those things would move."

As these things invariably go, miniweapons of destruction were soon the primary focus of interest. "Of course, back then there were no laws against firecrackers, the very notion would've been dismissed as foolish, so what we'd do is take powder out of a bunch of these things, make muzzle-loading cannons from pieces of pipe and fire marbles. Or else those solid balls they used to have in the middle of golf balls—they were even better, because they were full of white lead, and when they hit something they'd make a wonderful white splash." He laughs. "We also built really *powerful* crossbows that shot threepenny nails. And another time a friend and I built a good-sized catapult in my backyard from old medieval diagrams we found in the library, using stretched inner tubes instead of ropes. With that one, we'd fire rocks. I tell you, turn a couple of fairly bright kids loose with a couple of diagrams, and there's nothing you can't build. Now that I think back on it, it's fairly uncanny we didn't kill anyone."

In the midtwenties, when he was around eight or nine, Cooper became fascinated with radio after a friend of his brother's built a primitive set from scratch. "This was a pretty unique period in history, though of course we didn't see it at the time," he says. "It was really the start of a revolution, the first time ordinary people had access to the world beyond their surroundings through electronics. To me it was like magic. Of course, Galveston didn't even have a radio station at the time, but that didn't matter; we'd take this thing out and listen all night long to whatever we could pick up out there. I remember how excited we got one night when we got a signal all the way from Chicago!"

Before long, Cooper was building more sophisticated electronics equipment on his own. One of his first creations was a Tesla Coil he set up in the attic—a device which, practically speaking, did nothing, but made for one helluva light show. "I tell you, it had a secondary coil six inches in diameter and four feet long, and, man, I could get sparks off that thing ten or twelve inches long!"

Along the same useless but highly gratifying lines, he produced a static electricity machine—"two rotating circular plates which you'd turn with a crank to build up a static charge, and when you released it, it would be like a lightning bolt. It was splendid, just spectacular; people's hair would stand on end!"

Shortly after starting high school, he and his pal Shoomer Beamon found out the physics department was planning to throw away an old X-ray tube that didn't work. "I talked them out of it and took it home. Well, Shoomer and I got it going, all right, and started making X-rays of everything we could find"—he chuckles—"exposing ourselves to absolutely massive doses of X-ray."

That was one highlight of his secondary school career. The other was his exposure to Professor Patrick Underwood. Formerly chairman of the mathematics department at the University of Edinburgh in Scotland, Underwood had come to Galveston at eighty to be close to his grown children, and to keep busy he had started teaching part-time in the local high school. Cooper, a strong but often disruptive student, bored with the standard curriculum, had found his muse. "I started with old Pat Underwood taking plane trigonometry and solid geometry as elective courses; then spherical trigonometry and introduction to calculus. By now he was eighty-three and deaf as a post, but just a wonderful professor of the old school. He'd been teaching since the eighteen eighties, so here he was in this public high school in Galveston, using old texts from the English public schools. He really made us sweat blood—but, boy, did you learn your stuff!"

Cooper went on to the University of Texas, graduating in the heart of the depression. Fewer than half of his fellow majors in electrical engineering were able to find work in their field, but Gene was lucky enough to land a job with Dallas Power and Light, which at least afforded him the freedom to marry his sweetheart, Jody. Soon after, his old college faculty adviser told him about a teaching job opening up at Southwest Louisiana State.

It was there that Cooper put together his aircraft-tracking device, which led to the visit from military intelligence; and he was still there a year or so later when the Japanese attacked Pearl Harbor. In short order, Southwest Louisiana State was home to an assortment of military programs. Among them was the navy's V-5 program for naval air cadets, where Cooper's technical expertise was much prized, and he was given an exemption from military service.

Given the character of the times, this was very much a mixed blessing. "I was young and we didn't have children, and quite a few of the people I knew down there, friends of mine, were not too happy they were being called while here I was with this exemption. So I decided to ask for a commission in the navy. It was ridiculous in a way, because all I did was put on a uniform and essentially continue doing the same thing I was doing before."

Except he was doing it someplace else. The navy soon transferred him to a pre-radar program at Maine's Bowdoin College, then moved him on to the Radar School at MIT, and finally, to the Naval Academy at Annapolis. There he was assigned to Project Cadillac, designing search radar for what eventually became the airborne early warning system.

At the war's end, Cooper found himself entertaining a number of intriguing options, including a job from RCA and several others for teaching positions at prestigious East Coast colleges. He even considered, briefly, going into business with a couple of guys he had gotten to know while at MIT—they were named Tandy and owned a small Boston electronics shop they had dubbed Radio Shack. "It was just a hobby for them—their real business was leather goods—but when the war came along, they'd started building capacitators and a few other things for the government. Well, toward the end of the war, their manager approached me with an offer: 'We're thinking of opening a couple of other stores; interested in getting involved?' "

He wasn't. But despite his love of teaching, Cooper was also drawn to the possibilities in the field of postwar electronics. "It was a tremendously dynamic period," he recalls. "Electronics had just exploded during the war, and there were a lot of us just raring to go. Of course, most of the advances had been in military equipment, radar, absolute altimeters, navigational systems, and all the rest. So the question was: what now? What about consumer electronics?"

The answer for most in the era's version of the electronics industry was not exactly earth-shattering: radio. During four long years of war, so the thinking went, no new radios had been produced, so it seemed reasonable to believe there would be tremendous, pent-up demand. Never mind that there had been little appreciable improvement in the technology or that most older radio units worked just fine.

Rudimentary marketing research would have established what several years of dismal sales would eventually prove: customers wanted new products.

By then Cooper had gotten friendly with a manufacturers' rep in the electronics field who had always understood this. Milton Shapp had a radically different vision of the future, one which Cooper quickly came to share.

It was called television.

Working with Shapp even as he continued his teaching career at the Naval Postgraduate School, still located in Annapolis, he began designing and building pre-amplifiers for TV sets. "Then, just to satisfy my own curiosity, to know it personally, from the inside out, I built a TV receiver from scratch. I wound all the coils, built all the IF transformers, the whole bit. At the time, nineteen forty-six, there was only one TV station transmitting in the Washington-Baltimore area for a few hours a day—WTTG—and Annapolis was maybe twenty-seven miles away, but I managed to pick it up pretty good."

Soon, at the behest of another company, Cooper was designing an entire build-it-yourself-from-scratch TV kit. Costing $190 at a time when a commercial set retailed for nearly three times as much, it seemed a stroke of brilliance. "It was a pretty nice unit, and these people were pretty excited about it. But then they were bought out by a fellow who got convinced he should produce it as a regular commercial set, which isn't what it had been designed to be, and he went bust."

In short order, Milton Shapp came calling with an even more visionary notion: he wanted Cooper to design a distribution system that would bring TV to places where it was impossible to receive a signal. As a test case, they chose the isolated Panther Valley in Pennsylvania. "Basically," says Cooper, "these people were down in a hole. So what we came up with was building a receiver way high up on a mountaintop to pick up the signal, then feeding the signal on to a cable and running the cable down into the valley."

It was the first cable system anywhere.

Before long he was applying the same concept to a very different sort of assignment—"as a point-of-sales thing, connecting a whole bunch of TVs in Macy's in New York City to a single antenna." He smiles. "You go into a store now and there are fifty or sixty TVs all going at once, on the same channel, and you take it for granted. But until then it wasn't possible."

The go-getting Shapp soon began manufacturing distribution amplifiers and isolators to enable the spread of similar systems throughout the country, and his fortune was made. Twenty years later, he was the governor of Pennsylvania.

"Did you have a piece of any of that action?" I ask Cooper.

"Oh, a very small piece." He gives a small laugh, never much of a businessman and genuinely not caring. "Milt was more than fair with me. When the school moved out here to Monterey in 'fifty-one, and I told him there was no practical way I could continue to work with him, he sat down and wrote me a check for a pretty nice lump sum. It was enough to buy a house."

Around the same time he was working with Shapp, he found himself in yet another role that might have led to serious wealth. "See, at the end of World War II they were dumping everything, and people with a little foresight really cleaned up. Well, I made friends with a fellow in Baltimore, a sort of wheeler-dealer who'd sit there with a desk and telephone and buy surplus. This fellow was tremendously aggressive, but not really up on the technical end, so I served as kind of an unofficial adviser. Typically, he'd call and say, 'Hey, Coop, someone's offering a bunch of aluminum tubing.' I'd say, 'How much?' 'I don't know, about three warehouses full.' 'Well,' I'd tell him, 'I'm not sure what you can use it for—but I've got a sneaking feeling there's gonna be a place for that stuff before too long.' "

He chuckles. "I remember one time he called and said, 'Hey, Coop, they've got a whole bunch of synchros over at Martin they want to get rid of, a hundred thousand dollars' worth, but I can get 'em for practically nothing.' Now, a synchro's like a little motor, very precise, widely used in radar to transmit the rotational data of the antenna down to the display. 'Well,' I said, 'I don't know of anyone but the military that uses them, but they'll be technically sound for a while so I'd go ahead and pick 'em up.' Three months later, Korea comes along, and he sells them right back to Martin for five million dollars."

"I imagine he was pretty grateful."

"He was. When we got out here, and were building the house, he had all the appliances delivered."

For Cooper, all this money talk is beside the point. "Listen, I have no regrets at all about any of that. I enjoyed teaching. Besides, over the years I always kept a hand in with my outside consulting."

In fact, over his years in Monterey he worked on innumerable projects for both private industry and the government. Notable among them were the proximity fuse, which revolutionized antiaircraft by enabling the projectile to "read" how close it is to a target and so detonate without actually hitting it; and the project code-named Tinker Toy, which led to the placing of hitherto complex and unwieldy vacuum tube circuits on ceramic wafers, at the time an entirely new technology. "Man, it was really exciting," he says of Tinker Toy, with an uncharacteristic burst of excitement. "Way back, around 'thirty-six, I'd worked fairly extensively on analogue computers at the University of Texas, playing around with some simple digital stuff. But those things were massive; you could heat a building with the heat that came off the tubes; no way they were ever going to lead a consumer product. But now here was a standardized way to build a complex circuit with maybe two tubes about an inch square and an inch and a half high."

"Of course," he adds, "even Tinker Toy, which seemed so remarkable in its day, now looks primitive as the horse and buggy. With modern integrated circuits, you get maybe a million elements—and pretty soon they'll look just as primitive. We're going to see technology, perhaps organic, that will bring things almost to the molecular level."

For all the revolutionary technological developments he has witnessed in his lifetime, many at close hand, he also has a far, far better idea than most of how much remains to be achieved.

"It's true we had some pretty decent ideas," he says, "and some of them worked out all right. But probably the most important thing we did was break through the psychological barrier. Back when we started, there were just a relative handful of us who were competent in this area, and often we were just feeling our way. Now we know things that once seemed impossible *can* be done, and we've spawned a vast generation of highly skilled people with that whole different set of expectations. Back then, the attitude was 'only God can do this,' so a lot of people weren't even willing to try; today, it's 'why not?—all we've got to do is figure out how.'"

Yet, just as much to the point, his long experience in the field has left him more aware than many of those working today of the limits of technology. "People sometimes say complimentary things about what we did; that's what tends to happen when you get older. The fact is, we weren't visionaries, just damn hard workers. I don't think any of us could've visualized modern chips and integrated circuits—it was science fiction."

He pauses a moment. "Though I guess maybe we should've been able to guess, because nature's been doing this forever. Think about what you've got in your head, the complexity of the human brain, or the fact there's a program of an entire human being in a single cell— those things make everything we humans have achieved look like child's play. Man, a boll weevil walking around has more going on in its brain than any computer ever built. So, no, I can't say I'm all that impressed with what we accomplished."

At this point, Cooper is more than content to kick back and monitor developments in the field from a distance, leaving the heavy intellectual lifting to those fifty and sixty years younger. "Let's face it," he repeats with an easy shrug, "your abilities diminish, and there's no point getting upset about it. I have one old friend who in his time was one of the most brilliant engineers I knew, still is, really, but let's just say he's not aging gracefully. He's highly competitive with younger people, still thinks he has to prove something. So he keeps reading all the journals, keeps trying to stay on top of all the latest technological developments, and at our age it's just not possible. It's sad. Man, my feeling is, 'Let's coast a while.'

"Of course, then there's Moe—he's a different kind of bird altogether. He's not competitive in the least, never was, but for him the complicated problems are fun. Sometimes even now he'll come to me with one, and though at this stage I'm not all that interested, since it's Moe I'll work on it some. Only invariably, when I come to him with my answer"—he can't help laughing—"he'll have the same answer, only he'll have come to it in some totally different, needlessly complex way. But aside from that . . ." He points to his computer setup in the corner. "That thing there just sorta grew, like Topsy. But it's probably the last machine I'll ever build."

He smiles. "Of course, Moe'll probably be dragging me out to look at cars for him when I'm a hundred. Maybe I'll pass that assignment on to my grandson."

Indeed, a great deal of Cooper's focus these days is on his fifteen-year-old grandson, Augie, himself a blossoming electronics wunderkind. "Really, you should see this kid. He's just the same way I was. Even when he was tiny, he'd spend hours taking an old clock apart, or fiddling with a door to figure out how the latch worked. Don't ever let anyone tell you it's not in the genes—it just may skip a generation."

✦ CHAPTER 7 ✦

I can't explain it myself; there's no logic to it; I should've

been killed. But through the grace of God, when I woke up,

I was going up instead of down.

—Earl Godfrey

EARL GODFREY, FLIGHT TESTING AN F-4
PHANTOM, 1960.

"Lemme tell you," muses Moe, behind the wheel of the family Nissan, "women just throw themselves at guys like Earl."

Since I'm unfamiliar with this area—the Carmel Hills—my father-in-law's ferrying me to my introductory meeting with Earl Godfrey. The plan is for Moe to pick me up a couple of hours later, after running some errands.

"Oh, yeah?" I ask. "Why's that?"

"Well, first off, he's real good looking. And, you know, women are just impressed with these fliers. There's a reason those wings they wear are known as leg spreaders."

By now, of course, nothing Moe says or does surprises me. "You ever say anything like this to him?"

"Oh, no—Earl's a real straight shooter." He pauses. "It's not easy, being away from home as much as he was and being faithful when some woman's always throwing herself at you. Very few men can resist. But I'll bet Earl did."

"Would you have resisted?"

"No woman ever threw herself at me."

"But if one had?"

"Oh, no, I'd have succumbed. But ole Earl, he probably wouldn't even think about it. He's just a better man than me all around."

"I thought Moe was bringing you over," says Earl, greeting me at the door.

"Right. He did." I nod toward the curb, where Moe sits behind the wheel, hunched over a book.

"Say, Moe," calls Godfrey, "why don't you come in?"

Moe looks up. "Oh, no, that's all right; you two go ahead; I'm all right here."

Godfrey knows his man well enough not to argue. "Okay," he says, leading me inside.

A few minutes with Earl, and it's clear why even Moe wouldn't broach the subject of his friend's appeal to women in his presence. Earl is immensely good humored. But he is also a person of deep religious faith and a powerful, unapologetic sense of honor; in brief, someone long accustomed to thinking seriously and hard about large questions, eschewing easy (or even expected) answers.

Earl sometimes winces at Moe's more ribald jokes. But whenever the Girl Watchers end up talking about what is right and wrong in America, which they often do, it is invariably Earl who brings to the conversation a sense of urgency and passion.

Over coffee, Earl fills me in on his background. As he himself might have emerged from central casting, large, robust, and square jawed, so his early years have to them a quality that seems more out of the movies than real life. Born on a farm outside tiny Cozad, Nebraska, "right in the middle of the hundredth meridian," he attended a one-room prairie schoolhouse through eighth grade, with a single teacher presiding over children from ages five to fourteen.

"There were maybe thirty-five of us in all," he recalls. "You'd start over on the left row for first grade, and keep moving till you ended up on the far right in eighth. The teacher had a bench up front, in front of her desk, and she'd call up each grade in turn—talk to them about history or math or English. So even in the first grade, you were hearing a little bit about eighth-grade math."

Not, he is quick to add, that it worked very well. For all the misty-eyed nostalgia associated with this sort of thing, "I don't think I learned a whole lot. I wasn't much of a student to start with, and you certainly didn't get much individual attention. I'd have to say that today's education, even in the rotten public schools, is probably a hundred times better."

I ask him how his own kids, growing up as military brats on bases around the country, reacted to these *Little House on the Prairie* tales.

He smiles. "Oh, you know, they'd throw it up at me sometimes—how

I had to walk two and a half miles in the snow. It's easy to make fun of. But we would—if the school was open, we'd go."

Along with the war, the Depression was of course the other great formative event of the Girl Watchers' lives, and it is hard to overstate how powerful and enduring it was in shaping their view of the world. I think it's fair to say it left them all permanently wary about the future. They knew in their marrow, as few of those of us who followed could, how quickly things can change, and were determined never to be blind-sided again. Yet in the odd, often contradictory way the human mind and spirit work, they also emerged from that period with a profound sense of the need for human connection and the ultimate insignificance of material things; deeply compassionate but also impatient with that brand of human weakness—self-pity, whining, casting about for blame—that breeds helplessness and surrender.

Of all the men in the group, the Depression arguably had the greatest impact on Godfrey, for during those years his family was in truly desperate straits. One of six children, he lost his father when he was seven, just as the worst of it hit. "It was a struggle," he observes mildly now, "especially in those Nebraska winters. We had one stove in the house, and it got pretty cold. I had to go to work at a fairly young age to pitch in."

"How old were you?"

"Eleven."

He says this so matter-of-factly, you'd think it was the most natural thing in the world. "Eleven?"

"On a neighbor's farm. They didn't pay me anything, but I got to eat." He smiles, as if to show he realizes this might come off as a little melodramatic. "That didn't last long—by twelve or thirteen, I was getting paid. I'll never forget the first check I got; it was for fifty cents. But back then a dime was real money. The fact that something like that can happen to you and your loved ones . . ." He shakes his head. "I guess it gives you a certain seriousness. I honestly believe that struggle builds character in ways that prosperity really can't. I don't want to sentimentalize it; no one's saying poverty is good. But society really does function better when people think beyond themselves, and that's what those times made us do, pull together. Some people dismiss that as just nostalgia, but it's not. It's not just talk; it was true—bad as times were, nobody locked their front door." He smiles. "Not that there was much to take. You could've put a sign up: 'This Home Protected by Poverty.' "

As with so many others, those years fostered in Earl a fierce commitment to self-reliance. "Even during the worst of it, we didn't expect anything from the government. That was just the way we went about things, from generations back. My mother's father, who'd been a homesteader in South Dakota, built a store between two Indian reservations and started a town—Tuthill, named after him. Among other things, he was the postmaster. Well, he lived to be just a few days short of one hundred, and in his elder years my mother went up there to help take care of him. Looking through his desk drawer one day, she found all these government checks that he'd never cashed, dozens and dozens of them. He just didn't feel it was right to do so—after all, he was only doing his part as a member of the community.

"I think that's pretty admirable. Yet, here am I, a military retiree, and I think nothing about taking government retirement pay. I grew up accepting it was part of the pay package, and I do believe that. But I still have a hard time with some of those people I went to school with back in Nebraska explaining why that is right. I know my father would never have accepted welfare."

Self-examination is one of Earl's signature traits. Certain as he is of his values and beliefs—and in those his faith is absolute—his life's central challenge is to fully live up to them. In an age of nonstop self-promotion, he is profoundly antihype, playing down even those accomplishments he has every right to treasure. In high school, as he mentions a few minutes later, he was all-state in football, but "that wasn't all that much of an accomplishment at the time even in Nebraska."

To this day, he remains far more focused on his early shortcomings—especially the fact that he was a mediocre student. That left him, on graduating, with few prospects and no sense of his future direction in life.

Like Stuart Walzer and countless other prewar underachievers, he began to find his way, through no fault of his own, following Pearl Harbor. At eighteen, largely motivated by Jimmy Doolittle's thrilling raid on the Japanese mainland from the aircraft carrier *Hornet,* Earl applied for the navy's aviation program. The training was rigorous but, given the demand for pilots, relatively brief.

"How'd they teach guys to land at night?" I idly inquire, having read that the deck lights then were pretty primitive.

"Let's just say that was the last thing a guy learned—if he couldn't."

By the summer of 1944, he was flying F-6 hellcats off the *Yorktown* over Japan, dodging—and regularly losing friends to—antiaircraft fire. As the Japanese grew more desperate, there was the added threat of escalating kamikaze attacks and, as he puts it, "a new set of rules in the air." Among these was the fact that the Japanese had started strafing American fliers coming down in parachutes. "I didn't really think I'd get home alive," he says with a shrug. "I don't think anybody did. Our attitude was, 'If we can finish this thing off, great, there's a chance we might make it home. But only if it ends pretty soon.' Because one way or another, you were going to be there till the end. I'll tell you, though, that kind of thinking has one advantage; it makes you pretty hard to run a bluff on in a poker game. Come hell or high water, you're *gonna* call the other guy's hand. And we played a lot of poker."

"The other guys were telling me you had a few close calls."

"Some. One in particular. We were strafing a little field about halfway up the coast near Honshu. I got too low—had some branches in my face there—hit about twelve g's and blacked out completely. But when I woke up, I was going straight up."

"I don't get it. What happened exactly?"

"I can't explain it myself; there's no logic to it; I should've been killed. But through the grace of God, when I woke up, I was going up instead of down. Didn't even pop any rivets! All I can say is thank goodness for Grumman—if it hadn't been an F-6 airplane, I'd have had it."

Indeed, spiritually speaking, his war experience had precisely the opposite effect that Harry Handler's did. "I wasn't especially religious before the war. But it does something, surviving when you know you shouldn't have. When, really, you have no right to. Somebody else was looking out for me."

"Did that episode make you any more cautious?"

He seems surprised by the question—and I realize it was a pretty naive one.

"Well, you know," he says, with charitable patience, "caution has its place, but not in the accomplishment of a military mission. In the final analysis, if you're going to do it right, you have to want to be there."

"There had to be some guys who didn't."

"There were a few. But that wasn't a good thing. For them or anyone else."

"Were you ever scared?"

"Actually, it was kind of exhilarating. To know you were doing the right thing, and for the moment that truly being all that mattered. I'd say that's the great secret to happiness in life—feeling you're living a life with real and solid meaning."

Flying missions up and down the Japanese coast, both as attack aircraft and as cover for bombers, by early 1945 Godfrey and his buddies had a bird's-eye view of how badly the enemy was hurting. "Most of what they had left was in the north, around Okaido—railroads, steel plants, some mining—but by now you had to search for it. Mostly, it was complete devastation. In August, after we dropped the A-bomb, I flew over Hiroshima to see it for myself, and of course it was incinerated—everything completely blackened, with only a little piece of structure here or there. But the truth is, it didn't look any different from Tokyo after the firebombing, when the whole city just went up like matchsticks. I'll never forget that smell when we finally went ashore after the surrender, the smell of roasted human flesh just hanging over the city."

But like the other Girl Watchers, not for a moment did he doubt the necessity of the Allied response; he had witnessed firsthand the savagery and tenacity of the enemy. The depth of Japanese fanaticism showed itself even after the war's official end. "Some people in our squad were in the air, just about to make an attack over Tokyo, when word came in that it was over. Everyone was ordered to return to the ship. But as they were heading back, they were attacked by Jap aircraft, flown by the last of their fighter pilots. As far as those guys were concerned, the war wasn't over, not quite yet, and they came after us with everything they had. One of our guys got four airplanes in that scrap, but we lost a bunch of people ourselves."

As the formal document of surrender was signed by Douglas MacArthur aboard the USS *Missouri* that September 2, fifteen hundred naval aircraft flew above the ship in an awesome display of American might. Earl was "pretty much the last guy in the formation."

Only on the ship back to the States did he begin to seriously consider his next move. When the ship's skipper asked the newly minted vets if any might want to stay on in the regular navy, Earl decided to sign on. He had no other options.

In his unflinching self-analysis, he can sound surprisingly ambivalent about that choice today—though on paper his résumé is extraordinarily impressive. In the fifties he dueled Chinese fighter pilots over Korea and distinguished himself as a jet test pilot; a decade later, rising quickly through the ranks, he was serving in the Pentagon on the staff of the Secretary of the Navy. By Vietnam, he was captaining ships, culminating with the carrier *Kitty Hawk*. He retired as chief of staff at the Navy School here in Monterey.

But, looking back, he readily admits to his share of regrets. For one thing, he stayed in uniform years longer than he had planned, which cost him a shot at going to work for an airline. "The timing wasn't right," he explains. "Vietnam came along, and I couldn't leave. I would've felt like I was bailing out."

"Meaning?"

"I had too many friends in the Hanoi Hilton."

"Still and all," I say, "you obviously had a very successful career."

"No, I don't actually consider myself very successful."

I look at him in surprise.

"Well, maybe with the scholastic background I had, or the lack of one, I was more successful than I could've expected to be. Still, after you achieve a certain rank, you are expected to go all the way. And what's expected of someone who gets a carrier is that he'll make flag rank. I didn't. I never made admiral." He stops. "Except I do consider myself successful in family life. And when you get right down to it, that's really the hardest thing. I've got some pretty good people in my family. It's nice to think I might've had something to do with that."

As he describes it, the persistent conflict in his mind between his family's needs and the demands of a promising military career is one of the things that, in the final analysis, probably made him less than ideally suited for this career path. "I really liked being a father," he says. "I did everything I could to accommodate family first. In the military, that's not a good thing for your career."

When Moe arrives to pick me up, he asks, "Well, he tell you all about his exploits?"

"I think we covered most of it," says Earl.

"You were just a baby out there, doing all that stuff you did," says Moe. "How old were you at the end of the war, anyway?"

"Twenty-one. But I didn't consider myself all that young. There were a lot of people my age out there. George Bush was one of them."

"Boy, oh boy, some of my kids, when they were twenty-one, you'd hardly even trust 'em with the family car."

Godfrey smiles. "It does seem funny now, doesn't it? I have a grandson down in L.A. who just made twenty-one, and he's certainly still a kid." His tone changes slightly. "Maybe a little less now than before."

"Why's that?" I ask.

"He's going to be donating a kidney for his sister. She's seventeen and has a degenerative condition that's been coming on for about five years. The doctors thought it might go away, but it hasn't."

"Man," exclaims Moe, "you seem so calm about it. I don't know how on earth I'd ever deal with something like that."

"Well, no question it's stressful. My daughter's husband died two years ago, so my wife and I will have to go down there and pay close attention, 'cause she's gonna have two very sick kids on her hands. They say it's a lot harder on the donor than the donee. We've been hoping to hold off till next summer, when both of them are out of school, but it looks like we might not make it."

"How are the kids dealing with it?" I ask him.

"It sounds strange, but in a way it's changed everybody's life for the better. When my granddaughter Lauren found out about this, she dug in at school and is really doing well. And Jared—this has really tested him, and he's just come through. The first time he had to go in for a blood test, he fainted. But, boy, it makes you grow up fast."

"It sure must," agrees Moe.

Earl nods, not bothering to mask the pride. "He's just a very good individual. The way he looks at it now, he's just doing what he has to."

CHAPTER 8

Our aim with German girls was very simple. Man cannot

live by K rations alone.

—STUART WALZER

MARLENE DIETRICH. IN HER CASE, A GI COULD
ONLY DREAM.

"So," I throw out the question, as the guys move into my in-laws' dining room for my first meeting with the whole group, a buffet lunch of chicken and cold cuts, "what was it like suddenly finding yourselves back home in real life?"

To a man, they look at me in seeming bafflement.

"What are you talking about?" replies Moe, as if it's the dumbest thing he's ever heard. "You just did it, that's all. Everybody was trying to make up for lost time."

"I think what he's asking," Huff offers gently, "is how was it coming back from hell to find yourself up to your neck in dirty diapers?"

"Something like that. How hard was that adjustment after all you'd been through?" On the yellow notepad before me, I've underlined the words at the top of the first page: "The 'Best Years of Our Lives' problems: Hollywood bs or real?"

"Everyone was in the same boat," explains Harry, and though he too is entirely amiable about it, I get the idea he doesn't think all that much of the question, either.

I'm caught off guard, surprised at the complete nonreaction. After all, in a comparable situation, this is the sort of thing my fellow baby boomers and I might have hashed over ad infinitum. Had it been us, the war-to-peacetime transition would have been a full-blown generational obsession, the stuff of a hundred memoirs and made-for-TV movies and "My Turn" columns in *Newsweek*. Hell, it would have spawned an entire new subsection of self-help books (*The* Psychological *Bulge of the Bulge: Overeating to Suppress Memory; The War Inside: Getting Him to Finally Talk About It*).

But it's apparent that such a line of inquiry isn't going to work with these guys. They have spent their lives acting, not thinking about how they *feel* about it. Nor are they about to let themselves be herded into talking about something they don't feel like talking about. Clearly, if I'm going to get anything resembling answers to these questions, I had better come up with a new approach.

The brief silence that follows is probably more awkward for me than for the Girl Watchers.

"I got a joke for you," Moe abruptly announces, pouring himself an iced tea.

"Uh oh," says Harry, "I hope Benny's not in hearing distance."

"Don't worry; she's in the kitchen."

"Go ahead," says Huff. "You know damn well no one can stop you."

"Well, this gal's walkin' down the street, and she passes a pet shop with a sign advertising frogs for sale. 'Who'd want a frog for a pet?' she asks the proprietor, and he tells her, 'These are no ordinary frogs; they give the best head known to man.' 'You know,' she says, 'my husband's always demanding something from me I don't want to give; maybe this'll shut him up.' So she comes home and gives the frog to her husband. An hour later she finds him bangin' around with pots and pans in the kitchen. 'What the hell are you up to?' she wants to know. 'Well,' he says, 'if this frog can cook, you're gone.' "

Around the table, several of the others crack up.

"Very good, Moe," says Walzer with some surprise. "Well above your usual standard."

This is true. Moe is an inveterate joke teller—on the phone, he'll assault you with one he's just heard before even bothering to say hello—but his jokes are generally not my style. I'll take a convincingly written, funny character any day over a clever punch line, a wry, dead-on observation—Seinfeld, anyone?—over the best traveling salesman joke ever contrived. This is a matter not just of generation but of background. Moe, Arkansas boy that he is, is a product of something that now seems almost a misnomer: WASP American culture. It was the culture that at its finest gave us Mark Twain and Booth Tarkington, more commonly personalities like Rudy Vallee and shows like *Fibber McGee and Molly,* and until comparatively recently it *was* American culture. Indeed, our evolving sense of humor is one of many signs of the fundamental shift in the national personality that can be linked to the massive immigration from southern and eastern Europe that began at the tail end of the nineteenth century, and the ever fuller palette of ethnic influences on the mainstream it ushered in. I remember being flabbergasted to read the dialogue from the comedy *Our American Cousin* that John Wilkes Booth chose as his cue to shoot Abraham Lincoln, knowing the laugh would be so huge that it would drown out the crack of his pistol: "Heh, heh. Don't know the manners of good society, eh? Well, I guess I know enough to turn you inside out, old gal—you sockdologizing old man-trap."

Moe Turner could well be the only man I know who might well crack up at that line today.

But comic fashion is another means by which my generation has unceremoniously elbowed the previous one from the scene. Once the Marx Brothers, a collection of lunatic Jews, full of put-downs, show-offy literary references, and sly sexual double entendres, were an anomaly, an interesting change of pace from the norm of Bing Crosby and Bob Hope and screwball comedies about rich battling spouses; now we recognize them as the edge of a tidal wave that, breaking in the seventies, produced everything from *Saturday Night Live* and *The Simpsons* to Richard Pryor and David Letterman, and by the nineties had made *South Park* and *Jackass* standard-issue viewing for young teens. The older generation's humor tended to be gentle, targeting "human foibles" but no one in particular; we baby boomers, with our hip, ironic, urban sensibility, turned humor into a weapon, to mock, parody, and belittle— always doing so in the name of that most exalted of contemporary virtues, "honesty." To be sure, from our perspective, the new stuff is infinitely funnier than the old. But at what cost? As essayist Michael Long observes, "While overhauling American attitudes about sex, drugs and marriage," starting in the sixties we "wrested the definition of honesty from real life considerations to philosophical ones. Honesty was detached from its moorings of truthfulness and upright moral character. Honesty instead came to mean raw, rude declarations of personal opinion and observation, other people's opinions be damned. . . . This new norm was the idea at the heart of '60s humor, that ugly truths must be told regardless of whom they hurt."

The Girl Watchers are smart guys; they can certainly appreciate much contemporary comedy; Moe, for one, is a big fan of *Fawlty Towers*. Still, none is by nature cynical, let alone purposefully cavalier with people's feelings.

In brief, this is just one more way it is no longer their world.

"Tell me, Moe," I say, deciding to go with the flow, "how do you think Benny would react if she heard that joke?" My mother-in-law is no stick-in-the-mud (as she herself might put it), but she has a lot of class and a fully developed sense of propriety.

He looks at me in surprise. "Why on earth would anyone ever tell her?"

"May we never find out," agrees Harry.

"Not well," Huff speculates, "not well at all. A woman's way of looking at things is not at all the same. And *vive la différence!* I say that's all to the good!"

It hits me that we may actually be addressing my initial question—only in an indirect, less heavy-handed way. For more than anything else, what coming home meant was leaving behind the world of men and returning to a more civil one in which women set the rules of acceptable deportment. While decent men might continue to act as they always had among themselves, in the presence of women, they knew to keep certain aspects of their personalities under wraps.

The one thing the Girl Watchers will never be accused of is political correctness, and this is particularly apparent when it comes to sex and women. This is not a matter of politics—Stuart and Harry are unabashed liberals, Earl and Boyd libertarian conservatives, Moe and Cooper fall somewhere in between—but of biology. All the Girl Watchers are foursquare for equal rights and opportunities; but none even bothers pretending to buy the notion, so much in vogue in precincts of advanced thought, that it is just "social conditioning" that makes us think of the sexes as fundamentally different.

Having spent far too much time in recent decades in the company of guys my age who doggedly monitor themselves, lest a stray word or thought get them called "sexists" or "chauvinists," I find the Girl Watchers' attitude a blessed relief. Hell, it never even occurs to these guys that there is a party line correct thinkers are supposed to follow. For them, men are still men and women still women, and it is precisely this distinction that makes life worth living.

"Males are just hard-wired differently," Cooper now says, getting to the heart of the matter. "If you're a young man, and there's an attractive woman in the vicinity, there's an excellent chance you'll be interested. And even if you're an old one, there's still a pretty good chance you'll be interested in looking."

Handler nudges me. "In other words, there are very few *ex*–Girl Watchers."

"That reminds me of something ole Art Buchwald said," interjects Moe, who happens to have just been reading Buchwald's autobiography. "He spent the war on some little island in the South Pacific where he says they only had one woman. But he says she died 'and some sentimentalist went and buried her.' "

The others burst out laughing.

"There's a lot of truth to what women are always saying," he concludes. "Plenty of men only *do* want one thing."

Like the rest, this is an obvious and undeniable truth based on a lot of years of living. That anyone should challenge it, especially smart people on university campuses, is an absurdity.

"Oh, boy, you should've seen us at the end of the war," says Walzer. "I mean, here we were, a bunch of horny young guys occupying these German towns, and the army kept trying to scare the hell out of us to keep us in line. They actually told us German girls put razor blades inside their vaginas."

"I guess that'll deter you," says Moe, laughing. "Got you thinking about a second circumcision."

"Not for a second," Stuart shoots back. "I still have a photo of one of the girls I knew over there, Margaret from Dorheim. Only in her case there was a catch. She had a boyfriend who'd been a minor Nazi Party functionary. He had just snuck back into town, and in return for her favors, she wanted me to give him a little cover by being seen with him in public. The fact I was Jewish was a bonus."

"Did you?"

He nods. "Let's face it, hormones have a logic all their own. I'm afraid for a lot of us, our aim with German girls was very simple. Man cannot live by K rations alone."

"Gawd!" exclaims Moe. "So you maybe got a kid or two running around over in Germany . . ."

"Unlikely—I was so cautious, I'd always wear two condoms." As the others laugh, he looks from one to the other. "You guys think I'm kidding? My other great fear was VD. They had these pro stations— prophylactic stations—and it was a very painful process. You'd get a little tube of stuff, insert it in the end of your penis, and squeeze out the contents. I was so terrified, I did that even after I'd used my condoms."

"You must've really been something," says Moe.

"Just young—that's all it took. Actually, there was another girl who might be of interest to you. She was eighteen. And a virgin."

"Man, oh man, a dream come true."

"Not quite." Stuart laughs. "I don't mean to disillusion you guys, but it was completely humiliating. I couldn't get it in. I started yelling in my grade-school German, *'Es geht nicht! Es geht nicht!'* It doesn't go! It doesn't go!"

The others crack up.

"And to cap it off, I came in seconds! God, I was so embarrassed!"

"I would hope so!"

"Hey, remember yourselves at twenty."

This is obviously a point of connection among men that transcends generations. I sure as hell remember myself at twenty, and how the endless demands of my libido could mess up not only my judgment but, occasionally, my ethics.

"There were times you'd say anything," I say.

"*Anything,*" he agrees.

This is a major reason that I, for one, notwithstanding all the good the women's movement has done on the equity front, long ago started wishing it would drop this ludicrous idea that it's only conditioning by society that makes us think as we do about gender. Is it even possible to imagine these guys' counterparts, a group of eighty-something women, sitting around swapping yarns about getting laid in their salad days?

"Well," volunteers Moe, "Huff here was different. He was a good boy."

"I think I'm the only American soldier who can honestly say I was true the whole goddamn war." agrees Boyd. "Of course, Martha and I were already married by then."

"What does that have to do with it? In the navy the married guys were worse womanizers than the single guys."

"Christ, Turner, you make me sound like a goddamn virgin! You know perfectly well I'd already sown plenty of wild oats by then!"

"Oh, I know it, all right! And I respect that you were faithful." Still, Moe can't help smiling. "I remember one guy back then, he'd put *on* his wedding ring before he went out looking for girls. 'What the hell you doing that for?' I said, 'most guys take 'em off.' He told me, 'I want her to know going in there's only one thing we're gonna do, and that's the end of it.' " Moe cackles. "Pretty good thinking, I'd say."

"Well, it's never been a secret what men are after," says Harry. "But now we come to the age-old question: what in the world do *women* want?"

A long pause. For the truth is, in fundamental respects the ways of the other sex remain as incomprehensible as ever to these guys even after all the years of close observation.

"Well, I think you have to start with security," says Godfrey. "Women feel a lot more vulnerable in the world than we do, physically and emotionally—and often with good reason. They need to feel protected."

"While we need to be taken care of," says Moe. "At least I do."

"The word is *babied,* Turner."

"That's why a relationship between a man and a woman, if it's a good one, will be complementary," says Earl.

"And why if it's not, either or both will be so eager to get out of it," says Walzer, the divorce attorney. "It's foolish to generalize . . . but, oh, why not? Oftentimes women are more fickle. Talking about vulnerability, we men are the ones more easily hurt."

"Boy, isn't that the truth? A lot of women'll drop a man like that if something better comes along. I developed a theorem exactly along those lines, a quick-and-dirty explanation of how a lot of women work: 'Turner's First Law of Thermodynamics: the body closest to the fire gets the heat.' " He grins. "I remember one time during the war, me and this buddy of mine went to a dance at the officer's club in Boston. All the local girls were hanging around out front, so I took one of them inside. She was quite pretty, real sweet and everything, and we're having a great time, dancing and talking. But all of a sudden some photographers show up and start snapping pictures—they were doing a spread for *Life* magazine, "Life Goes to a Party." And then I realize my date's disappeared—she's dived under the table." He laughs. "Turns out she was married to some poor wretch overseas."

"I imagine wartime must've been quite disorienting for a lot of women, since they'd always more or less lived under the jurisdiction of men," notes Walzer. "During the war, all those rules were suspended, and for the first time many women were on their own, both in the workplace and their personal lives. And a lot of them liked it that way."

"Well, a lot of their husbands didn't," counters Moe.

"They were only doing what a lot of guys were doing overseas," says Harry.

"Right, but we want women to act differently. *Better.* Because they're the first line of defense for children."

"Let's just say consequences were probably mixed," says Godfrey, "the same as with women's liberation later on."

I think Earl has it just about right. Entering manhood as the women's movement came of age, I have seen almost every woman I know struggle with the push-pull between the new imperative of being out in the world and the traditional one of family; and now, in the age of the emotionless, no-strings-attached adolescent "hookup," I watch some of my twenty-one-year-old daughter's contemporaries pretending, against their every instinct, to be as cavalier about sex as young men.

Yet if I'm straight with myself, I also have to acknowledge the continuing battle within myself—between the kid I was who loved it that women were as up for no-consequences sex as we were, and the more sober, conservative, and, yes, censorious version of today, looking out for society's greater good. In a discussion like this one, I can move seamlessly from one to the other, and at times actually be both at once.

"My God," exclaims Moe, "when I was in college, just a few years before the war, things were still so innocent."

"Even after the war. When I started at Harvard Law School in 'forty-eight, you could get expelled for having a girl in your room. Even in a motel, if they found out!" Stuart agrees.

"I visited a friend's daughter at Harvard in the seventies, and they not only had co-ed dormitories, the bathrooms were co-ed," he adds.

Moe nods. "I'll tell you, my son Jonathan, when he started at UC Santa Cruz in the eighties, they put him in a suite with five girls, and he found it pretty shocking seeing them walking around naked. He was innocent, just like I was."

"It should only have happened to me," whispers Harry.

"That's all a result of the sixties, when in loco parentis disappeared," says Cooper.

"When he went to college," says Moe, nodding my way.

"Listen," I say, "I'm no defender of the sixties; I think there were plenty of excesses that did a lot of harm. But, I gotta tell you, it was a *great* time to be a guy."

"I can certainly see that," replies Stuart. "But I've got to say, it seems to me once you share a bathroom with a woman, things get a lot less romantic."

Earl and Stuart rarely agree in this kind of discussion, but this is an exception. "We're all for equality of opportunity and all that," says Godfrey, "but some of this other stuff, I just don't know. . . . And I don't think you can look at it just from the male perspective. A lot of women now feel under pressure to act in ways they're really not all that comfortable with."

"There's just so much pressure from popular culture," adds Harry.

"You turn on the TV these days, there are things you wouldn't find in the raunchiest nightclub fifty years ago!" interjects Moe.

"That's right, Turner—and you watch every one of 'em!"

As long as we're more or less on the subject, I ask Earl about some of the supposed problems aboard navy ships since they went co-ed.

"Oh, boy," he says, "don't get me started. It's just been an administrative nightmare. The majority of women in the military perform well; they're as capable as the men. But on these long cruises there've been serious problems, with women getting pregnant right and left. It's led to a whole different set of standards for women."

"Nothing worse for morale," says Huff.

"Exactly right! If a woman's bored after being out there six months, or she's mad at somebody, she can just ditch the whole thing without any penalty whatsoever. All she has to do is say, 'Uh oh, I'm pregnant,' and the commanding officer will ship her out. It's just devastating to cohesion. I'm all for fairness, but you can't let military necessity take a backseat to social engineering."

"Don't they check it out if she actually is pregnant?" wonders Moe.

"Sure. But even if she's lying, you've got to figure the commander probably wants to ship someone like that out. This whole system was imposed on them by politicians."

"Can't a guy get out by saying, 'I made her pregnant'?" suggests Harry.

Earl laughs. "I'm sure it's been tried any number of times."

"Have there also been problems with gays on ships?" asks Walzer. "After all, we know that gays have always served on ships."

"That's a complicated situation. My feeling is that any sexual behavior, homosexual or straight, can be disruptive. As far as the military is concerned, we're better off when the whole thing is kept in the closet. It's a private matter that's gotten way too public in this country."

"I'll tell you what I find so amazing about this gay stuff," says Moe, "on our ship we were gone for a year with a thousand men on board—"

"Hold on," Huff cuts him off, laughing. "Where's this going?"

"And I never heard of a single case of homosexuality."

"Christ, Turner, you wouldn't've recognized it if you saw it."

"That's true, too. Growing up, I didn't have the slightest idea that homosexuality even existed. For years you never heard a thing about it; now it's about all you hear."

"I was as ignorant as you, Moe," Walzer says, "until the supply sergeant volunteered to be my tent mate and offered me extra blankets. I was very flattered—for a little while. I had to keep him away all night with a bayonet. And the next day he took back all my extra blankets."

"Cold but secure," says Handler.

"But, you know, my views changed a lot after one of my brother's sons died of AIDS," adds Stuart. "This was back around nineteen eighty-six; he was one of the first people to get it. My brother—his father—couldn't even acknowledge his son's homosexuality for a long time. Of course, now we understand there's always been a certain percentage of homosexuality in the population, and that it might well be genetic."

"Like having blue eyes," Moe agrees, "that's about what it adds up to. I know a guy like that. His son's queer as a three-dollar bill, and he goes around cracking 'faggot' jokes. It's pretty awful, when you think about it."

"Well, I'm with Earl," says Huff, "it should be private. I was flipping through the channels the other night, and I couldn't believe my eyes. All these guys were naked and they were doing things you couldn't imagine on one of those cable channels."

"Probably Showtime," I say. "There's a show called *Queer as Folk* that's pretty explicit."

"That's it! Fortunately, Beverly was there; she changed the channel very fast. Excellent woman—she's concerned about my heart."

"I'll tell you," says Moe, in his quirky way inadvertently steering things toward safer ground, "you see all kinds of things these days that would have seemed impossible back then. Not long ago this friend of mine told me he was on a nude beach and he saw a couple of seventy-year-old three-hundred-pound women slathered in oil."

"I imagine something like that can really do a number on your libido," observes Harry dryly.

"Think about it this way," says Stuart, "these are the very women that fifty years ago we were lusting after."

You can bet that little of this will be repeated to their wives over dinner this evening. Raised with the old-fashioned notion that women are literally the gentler sex—and so innately more civilized than men—in their presence the Girl Watchers have always taken care to be on their best behavior. Indeed, most would have no argument with Katharine Hepburn's prim observation to the hard-drinking, foul-mouthed Humphrey Bogart in *The African Queen,* that "human nature is something we must strive to overcome."

At least, that is, around women. With one another, all bets are off. When they get together, in all sorts of ways it really is as if they're still part of the world they inhabited so long ago, before they came home.

"Well," says Harry now, "at least *we're* still as attractive as fifty years ago, give or take a few extra trips to the bathroom," and the others laugh.

"This is the paradox of life, isn't it?" says Stuart. "When you're young, you can get it up but you go off like a shotgun. When you're old, you can hardly get it up at all. So at both ends, you're screwed."

"Well, you know what Ben Franklin says," observes Moe, who's been reading a biography of the statesman and philosopher along with the one of Art Buchwald. "That women deteriorate from the top down—even when they're old, they're still good down below."

"Yeah, but what about us? We're no good down below."

"Stuart, you should do what I do," advises Harry. "I take two Viagras before I go to bed every night—it helps me dream about it."

"Actually, I have," says Walzer. "I was talking to my neurologist just the other day, telling him Viagra isn't so great after all, not for me, anyway. It gives me an upset stomach. So I said, 'Tell me honestly, Doctor, are there still men my age as interested in sex as they used to be?' And he said, 'Yes, there are some men who still carry on a very healthy sex life.' And—I didn't even intend it this way; it just burst out of me—I said, 'At *home?* With their WIVES?' "

There is a tremendous burst of laughter—laughter of recognition.

"That reminds me of a joke I heard . . . ," says Moe.

"Oh, Christ, Turner, what doesn't?"

"Now, just hold on; you'll like this." He pauses a beat. "This gal went over to visit her daughter-in-law, and when she opened the door, she was standing there naked as a jaybird. The mother-in-law says, 'What's going on?' She says, 'I'm waiting for my husband; he calls this my love suit.' So the gal goes home, and when her husband shows up, there she is, waiting for him—and his eyes pop out. 'My God, woman, you're naked!' 'No, she says, this is my love suit.' 'Well,' he says, 'it needs pressing.' "

Moe laughs a little harder than the others.

"Well, Moe," says Harry with mock weariness, "there's another one you can be sure I won't be telling my wife."

CHAPTER 9

It was such an old-fashioned courtship, so romantic and respectful. The flowers, the candy, the theater, the dinners, the dancing. . . . And nothing was ever asked of me. Ever.

—BEVERLY HUFF

BEVERLY AND BOYD HUFF ON THEIR
HONEYMOON, 1998.

I realize there are some who will take the way the Girl Watchers talk about the differences between men and women as backward and, yes, even insulting. Not long ago, Andy Rooney, who by age, experience, and demeanor would fit into the group without missing a beat, once again got in hot water by telling an interviewer that the thing that bugs him about televised football "is those damn women they have down on the sidelines who don't know what the hell they're talking about." "Oh, this poor man," Fox Sports' Pam Oliver, was quoted as reacting. "He speaks probably for his generation of people, but that doesn't make it right."

Leaving this little contretemps aside, there's a larger point here worth making: the assumptions—about gender and age—cut both ways. When today's self-assured young women talk about men of the World War II generation, it is often with a kind of bemused scorn. The attitude is that these old guys are relics of an antediluvian age rife with gruesome inequities, and good riddance to it. Yet such thinking fails to recognize the many aspects of that age which would be well worth preserving, even in their own self-interest.

It is no coincidence all the Girl Watchers have been so spectacularly successful at marriage. True enough, they and their wives have operated over the years largely in different spheres; the women at home, at least while the children were around, as their husbands took on the larger world. Yet far from causing friction, this supposedly antiquated view of relations between the sexes has mainly promoted balance and harmony in their relationships. For in its very clarity, the arrangement bred peace of mind. The modern notion, a given everywhere from college women's studies classes to Lifetime TV, that such a social arrangement resulted in the mass production of patriarchal bullies daily returning home to pathetically docile spouses (probably self-medicated in their lonely distress) is self-congratulatory hyperbole. Like millions of middle-class women of their generation, the Girl Watchers' wives— smart, engaged, with passions of their own were satisfied with their lives, and were their husbands' life partners in the fullest sense.

This is not to suggest there weren't many women, as well as more than a few men, who were unhappy with the arrangement, or that some of these don't also make a compelling case. But while these days it is easy (as well as fashionable) to dwell on the drawbacks of the old-fashioned division of labor, there are also, heaven knows, plenty of problems that have come with living in a time when *nothing* is clear and roles are constantly confused; when both men and women are expected to be everything at once: professionally successful, superparents, in fantastic physical shape, *and* great in bed. Think it's a coincidence that we talk so much more about stress—not to mention impotence—than they used to?

Just as much to the point, for all their supposed social backwardness, men of the Girl Watchers' generation were acutely sensitive to a reality that for many of their sons and grandsons seems to have become a deep dark secret: women respond to men who treat them with respect and courtesy.

For the Girl Watchers, courteous—even chivalrous—behavior was inbred, just the way things were supposed to work between men and women. It still comes as naturally to these guys as breathing.

In fact, this is the one area where I have to watch myself in their presence. With men around my own age, guys in their forties and fifties, there is an implicit understanding that you can gripe about your wife—good-naturedly or a little less so, depending on how well you know the guys—bringing up her assorted irrationalities or her overprotectiveness toward your son or even the sad fact of her squeamishness about certain kinds of sex. But with the Girl Watchers, such a thing is unthinkable; and not only because I'm married to one of their daughters. (To the contrary, Moe is the one member of the group who might actually encourage such a conversation.)

Maybe the most striking example of this reticence is Boyd Huff, precisely because in other respects Boyd is so gruff and plainspoken. Yet when it comes to the women in his life, you will never find so thorough a gentleman.

I first met Boyd shortly after his first wife, Martha, died. Before I knew anything about his exploits in the war, I heard my mother-in-law marvel at his extraordinary devotion and gentleness during Martha's long, heartrending illness. He would often bring her with him to lunch at the Turners', and though by then her Alzheimer's was so far along she could scarcely recognize anyone, he would treat her like royalty. "He'd pull out her chair for her," my mother-in-law said, "and hold her hand, and make an effort to include her in every conversation."

By every account, their fifty-two-year union had been rock solid, based on common interests and deeply held mutual values. Having met on a boat from Alaska to the lower forty-eight, over the years they shared a passion for travel, as well as tastes in music and art. Martha, who had an advanced degree in accounting, was also in uniform during the war, as a dispensing officer in the navy. She shared with Boyd a sure eye for real estate and managed the family finances, providing what they were both sure would be a comfortable and secure future. Once they settled in Monterey in the midfifties with their two young sons, Jerry and Andy, they both fell in love with sailing.

"We had a twenty-five-foot cabin cruiser to start with," Huff tells me one evening over drinks at the Monterey Yacht Club, a favorite haunt since those early years. "Christ, we used to go up and down the coast, all over the damn place. It had a little galley, could sleep four. Just perfect." He takes a sip of his Old Crow on the rocks, remembering. "Christ, Martha was just wonderful; she was the first mate and chief bottle washer. I'd beat it home from work at around five, and she'd have the boat all rigged out, and off we'd go with the boys."

Of course, that's something else they would come to share: the heartbreak when, in different ways, both the boys were lost; Andy killed in the shooting accident and Jerry diagnosed with schizophrenia.

Boyd takes another sip of his drink, glances toward the entrance to the club. Beverly, his second wife, is due to join us any minute.

"But then, after Martha died, I traded in the cabin cruiser for the *Stillwater*. That's when I got so fanatical about sailboat racing."

I also remembered this from the time I was first getting to know Boyd—how, at eighty, he was racing his sleek Shield sloop with a single-minded purpose, as many as four and five times a week—manning the tiller himself and commanding a crackerjack crew that included a former sailing coach at Annapolis and, his secret weapon, a fellow oldster who was an expert on the ever-shifting conditions in Monterey Bay. At the time the *Stillwater* dominated local competition, which pleased Boyd beyond measure.

"Some of the other fellows got rather bitter," he happily recalls. "They'd say, 'What the hell does that old bastard have?' Hell, what that old bastard had was brains."

Still, he was bereft of Martha, and it was impossible back then not to note a distinctly aimless quality about him. When he would turn up at my in-laws' in his decrepit Honda Civic hatchback, predecessor to the Daewoo, he was bluff and engaging as ever. But there was no one waiting for him at home, and he rarely seemed to have anywhere he needed to be. Despite his many friends, Boyd's closest companion then was a sweet, extremely aged collie named Mack, who drooled so uncontrollably and in general was so malodorous that even Moe sometimes objected, referring to the dog as "that dumb blonde." No matter; Boyd was fiercely protective of Mack and insisted on taking him everywhere. On racing evenings, he would leave Mack in the hatchback parked on the wharf outside the Yacht Club; then, returning after many hours and more than a couple of drinks, for often as not he'd close the place, they would drive off together into the night.

"I suppose that's why I got so involved with racing in the first place," he says now. "I needed the diversion."

Today so much has changed that all that seems far more distant than a mere six years. Huff has exceeded what even his friends saw as his remarkable capacity for resilience, emerging from the depths of mourning into a whole new life.

Mack is gone, along with the Civic, and though Huff still races, so is his old crew. His new one—which includes a Navy School aeronautics professor and his teenage daughter, as well as a female court translator fluent in French—rarely sails the *Stillwater* to victory. At a four-mile race I joined them on earlier this evening down to Point Magoo and back, she finished fourth in a five-boat field.

Yet—further proof of how much has changed—Boyd can't even pretend to give a damn.

"Better not tell Beverly we lost," he warns me now, grinning. "She'll lock me out of the house!"

Of course, this is the most significant change of all: marriage to a boisterous, loving woman, who is Huff's match in every sense of the word.

"Does Beverly ever come out sailing with you?" I ask.

"Oh, no, she just loves to come down here, sit at the bar, and talk to guys." What a great wife!"

When Beverly shows up five minutes later, she nods toward the table where the captain of the winning boat and his crew are celebrating. "Looks like someone did well."

"Oh, what the hell difference does it make? I always say the object is to have fun."

She bursts out laughing and gathers him in a fierce hug. "I should be ashamed to be seen with you."

Twenty years younger than Boyd and still plenty good looking, Beverly is as straightforward as she is ebullient: "just a great gal," as Moe enthuses, "a real live wire. God, did Huff ever luck out!"

"These days I'm the envy of all my friends," Huff boasts, out of Beverly's earshot. "They can't figure out how I did it."

It's not such a mystery, really—not if you believe, as Huff always has, that you make your own luck. His courtship of and marriage to Beverly—which helped him bounce back to begin living life anew in his mideighties—reflects the same purposeful optimism that helped him survive the war in Europe and all the trials since.

Think of it as vintage Huff: a remarkable mix of old-fashioned gentility and sheer chutzpah.

"He just swept me off my feet," Beverly explains a few days later. "That pretty well sums it up."

The moment we settle down to talk in the living room of their home in Hidden Hills, a development of elegant homes on the outskirts of Monterey heading toward Salinas, a golden retriever puppy comes bounding into the room and leaps into her lap.

"Down, Scarlet!" she orders her off the couch.

The dog responds by going for Beverly's face and licking wildly.

"Scarlet, down!!" she repeats, her authority dissolving in laughter.

"So this is Mack's successor . . ."

"But a lot less well behaved."

Beverly grabs the dog and wrestles her to the floor, literally pinning her down. "Can you believe this?" she says, looking up at me. "And she just got back from obedience school!"

Getting to her feet, she drags Scarlet outside.

"Lovely furniture," I observe, when she returns and takes a seat, for the room is full of antique pieces.

"A lot of it came from Boyd's mother. That"—she points to a straight-backed leather chair, the least comfortable looking in the room—"is his favorite. He says it reminds him of when he used to have to sleep sitting up in a Jeep in French barns. He'll sit there for hours reading, and I'll find him snoring away."

She leans forward. "So, you want to know how we got together? Well . . . I used to go with a friend of his—did you know that?"

"Boyd told me. He says he stole you from him."

"I know, that's his version." She laughs. "The truth is, as Boyd well knows, it wasn't going anywhere."

In fact, says Beverly, Boyd's friend was only the latest in a string of single men she had gone out with since the death of her husband, a vice president at Hewlett-Packard. Along the way, she had learned more about the changes in the dating scene since her youth—and about the expectations of the crop of available men her age, along with their amazing self-centeredness and the crystal fragility of their egos—than she ever wanted to know. She had gone so far as to make for herself the commonsensical rule that she would not commit to remarry without waiting at least a couple of years because "it's awfully hard to hide your real self that long."

Boyd, who got to know Beverly through his friend, began joining them occasionally for dinner or drinks; then more than occasionally. Knowing his friend's erratic history with women, he bided his time.

One day, he called the friend saying he had an extra ticket to *Carmen*. Could he borrow Beverly for the evening?

Describing that first one-on-one quasi date four years later, the second Mrs. Huff can scarcely stop smiling. "It was miserable out that night, just pouring rain, and Boyd picked me up in that old Civic hatchback with that soaking-wet collie dog in back stinking to high heaven. The windows were so steamed up he couldn't see, so he kept wiping them with his fedora. I mean, talk about a man comfortable with who he is! So then we're watching *Carmen*, and right in the middle he leans over and says, in that big booming voice of his, 'She's such a slut!' The whole theater cracked up."

Remembering, Beverly does too.

After the opera, he took her to the Yacht Club for drinks and dinner; then on to another restaurant that featured a pianist. "He was so attentive. Every time I went to the bathroom or turned to look out the window, there'd be a fresh margarita. And he kept paying the piano player ten bucks a song to play my favorite songs—'I Could've Danced All Night,' all the old show tunes. It was heaven."

"When I got home that night, I called my daughter and told her, 'I have just had the best date of my whole life!' I went on and on. And it wasn't even officially a date."

A couple of months later, when Boyd learned Beverly and his pal had had the inevitable falling out, he wasted no time. Calling Beverly, he asked if there was anything he could do to patch things up between them. "I was pretty upset," she recalls. "I told him, 'No, I'm afraid not.' "

"Good," announced Boyd, without missing a beat, "then quit this bawling and let's have dinner!"

Describing this phone conversation, Beverly looks at once sheepish and amused. "I was so naive; I really had no idea—I actually thought he was just offering me a shoulder to cry on."

Nor did Boyd, ever the gentleman, give her any reason to suspect otherwise for some time. "Looking back, it was such an old-fashioned courtship," she says of those first few months, "so romantic and respectful. The flowers, the candy, the theater, the dinners, the dancing. This is a man who still opens doors and does all the other little things. And nothing was ever asked of me. Ever.

"Then, on Valentine's Day, he took me to dinner at a fabulous restaurant, and all of a sudden he pops the question. I was stunned, completely caught off guard. I told him to ask me tomorrow when he was sober. At seven-fifteen the next morning the phone rang. 'You thought I wouldn't remember? Well, I'm sober, and I'm asking.' "

She didn't agree immediately. Not only was there the twenty-year age difference, but, at least as troubling for Beverly, there was what she saw as the discrepancy in their life experiences and levels of sophistication. Beverly is a Berkeley grad with a degree in elementary education, but she had worked only as a secretary, to put her husband through school. ("That's what we called ourselves then," she says, laughing. "Now we're administrative assistants.") Boyd, on the other hand, was a respected scholar who spoke several languages and had traveled the globe.

Of course, Huff was impervious to age. As for her alleged lack of worldliness, he said that if that really bothered her, he would be happy to "be Henry Higgins to [her] Eliza Doolittle."

Beverly ended up breaking her own rule about the two-year wait and saying yes.

"How could I not?" she asks. "This breath of fresh air had come along, this completely original, confident man—and, really, I didn't see his age at all." She laughs. "The instant I accept his proposal, he marches me downtown to buy a ring. As soon as he puts it on, he says, 'Now it's official!' and suddenly, right there in the jewelry store, he bends me over and gives me this big walloping kiss, just like in an old movie!"

Then the gossip started.

"One woman at the Yacht Club actually said it to my face: 'You can't possibly love an old man like that; you're after his money.' " Beverly shakes her head in disgust. "I mean, a few drinks and people's tongues really get loose, don't they? And I'm thinking, 'Is that really how all you people are looking at this?' "

To anyone who knows Beverly even a little, the whole idea is beyond ludicrous. Aside from the fact that she came to the union with money of her own, it would be hard to find anyone so clearly less mercenary.

Yet it wasn't just women at the Yacht Club who initially found the match unseemly. So did her own children, along with a number of Boyd's friends. "Not Moe, of course," she smiles. "His comment was, 'Just live with her; don't marry her!' Of course, Boyd, being Catholic, said, 'There'll be none of that!' "

The talk got so nasty that Beverly began to think seriously about breaking off the engagement—until a navy chaplain set her straight. While his advice was simple, in her distress it was what she needed to hear: if anyone else had a problem, tell them to back off.

In retrospect, all the fevered objections must seem absurd even to those who made them. Boyd's friends adore her almost as much as Beverly's kids have come to adore him.

Indeed, for all the gifts she has bestowed on her husband—love and security in equal measure, an instant family—the worldly Boyd has in fact reciprocated by exposing her to a range of new ideas and experiences. They regularly attend classical concerts and the theater, they've already traveled to Germany, Britain, Scandinavia, and Russia, Beverly has gotten interested in history. "Especially Henry VIII and the Tudors," as Huff has told me, with no little pride. "She likes the gory stuff. Now she tells me, 'Shape up, or I'll behead you.' "

Nor, Beverly adds now, has Boyd ever stopped surprising her. "You never know what's going to come out of his mouth," she says, "and his generosity will get him in even more trouble abroad than at home. When we were in China a few months ago, we met a very nice young girl, and before I know it here was Boyd, telling her mother, 'Send her to Monterey. I'll take care of her education.' " She shakes her head. "A heart of gold. 'What else is money for?' he says. 'We're buying her a future!' The problem is, where money is concerned, he still thinks it's nineteen fifty. He thought he could get the girl two years at Monterey Peninsula College for ten thousand, including room and board, when it's actually closer to thirty thousand. But of course that hasn't stopped him; he's following through."

The one thing she hadn't fully anticipated was how large Boyd's son Jerry would loom in their shared life. "This was all brand-new territory for me; I really didn't understand at first how hard it really is." This woman is no complainer, but the reality of dealing with a heavily medicated adult schizophrenic is simply not something you can prepare for. "I don't mean that the way it probably sounds. It's just that when he comes home, which he doesn't often, he gorges food, just stuffs it down, then throws up. Well, Boyd doesn't clean it up. I have to take all the quilts and hose them down. And he doesn't clean up the bathroom when Jerry can't hit the toilet."

"Does Boyd understand how you feel?"

She nods. "But he's so used to his behavior, he doesn't see a lot of things other people see. Jerry was here one Christmas, out in the backyard with my seven-year-old grandson, having a catch. And after a minute this little boy comes running in, saying Jerry broke his hand— he just burned the ball in. But I also understand how much Boyd loves his son." She stops. "And have you seen Boyd with my grandchildren? He's wonderful with them. It's part of the life he's never had before."

I know that just from the way Boyd talks about them. This is a man born to be a grandfather, someone with vast stores of knowledge and lore he's desperate to pass on. And now, finally, he has the chance.

"I've been with him at garage sales when he buys them history books."

She smiles. "And toys, and sports stuff, and puzzles. God, it's getting to be a problem, the way he spoils them!"

A moment later, Boyd comes bursting through the door, followed by Scarlet. "Ah, my wife and my Boswell!"

In an instant, the dog is back on the couch, all but pinning Beverly back down, frantically licking her face.

"Boyd, get him off!"

"What the hell you want me to do, for chrissakes? Boot her off yourself." He grins my way, then goes to the couch and yanks Scarlet to the floor. "Amazing! Beverly keeps sending her to this special school. They claim she's cured, and soon as she's back home, crazy as ever. Kinda like sending a kid to Berkeley these days!"

He takes a seat beside his wife on the couch. "So what've you two been talking about?"

She slips an arm over his shoulder and, drawing him closer, kisses his cheek. "I've been telling all your secrets."

"I'll bet you have. If only you knew the half of it."

Already Scarlet is back up with them, licking away.

"Oh, good Christ!"

"Off, Scarlet!" commands Beverly, and yanks her to the floor. "Now stay!"

"Back when I was in Alaska, I had a dog team," muses Boyd. "I used to have to beat the hell out of 'em."

I've heard about the dog team before—it was just before the war, when he was earning money for his graduate education by driving an aerial tram at a gold mine—but this is the first time he has said anything about severe disciplinary measures.

"Why'd you do that?"

"You had to beat 'em to get 'em to go! Out there in the goddamm tundra, they had to know who was boss! Your life depended on it."

"No, you didn't," says his wife. "You didn't beat them."

"You had to—they were just savage as hell." He pauses. "It used to take me three hours just to drive 'em down to pick up the mail."

"The mail was at the Fish Hook Tavern," explains Beverly, "which was a bordello."

"It was a mail stop," insists Boyd.

"Right—M-A-L-E."

They both laugh.

"So I'd arrive at the Fish Hook Tavern, cold as hell, and I'd find a nice warm corner and snuggle into a ball on the floor."

"And the girls would snuggle with you."

"Like hell they would; they were nice girls."

"Well, they had good hearts," concedes Beverly. "They'd bring the dogs in."

"And I wouldn't even touch them."

She laughs. "That's only because all the miners had gotten there first."

"Exactly! Out of respect for my predecessors!"

Beverly rises from the couch and seizes the dog. "C'mon, Scarlet, you've had your fun." She starts dragging her toward the door again. "Can you believe it? Now he wants to get another one. He found a collie on the Internet."

"Mack II," booms Boyd, watching them go, "that's what we're gonna call him."

CHAPTER 10

I just think of you, honey, and feel all good and warm

inside. Golly, if you were here now, I betcha I'd walk down

a dozen piers and kiss you from head to toe!

—"BENNY" TURNER IN A LETTER TO MOE, 1946

MOE AND BENNY TURNER AS NEWLYWEDS, 1946.

The odd thing about my relationship with Moe is that the closer we've grown over the years, in some ways the more impenetrable I find him. It is easy to take him as a character and leave it at that. But, as his friends know, that's only what he chooses to put on display. The question is why he often seems almost to go out of his way to keep the rest of it—the generosity and compassion; the depth of his feeling for those in his circle—so carefully under wraps. It is the single subject that is nearly impossible to get him to talk about.

One afternoon, I go out to the little greenhouse out back that Moe has turned into his sanctum sanctorum. Comfortable in a chaise lounge, surrounded by hanging plants and (for some reason) an array of copper pots, a pile of books within reach on the floor, and the local classical station, K-Bach, playing on the radio, he is reading *Great Prison Escape Stories of the Civil War.*

"Got a few minutes?"

Looking up, he eyes me skeptically. "What for?"

"I'd like to talk about your marriage to Benny and what you think makes it work."

The fact is, of all the Girl Watchers' contented marriages, my in-laws' is by far the hardest to figure. Several of the men readily describe their wives as their best friend. Every one of the other couples share passionately held interests. Stuart and his English-born artist-wife, Paula, run book discussion groups together at the Monterey Library, for instance, and attend classes at Monterey Peninsula College with kids little older than their grandchildren; Harry and his wife, Pat, are both serious amateur musicians; a full wall of the dining room in Gene and Jody Cooper's home is taken up by their black-and-white photographs. But to the naked eye, it would be hard to imagine two people less obviously well matched than Moe and Benny. Deeply and thoughtfully spiritual, Benny spends much of her free time down Jocelyn Canyon at St. John's Episcopal Church, a place that Moe, the scientist and confirmed skeptic, has visited only once during all the more than two decades I've known him; and then only to attend the baptism of a grandson. While Benny is down at St. John's, he is likely to be here in the greenhouse, classical music blasting away, with a pile of books beside him—almost none of which he ever discusses with her.

"Benny and Moe are about as different as two people could possibly get," as Cooper puts it. "The fact is, there's probably only one woman in the whole world who could live with him. And somehow he found her."

Moe wearily sets aside his book. "I have no idea—what kind of a question is that?"

"C'mon, think about it."

As I know he knows, I'm not asking merely why the marriage has stayed together. That one's simple. Like so many of their contemporaries—and in such contrast to so many couples today—he and Benny went into it with the firm and unshakable conviction that this was for keeps, literally till death do them part.

But of course, even such a powerful philosophical commitment to the institution is no guarantee of compatibility. The real question is the one a stranger might pose, happening upon two people leading such separate and distinct lives—yet living in such evident contentment: what makes this marriage work?

"She just must be easily satisfied, that's all," says Moe, dismissing it out of hand. "Poor Benny, she's looking for her reward in the next life, 'cause she damn well knows she's not getting it in this one."

I ask him if he believes that.

"Course I do. She's definitely the loser in this deal. If I'd've been like Cooper or Godfrey, I'd have smothered her with kindness, which she deserves. The slightest little thing you do for her—just crumbs—and she's so delighted." He shakes his head sadly. "I'm telling you, it's really a shame. She'd've made some goody-goody guy a great wife."

This is all too typical of Moe when the topic is emotionally dicey: the illusion of honesty but not the substance; self-denigration as a defensive tactic as he buys time to move out of range.

"I really don't think that's it. She certainly doesn't feel that way about it."

"She should—that's another one of her weaknesses: she's too soft-hearted."

Not, it must be said, that Moe has ever been shy about discussing a large part of Benny's appeal for him, at least at the start: that she was the best-looking woman he had ever met. "I got the best of 'em all, no gettin' around it," he tells me again now, not so much an expression of sentiment as a matter of statistical fact, "a vest pocket Venus with an hourglass figure: thirty-four, twenty-three, thirty-three; a hundred and three pounds. My friends were incredulous. But like I always say, it's just as easy to ask out a beautiful one as an ugly one. Easier, 'cause your heart's in it."

"Your friends thought she could've done better?"

"Of course she could've; all kinds of guys wanted to marry her. She was so great looking, they'd propose to her on the first date. But she was so classy, none of 'em ever tried to go to bed with her."

"So what do you think your appeal was for her?"

He hardens slightly. "How should I know? Ask her. She said she married me 'cause I didn't put her on a pedestal like all these other guys. Then she got bitter 'cause I wouldn't put her on a pedestal. I was also lucky. I was stationed at the time in Washington, at the Bureau of Aeronautics, and most of the competition was overseas."

"In other words, you were her only option."

"Just about. There was one other person she'd been going with, some guy who'd studied over in England, at Oxford. But he was kind of goofy—ended up one of these swami types—so she'd probably have been even worse off with him than with me. That answer your question?"

"Tell me about the first time you met."

"I was at this party with a little Catholic girl whose fiancé had been shot down in Europe, and I saw Benny there. That's pretty much it."

"Do you remember what she was wearing?"

"A dress. I think it was maybe black and white." He picks up his book. "You'll have to ask her."

"It was a black-and-white party dress," Benny immediately answers later that afternoon.

"That's what he said."

"Did he?" she says, pleased. "I didn't think he had any idea."

Temperamentally, it is hard to imagine a greater contrast than with her husband. While Moe, erratic and impulsive, is quick to irritation and just as quick to forget all about it, the demure Benny is a walking island of calm. He has an insatiable need to connect with everyone he meets; she's so self-contained that strangers might consider her remote. He is irredeemably disorganized; she so craves order she sometimes seems close to despair surveying the chaos her husband has imposed on their home.

And while Moe, in the right mood, will rattle on about just about anything, Benny's words are always carefully considered.

"I remember I almost didn't go that night, because it was so far from where I was living and I was worried about getting home," she says now. "But what really made an impression was how easy it was to be with him. There was a Victrola at this party, and a fireplace, and we just spent the longest time talking, and there was no need to put on any pretenses." She smiles. "He wasn't quite so far out as now."

"I gather your mother wasn't crazy about the idea of your marrying him." According to my wife, they actually waited until Christmas Eve to break the news to Benny's mother, hoping she'd be so emotionally depleted by the holiday she would only have the energy to cry a little. It didn't work; she wept piteously.

"Well," allows Benny, protective even in retrospect, "he tried his best. The whole time he was with my family he was on his best behavior. He was polite to everyone and didn't try out any of his wacko ideas."

"Why do you suppose you were so drawn to him?"

She thinks about it a full five seconds. "I suppose his unpredictability was part of the attraction. I had a very sheltered, very traditional background, and so much Moe did was unexpected. I certainly wasn't going to be able to be a little girl anymore. No one could have made me grow up faster than he did."

"I imagine he was a lot more entertaining than most guys."

She smiles—that one doesn't even require an answer. "And believe it or not, he was also a marvelous dancer."

"Really?" It's hard to even imagine Moe on a dance floor.

She looks at me closely, realizing how inadequate such an explanation must sound. "We love each other enormously," she says. "We don't say it all the time, but it's very deep. I remember how moved I used to be by his letters. That's really how we got to know each other, through our letters. Would you like to see them? I haven't looked at them myself in years."

Until now, I didn't know these letters still existed.

She hurries into a back bedroom and returns a few minutes later with an old tin box, crammed full.

The correspondence begins soon after that first evening in late 1944 and ends in mid-1946; it reveals a pair of flat-out romantics, improbably innocent even by the standards of the day. The young Moe is so endearingly love-besotted that he's almost impossible to recognize in the flinty curmudgeon I've come to know.

His letters are full of the kind of rhapsodic language that within mere decades would seem hopelessly cornball even to similarly ardent young lovers. He even tried his hand at love poetry. One poem, posted from Philadelphia on January 8, 1946, was on an illustrated card featuring a young woman in a forest, surrounded by cherubic children and assorted woodland creatures:

If I, a dream, adrift on evening's wind
had a choice of just whose heart I would enter in:
I think of all the hearts this world does boast
your heart is the one I care to enter most.

Moe was full of dreams and promises to Benny about the shape of their future together, which he confided with eager tenderness. "It seems as if every beautiful song I hear was written about you," he writes from the Naval Radar Training School in St. Simon Island, Georgia, early in the series. "You are as much a part of me as the dreams that you replaced. I am looking forward to the day that I am out of the Navy and we can seek our fortune together. A nice little place out in the country with lots of little interesting places within walking distance. Places to dangle your feet in the water and places to lie in the grass and feel the warmth of the sun in your face and to hear the wind in the grass. A place where the talk is not of war but where people are filled with the wonder of life and God."

Nearly as stunning as his frequent religious references is the intensity of young Moe's ambition. Already in his late twenties by war's end, he wrote over and over of his need to make up for lost time and succeed in life; not merely financially but by the size of his contribution to the world.

Moe and Benny married on March 21, 1946, the first day of the first spring after the end of the war. But a couple of months later, he was back in the South Pacific as part of the team for the A-bomb tests code-named Operation Crossroads, and the correspondence resumed. Stationed on the island of Eleye that summer, Moe wrote letters that alternate between shoptalk about test preparations—his job was, of all things, to fly through the mushroom cloud and measure radiation—and insistent, sometimes desperate, professions of devotion and longing. Even now, he can scarcely believe his good fortune—"It seems impossible that anyone so wonderful as you would fall in love with me" was a typical sentiment—and when she didn't write back fast enough or, especially, if her letters weren't ardent enough when they did arrive, he would immediately fear the worst.

During this postnuptial separation Benny was living in a women's dormitory on Sutter Street in San Francisco, trying and failing to put away some money doing clerical work. Her letters to Moe reflect the sweetness and naïveté of a twenty-two-year-old unsophisticated in ways no young American woman this side of the Amish country could possibly be today. "It's such a good feeling to be married," she writes, a couple of weeks after his departure. "Before, I sorta had no real feeling of belonging, but now I just think of you, honey, and feel all good and warm inside. Golly, if you were here now, I betcha I'd walk down a dozen piers and kiss you from head to toe!"

On her own for the first time, she is sometimes innocent in ways that strain credulity. "I dropped by Leo Killian's office during my lunch hour today," she writes at one point, referring to an acquaintance of Moe's. "He took my telephone number and address and said he'd like to get another couple and have the four of us go out to dinner some evening. I told him I didn't drop by with that in mind, but just wanted to be able to tell you I had seen him. What do you think of it?" And, little more than a week later: "Tonite as I was up in the laundry room ironing, there was a phone call for me. It was Leo Killian, who invited me to go with him tomorrow nite to dinner. I said I would, but I don't feel at all keen about it. I don't feel right doing it—and not knowing if you'd want me to, is another thing. It's very nice of him to do it, tho. I told him I had 2 letters from you today, and he said, 'Gee, I know that makes you happy,' and it certainly did, honey."

There exists no record of how happy Moe felt about the information in *her* letter.

But mainly, continually, she offers him reassurance that her devotion is equal to his. "Ever since reading your letter today, I have felt so ashamed of myself, as I've caused you to worry by not writing. Please, honey, don't ever say that I miss you less as time goes by. I miss you so doggone much that I go to bed each nite reliving in my mind some little incident of our life together."

If such heartfelt remorse didn't lift his spirits, what she went on to say surely did. "Believe me, honey, every time I look at my nighties in their little green box, I just feel like hugging them to me, as they are part of such perfect happiness, and I'll be the world's happiest little wife when I again have cause for putting them to use."

In his return missive, a delighted Moe professes shock: "'Cause all this time since I left you my mind has been on religious subjects. . . . Honey, although it's pretty hot and I have only a cot, I would love to share it with you. It won't be too long now."

Yet of all the letters, the one that is most unexpected in both tone and content is the note Moe wrote Benny in the closing moments of the momentous year 1945. "Well, in thirty minutes it will be 1946. Seems that all in one day people realize that there was a past and there will be a future, yet how soon in the effort of living in it will they forget? I write late at nite and all is black out and the otherwise stillness is accented by the sounds of the wind in the trees. Tonight they could suggest anything. Maybe the sound of the souls of all the people who died this year leaving the earth. But maybe it could be the sound of storks' wings as they bring new life and hope to a world that needs it."

Late that day, after I have returned the letters to Benny, I find her reading them over herself. I tell her how much they surprised me, especially Moe's.

"They remind me all over again why I love him so much," she says evenly. "He's a very decent and honorable person, and nothing is more important than that. In the end, knowing that about one another is what gets you through the hard times."

There is no trace of maudlin sentiment in this; it's just something she has been thinking about.

"Why do you suppose he has such a hard time showing it?" I ask.

"He's always been that way. Even then he had a hard time expressing emotion face-to-face; it's just the way he grew up. But you've seen how generous he is."

"Of course."

"Well, you know, then," says his wife. "He's found his own way of showing his love without the physical contact."

A few minutes later, I find Moe, still in the greenhouse. Now he's reading *Elementary Particles and the Laws of Physics*.

"You ever read this?" he asks, looking up.

"I don't think I'd understand a word."

"What's wrong with you? Sure you would." He snaps the book shut and thrusts it my way. "You should know about this."

"Moe," I say, taking it, "I've been reading the letters you and Benny wrote each other during the war."

He looks at me with interest but says nothing.

"Fascinating. You had all kinds of stuff in there about the atomic tests. Did you end up wearing sunglasses when you looked at the blast? It wasn't clear in what you wrote."

"Of course I did. I also had a pair of Japanese military artillery glasses. I tell you, a second or two after the flash, it was like someone hit that plane with a baseball bat."

"You must've gotten quite a dose of radiation."

"Oh, yeah, lots more than we should've. When they dropped the second one, I was sitting up front with the pilots in the B-29 with my Geiger counter. The head pilot was one of these real macho guys—I warned him not to, but he really flew straight through the plutonium cloud. That needle jumped right off the chart. 'Well,' I told the pilot, 'that does it; you're on your way to being sterile.' Man, you should've seen how he almost jerked the wings off the plane getting out of there. Afterward we made up a little poem about that: 'If your daughters have two heads / and your sons are quadrupeds / you're a veteran of Bikini.' "

"Funny, there was a poem Benny wrote you about the tests at the time."

I had jotted down Benny's poem, because it struck me as such an artifact of that infinitely more innocent time, expressing not the trepidation we feel about nuclear weaponry today but only awe and wonder.

Into remote Bikini lagoon
The target ships assemble
For they will face the atom soon
To sink—to list, to tremble

July the first—a perfect day
The bomber hits the air
The time has come—so bombs away
A hush—a blinding glare . . .

But Moe doesn't ask about Benny's poem, or anything else about the letters.

"You interested in taking a look at them?" I ask.

He shakes his head no. "I don't think so."

"Why not?"

"I just don't—Benny can; it's more her speed."

He picks up a new book from his pile: the library copy of a recent biography of Mozart.

"Think my children would have a different impression of me if they read those letters?" he asks suddenly.

"I think so. They're very warm—sentimental even."

"Benny's a really good writer, don't you think?—not like me. That's when I could tell how sharp she is, after I saw her letters. She's so quiet; before that I had no idea she was such a remarkable person. They really impressed me."

"I think yours impressed her, also."

"You think so?" For a moment, from the delighted expression on his face, he could almost be twenty-five again. "Till her, I'd never told any woman I loved her, did I ever tell you that? A lot of guys tell every woman they see."

✦ CHAPTER 11 ✦

Remember how it was? One minute all these students are getting married, and, Christ, nine months later you could hardly walk down Telegraph Avenue for all the baby buggies!

—BOYD HUFF

THE TURNER FAMILY, 1953—WITH TWO MORE
STILL TO COME.

The next time the full complement of Girl Watchers gathers around Moe's dining room table, Walzer returns to where we started last time. "Weren't we going to talk about coming back from the war?"

"We got sidetracked. We ended up talking about women."

"Always a pleasant diversion," observes Huff.

What I'm hoping to hear about is what it was really like back then. How great was the sense of urgency to make up for lost time and get their lives rolling?

And—though for the moment I leave this part aside—was that time really the way it is so often portrayed today? For while the postwar baby-boom years, roughly the mid-forties to the mid-fifties, generate far fewer best-sellers and documentaries than the war itself, they too are now regularly described as a turning point in our national story. That period produced its own set of assumptions and myths—and few of them are positive.

Only a month or so ago, looking over my seventeen-year-old son's reading list for an eleventh grade course titled "Post World War II America," I discovered that almost every one of the books stressed a single theme: conformity. The list included *The Man in the Gray Flannel Suit*, Sloan Wilson's 1955 best-seller about a young man caught in the post-war corporate rat race; an excerpt from Vance Packard's *The Status Seekers*, describing what he saw as the spiritual emptiness resulting from Americans' obsession with material acquisition; and *The Feminine Mystique*, Betty Friedan's revered 1963 book that "exposed" the "problem that has no name," the purposeless and deeply unhappy lives of American housewives before the feminist revolution. For good measure, the teacher also tossed in Allen Ginsberg's famous poem "Howl" (opening line: "I saw the best minds of my generation destroyed by madness . . ."), as well as a couple of essays taking aim at that other convenient target of recent years, fifties TV sitcoms like *Father Knows Best* and *Leave It to Beaver*, with their supposedly fraudulent idealization of family life.

"Damn right there was urgency," Boyd replies to my question. "Christ, I was almost thirty years old; it seemed to me like I was already approaching middle age! You just felt this awful pressure to get a family going and complete your education and get out there." He laughs. "It was good-bye to the good life."

"And hello diapers!" tosses in Walzer.

As they begin batting the subject around, I quickly realize something that almost never gets factored into the way we think about that time: how unbelievably *hard* it was to build a life from scratch, as so many veterans had to. Finding themselves far less well along professionally than they had expected to be, often—having been away in uniform during the years young men normally go through the more subtle maturing rituals of dating and courtship—even less prepared than men of prior generations for life's other great challenge, fatherhood and children, they attacked the task of catching up with the same grit many had brought to the beaches of France and the jungles of the Pacific.

In retrospect, what is so impressive is not just the extent to which so many succeeded; but the way, over the decades that followed, all those individual success stories came together to foster unprecedented levels of prosperity for the country itself.

"When I got to Berkeley after the A-bomb tests in the Pacific, I could hardly believe how much drive people had," Moe says. "I mean, there was never a bunch of students like that in all history. These guys had all this experience in the war, and they were *serious*. Man, talk about competitive!"

"Thank goodness for the GI Bill," says Harry.

"Best money the government ever spent," Stuart completes the thought. "It's an investment in human potential that's paid for itself a hundred times over in taxes and revenues generated. It's *still* paying off."

"That's one of the things Martha and I had going for us," says Huff. "Since she'd also been in the service, both of us were on the GI Bill of Rights."

"Ninety-five dollars a month times two," says Earl dryly. "Just to put it in perspective."

Huff laughs with the others. "Well, it helped *some*. I wouldn't accept money from my father, and it was one helluva thing, trying to get a degree and support a new family at the same time. I don't believe I ever worked like that in my life."

"My goodness," says Gene Cooper, "the *energy* people had! But then it was just natural."

Sitting there, I can't resist a smile—it sure doesn't seem natural to me. Finish school, launch a career, start a family *all at the same time?* When I was in college, between attending antiwar demonstrations, chasing women, and smoking the occasional joint, it was more than enough trying to keep up a low-B average. In my circle at least, a career was something you maybe started thinking about midway through your senior year. Marriage? Kids? If you were on the mature side, you got to that around thirty; and even then generally with extreme trepidation. It's not for nothing we got known as a generation of commitment-phobes.

"Man, oh man, money was tight," adds Cooper. "The truth is, you never felt entirely secure, especially once you had children."

"I really don't think a lot of younger people can appreciate what it was like, even with the current economic troubles. It was just dog-eat-dog, fierce competition for relatively few jobs," says Harry. "I was with you, Boyd; I wouldn't accept any money from my parents, either—it was a matter of pride."

"Christ, that's why I didn't get my Ph.D. until 'fifty-three, because when the kids came I could never really ease off. It's funny, that whole time I don't remember the term *work ethic* ever even coming up."

"Growing up in the Depression was part of that, too," agrees Earl. "We learned young that necessity is an awfully good motivator."

"Heck, that's why the ninety-five dollars from the GI Bill meant something," says Cooper. "I was able to have two kids for about two hundred and fifty dollars each."

Earl nods. "That really was the payoff, wasn't it? Here we'd fought a war. Now we got to come home and make a life and a family."

✦ ✦ ✦

I knew Joseph Heller, the late author of the classic *Catch-22,* and I remember him talking once about his experiences in the postwar period. Heller was in school three thousand miles and a cultural mindset away from Moe, at New York University, but his description of the frenetic energy and ambition on his own campus, the desperation to make up for lost time, was nearly the same; for what their generation had been through and how it left them feeling about themselves transcended background or region.

Heller has one of his characters observe to another, with the uncanny blend of poignancy and cynicism that make the book so memorable: "A second ago you were stepping into college with your lungs full of fresh air. Today you're an old man. . . . You're inches away from death every time you go on a mission. How much older can you be at your age? A half minute before that you were stepping into high school and an unhooked brassiere was as close as you ever hoped to get to Paradise. Only a fifth of a second before that you were a small kid with a ten-week summer vacation that lasted a hundred thousand years and still ended too soon. Zip! They go rocketing by so fast."

Years later, when I heard Heller was finally writing a sequel to *Catch-22,* I hoped and half expected he would set it on campus in the immediate postwar period—maybe even using some of the same characters. It seemed a natural: Milo Minderbinder, the unscrupulous wheeler-dealer, using the names of dead former comrades to rip off the GI Bill or cornering the market in baby food; sweet, awkward Major Major, majoring in accounting despite being completely befuddled by numbers; the despised Havermeyer, looking to win the academic race by kissing every available ass; and of course Yossarian, Heller's alter ego, maybe with a wife and a baby and another one on the way, taking it all in with sorrowfully bemused lucidity, reflecting (with the benefit of forty years' hindsight) on the America such men were about to build.

✦ ✦ ✦

"My God, remember how it was in Berkeley, Turner? One minute all these students are getting married, and, Christ, nine months later you could hardly walk down Telegraph Avenue for the baby buggies! You'd come out of class and see all these kids running around all over the campus, waiting for Dad."

"Do I remember? I was one of 'em!" Moe looks around the table at the others. "Here I'd got back from the Pacific figuring I'm set! I'd landed this teaching job while I'm going to grad school, and ole Benny's gonna bring in extra money with a job as a clerk in San Francisco. Well, the very first day, she comes home from work saying she doesn't feel well."

"One day?" laughs Walzer. "That's gotta be some kind of land speed record."

"With Benny, all you had to do was walk by her. Before we were done, we had diaphragm babies, pill babies, babies by the rhythm method. We had two children almost immediately. Larry and—" he looks at me— "your wife."

"I'm aware of that, Moe."

"Well," Moe continues, "just speeded up the schedule a little, that's all. Long as they look like you, I say. I'd rather have my kids look like me than the best-looking guy in town."

Later, recounting this part of the conversation to my wife, she tells me that she has heard the line many, *many* times before. What interests her more is Boyd's description of the buggy-choked Telegraph Avenue of those years. A Berkeley grad herself, class of 1972, she remembers the same stretch of road crammed with VW Bugs and mini-vans. "What a difference! In our day, getting pregnant was everyone's greatest *fear.* Aside from a few hippie chicks, no one *wanted* to be a parent. Have kids? We were kids ourselves!"

Moe and Benny were just one of hundreds—maybe thousands—of young couples in those few square miles alone for whom parenthood was less planned than something that happened to them. Yet, also typically, it was something they welcomed without a second thought.

When you have just gotten through a world war, taking on kids just wasn't that big a deal.

"Christ, Turner," says Huff, laughing, "remember that back apartment you had in that old house? It was so goddamn tiny, I don't know how the hell the three of you survived in there."

"Well, it was a step up from the first place we were in: just one narrow room, with a little niche behind a curtain. In the next one over, some guy hung himself while his wife was in the same room, and she didn't even know he was doing it."

"What a lovely little anecdote," muses Harry.

"There'd been a Communist cell in that place before you got there," adds Huff, who was managing the building and met the Turners when they moved in. "I didn't give a damn about their politics, but they were bad tenants. Always creating an uproar, cars coming and going at all hours, strange women staying overnight!"

"Berkeley!" says Earl, smiling. "Some things never change."

"Let me ask you guys a question," says Walzer, glancing around the table. "Can you even imagine acting like these husbands today, being right there in the birthing room with your wife?"

"My God," exclaims Moe, "I would've been so embarrassed!"

"When my kids were born, I'd bring a briefcase full of legal work to do while I sat there. I mean, if someone was perverted enough even to want to go in, they wouldn't let you, anyway."

"Especially the nurses," says Earl. "They had *no* use for males. They didn't even want to see your face."

"Well, he was in the room when both his kids were born," says Moe, jerking his head in my direction, "weren't you?"

"Of course I was. These days, you'd almost be embarrassed *not* to be."

"How'd you feel about it?"

"It was fine. It was easy."

"Did you find it a beautiful experience?" asks Huff, without any discernible hint of sarcasm. "That's what you're always hearing."

I hesitate. Once again cast as an emissary from across the generational divide, I don't want to mislead. "It was okay. I didn't get all goo-goo eyed like some guys—no videos or anything like that."

"Didn't you find it has an effect on the romantic angle, seeing it all so closely?" asks Stuart.

"For some people I guess it can. It is pretty raw."

Moe physically shudders. "All that touchy-feely stuff they do nowadays. *My* wife wouldn't have wanted it, I can tell you that."

"You can't say that, Moe," cautions Cooper. "Times change, and people change with them. If we've learned anything, it's that the human animal is infinitely adaptable."

"Well, I'll tell you this much," declares Moe, "we were complete babes in the woods, didn't know the first thing about babies! It wasn't like when we grew up, where you had grandmothers and cousins to tell you what to do. Most of us were far from home, totally on our own. If it wasn't for some other graduate students who already had 'em, Benny and me might've killed our first one."

"Kind of gave you a new appreciation for the extended family," says Stuart. "Suddenly, even the most annoying relatives had their uses."

"Of course there was Dr. Spock," points out Earl. "But then he went off the deep end."

What Earl is of course referring to is the widespread notion during the sixties that it was the "permissive" parenting advocated by Dr. Spock, at the time a noted antiwar activist himself, that had produced the generation so contemptuous of their elders.

Spock himself bitterly resented the charge, pointing out that his best-selling book urged discipline and structure along with generous helpings of love and understanding. But regardless of his intentions, his book was such a sharp break with the harsh and regimented brand of child rearing recommended by his predecessors that many new parents were bound to overlook the parts urging firmness.

Yet it is also the case that fathers were always far less likely to fall into that trap than were mothers, who, indeed, tended to be more sympathetic toward Spock and his approach in general. It is no coincidence that in 1968, when Dr. Spock was put on trial for counseling resistance to the draft, the government used summary challenges to dismiss every prospective woman juror.

"It isn't popular to say these days," Moe declares flatly now, "but some things are just built into the genes. I never changed a diaper in my life."

This is something I've never heard from any male contemporary; none would dare. "You sound proud of it."

"I'm not *not* proud; it's just how it was. I was the one who had to go out and make a living, and that was plenty. It wasn't easy."

"I'm with you, Turner," says Boyd.

"Of course you are! My wife could play with a little kid and bill and coo all day long; if I was watching it more than a few minutes, I'd get bored. I wouldn't start getting interested at least till they started to talk. But I could do other things for them."

"Like explain the theory of relativity," says Harry. "At least once they're talking."

"That's right! And believe me, I tried!"

Never mind having nothing to apologize for, these guys are damn proud of what they did. By their late twenties, having survived the darkest depression in our history and a terrible war, each went on to succeed in providing his loved ones with a level of material well-being far beyond anything that seemed possible at the start.

And if along the way it was their wives who did almost all the cooking and cleaning, not to mention the comforting after playground injuries and most of the homework supervision, that was the bargain everyone agreed to. Easy as it is today to deride such an arrangement as backward, at the time it seemed to work remarkably well, for their families and, yes, even for society at large.

"Anyway, I could do all kinds of things my wife couldn't. I could build things! Remember, Boyd, how we fenced in the backyard of that Berkeley house?"

"Right. We put up that little playground for Larry and Jerry, so they could play out there while the wives watched 'em from inside the house."

"Martha also stopped working?" I ask with some surprise, for Huff's first wife had a reputation as a relentless go-getter.

"She worked until Jerry arrived. After that, I wanted her there with the children. And she wanted to be there, too."

"Which in retrospect was a wise decision," says Stuart, the most liberal member of the group and in general strongly sympathetic to the feminist view.

"It was," agrees Earl, the most conservative. "It was better for the kids all around."

"Jody and I felt the same way," says Cooper. "I was always involved, of course, but not quite to the extent she was."

"I don't have to tell you that a lot of people these days would be upset by your position on this."

"Look at it from the kid's point of view!" says Moe. "I know how much it meant having my mother there for me when I came home from school. I remember the one time she wasn't, I got so upset I couldn't stand it. Just one time!"

Stuart laughs. "You still haven't gotten over it."

"That's just about right. Little kids need their mothers; it's pretty much that simple."

Though I see part of my role here is playing devil's advocate, once again I can't help finding this indifference to the dictates of contemporary orthodoxy incredibly refreshing. For today it is everywhere a given that the fifties were a grim and joyless time when hypocrisy flourished behind every pleasant suburban facade and all but the most daring were straitjacketed by convention. When my son was taking that course on the postwar period, he was hardly alone in thinking the movie *Pleasantville,* wherein the uptight fifties characters appear in black-and-white while the liberated contemporary ones laugh and dance in color, got it just about right.

How even to begin deprogramming a kid raised on today's education and popular culture?

Look, I told my son, there absolutely *were* terrible inequities back then, things which should embarrass us as a country. But frankly, in some ways, at least from the perspective of a middle-class kid growing up in that time, things were actually *better* than they are today. Our dads may not have been around much, but most of our moms were. Most of us felt secure and powerfully loved. Moreover—this was something that took an extra bit of explaining, since the concept was alien to his experience—part of that security had to do with the fact that we were allowed to be *innocent* for so much longer; protected by our elders and society itself from the worst of the adult world and so happily ensconced in one of our own. Even at twelve or fourteen we would be unembarrassed to love *Old Yeller* or *Swiss Family Robinson* or *Journey to the Center of the Earth,* and the World Series (all day games!) was an annual event understood to be so colossally important that some teachers cheerfully overlooked our transistor radios.

As for those much-mocked family sitcoms, the "traditional" moms were not nearly as passive as a lot of people seem to think today, or the "traditional" dads nearly so—to use another favorite put-down word—patriarchal. Lots of times, in fact, they made mistakes, and their wives and kids had to straighten *them* out. Thanks to cable, this should be obvious to everyone, yet somehow it's not.

Not long ago, for instance, I caught an old *Leave It to Beaver* episode in which Wally is nominated to run for class president against Lumpy Rutherford, and Ward intervenes when he thinks his son is taking the race too lightly. Following his dad's advice, Wally turns into the consummate glad-handing, phony politician and loses as a result. The show ends with Ward talking to the boys in their room:

Wally: Heck, Dad, I'm not sore at you.

Ward: I wouldn't blame you if you were, Wally. I'm afraid I made you look pretty silly with all my advice . . . I'm sorry, I really gave you a bum steer.

Beaver: How come you gave him a bum steer, Dad?

Ward: Oh, I guess it's all just part of being a father, Beaver. Your boy makes the football team and you visualize him scoring touchdowns all over the place. He gets an A in mathematics and you see him as an atomic scientist landing on the moon. Maybe even picture him marrying the banker's daughter.

Beaver: Gee, Dad, I thought only kids had goofy dreams like that.

Ward: Oh, no, Beaver. Parents have their share, too. You see, as you grow older, you realize some of the dreams and ambitions you had are just not going to come true. So you begin to dream through your children.

Wally: (incredulous) You mean Mr. Rutherford dreams through Lumpy?

Ward: Of course he does. I don't guess there's a father anywhere who doesn't want things to be a little better for his children than they were for him.

The fact is, allowing for the assorted lunacies unique to every family, such a dynamic was really not all that far from what was going on in lots of our actual homes. If it was our mothers who were always (sometimes too much) *there,* driving us to the dentist, checking in with our teachers, eyeballing our friends, it was not as if our fathers' physical absence was to be confused with absence of interest. That our fathers worked all the time was not something to be resented; it was simply part of the way things were. For we also knew, though we didn't give it a moment's thought at the time, that they were working for *us.*

"I'll never forget, in nineteen fifty-one, we had quite a crisis," Cooper is saying. "We were about to move to Monterey from Annapolis, and I was out here setting things up. Jody and the kids were staying with my mother in Galveston, and she had Kenny, who was five, in nursery school down there. And he came down with polio."

Polio? The very word still evokes terror. Obviously, the story has a happy ending: I've met Kenny, thriving as an artist in San Francisco, the father of Cooper's beloved grandson. Still . . .

"He was losing control of his limbs, a steady downward progression," Cooper goes on. "He'd try to walk, and he would fall. It was a pretty tough deal all around."

"Might've ended up in one of those iron lungs," says Moe, Mr. Sensitive. "Little girl we knew, she got it around the same time as Kenny and ended up having to wear a brace." He pauses, then tosses in, "She's a lesbian now."

"It took a while in the hospital and a lot of physical therapy, but he made a pretty good recovery. It tore us up quite a bit, but Jody really held it together."

"Lots of men go straight to pieces in those situations."

"My God, what a thing to go through," says Stuart. "And they say the war is scary!"

Earl nods meaningfully; he's going through some of that himself now as two of his grandchildren ready themselves for the impending kidney transplant. "There's no more frightening feeling; that's when you really understand the meaning of powerlessness. In the grand scheme of things, family is really all that matters."

"Can you imagine what it must have been like in earlier times, when medicine was so primitive and you just watched your children die left and right?" says Stuart. "Really puts things in perspective, doesn't it? It seems like a hundred years ago that you had to worry about polio."

"It *was* fifty," Harry points out, truly putting things in perspective. "It was a *long* time ago"—he laughs—"when the dinosaurs ruled the earth."

I can certainly understand the impulse to trash the recent past. Let's face it, nothing inspires so contented a sense of moral superiority than the certain conviction you're more enlightened than those who came before, even, *especially,* if they're your parents. Still, isn't it the very definition of irony that we so readily belittle the values of that time only because they gave us the security to do so?

Not that the men at this table give a damn about any of the criticism in the first place.

"Well," I say, as we start to wrap things up, "I certainly don't hear anyone being defensive about the nineteen fifties."

"Defensive?" demands Huff with surprise. "Why on earth would we be?"

"You want to talk about the fifties?" says Cooper evenly. "Back then we were still building the best cars in the world, devising the best agricultural machinery, building the best steel mills, manufacturing just about everything you can think of from textiles to nuts and bolts. We developed the tape recorder in this country and TV sets and created whole new categories of cameras. Look around today, and about the only original complex engineering we do is on weapons systems."

"Well, you know," I say, starting to feel a bit foolish even pressing the point, "there's all this talk today about the conformity and the materialism of that period—of how America back then was a cultural wasteland. The suburban tract housing and all that. Remember that song 'Little Boxes'?"

"What?" Huff erupts again. "We're supposed to be upset because we built suburban tracts that snobs don't like, so that the families of ex-soldiers could have a better life?"

"I don't think it was a cultural wasteland at all," says Godfrey. "Well, maybe to some people out there in New York, but not to anyone I know."

"Even with those little tract houses," chimes in Cooper, "every one of the dads worried about how to pay for them. That's why a lot of vets ended up going back and joining the reserves; it seemed a pretty nice way to make a few extra dollars."

It always seems to get back to responsibility with these guys—doing the right thing even when it wasn't the easy thing. Lest we forget, theirs was the only American generation that found many of its members at risk of the ultimate sacrifice not once but twice.

"That was my story," says Walzer. "I decided to go in the reserves because I was in my last year of law school and pretty short of money. So I enlisted in the intelligence unit. Well, my commission arrives—and I see they've put me in the armored cavalry. Tanks!"

The others laugh.

"And *then* the Korean War starts! And I'm remembering how it was in France—how as we'd be walking back to the rear, these poor guys in the tanks would be going forward, white as sheets. I really wasn't sure I was up for that. The idea of being set on fire really bothered me."

"Where was your patriotism?" asks Handler, grinning.

"Well, as an amateur lawyer, I read this form over more carefully than I've ever read over any legal document in my life. At the bottom there was something called a 'declination.' Well, that was my escape hatch—I declined."

"I also joined the reserves," says Harry, "but then found I really didn't have time to make the meetings, so I sent in my resignation. This was two months before all hell broke out over there and they closed that loophole." He pauses meaningfully. "The other guys I was with—all World War II vets like me, just guys with young families looking for a few extra dollars—they all ended up going over to Korea. I don't think a single one of them made it back."

CHAPTER 12

Moe has pointed out that traditionally schizophrenics choose to identify themselves as Napoleon—Alexander the Great's a far less common choice. I remind him that Jerry's a lot better read than most.

—BOYD HUFF

JERRY, MARTHA, AND BOYD HUFF; ANDY HUFF IN INSET.

"*It's very gracious* of you to do this," says Boyd Huff, as we pull out of the Turners' driveway and start down their hilly street, a little before ten on a brilliantly sunny Tuesday morning. "Jerry will be most grateful."

The truth is that knowing how much Jerry means to his father, I've been eager to meet him for some time.

I've come to like Boyd tremendously. It's impossible not to. Generous-spirited and endlessly accommodating, he is blessed with what a therapist acquaintance of mine would call "up energy"; yet this is balanced by a cool, clear mind that once made him so adept a foreign policy analyst.

Still, for all Boyd's bluff candor, I've wondered about the toll taken by the succession of terrible psychic blows he has endured over the years, any one of which might have destroyed someone else.

He has never gone into much detail about Jerry, living in a halfway house for schizophrenics up in San Jose. Not that I've pressed him, any more than I have on the subject of Andy, his second son, killed in a shooting accident. My reluctance to bring up his sons has almost as much to do with Boyd's impatience with the woe-is-me confessional mind-set as with the subject's obvious delicacy. Moe has more than once observed he never worries about Boyd because "he's so ornery, he'll survive anything," yet it strikes me this slightly misses the real point. It's not that Huff is impervious to emotional distress, just that—a far different thing—he refuses to surrender to it. His attitude—and it has served him well—is that there's simply no purpose in dwelling on that which can't be undone.

I have seen only one picture of Jerry Huff. In the shot, taken with his parents, he is maybe sixteen and appears to be the prototypical all-American California kid, circa 1965, good looking and upbeat. My wife, who is a couple of years younger than he is, remembers the Jerry of those years as the highly promising young man he was: a gifted athlete and a voracious student of classical history, very much his father's son. "We all thought he was going to be a star," she says.

Jerry's schizophrenia hit, as is typical of the disease, in early adulthood—during his first year at the University of Arizona. Arizona is a perennial baseball powerhouse, and, as a pitcher on the freshman team, Jerry was evidently viewed as a serious prospect. But, so the story goes, one day he stood up on the team bus and announced to his fellow players that he was Alexander the Great. "That's how it started," Moe says, "and it was all downhill from there. After that he started doing stuff like that all the time."

Before long, his parents had to bring him home. They enrolled him at the local junior college, Monterey Peninsula, but Jerry's downward spiral only accelerated. Over the ensuing years treatment by a legion of doctors and psychiatrists failed to arrest it. Today, in his mid-fifties, Jerry passes his days heavily medicated, wandering the San Jose streets from early morning until evening, when he returns to his halfway house to sleep.

Like many schizophrenics, he also hears voices. Beverly Huff told me that on Jerry's last visit to Monterey, her grandchildren ran to her reporting that someone was with Jerry in his room. They had overheard him in conversation with a real tough guy whose voice was a lot deeper than Jerry's and who seemed furious with him. This imaginary being kept ranting and cursing, telling Jerry what a mess he was, and "poor Jerry just sat there and took it."

Driving north on Highway 101, Boyd is in excellent spirits. Pretty soon he is reminiscing about the old days—specifically, the moment he first spotted Martha, his first wife and Jerry's mother, on the boat heading home after one of his stints working in Alaska.

"Christ," he says, "there she was in the dining room, on the side of the rope reserved for the swells, and there I was on the other, with the working stiffs. But, Christ, I liked what I saw, so I sure as hell wasn't about to hold back. I jumped the rope and gave the headwaiter five bucks to seat me next to her. Never regretted it a moment; we had a great life together."

"You get along well with her family?"

"Eventually, eventually." He laughs. "Her father was the largest rose grower in Denver, a fact of which her mother was extremely conscious. The old lady accused me of marrying Martha for her money." He's still amused by the sheer absurdity of it. "Christ, I should've said, 'I wish I did,' 'cause we had a helluva time after the war making ends meet."

"They didn't help you out?"

"Oh, no, not a bit, any more than my parents did. My father had his convictions; it's one of the things I so admire him for."

"So you still think he was right?"

He reflects on it a moment. "Oh, I don't know, if it was my kids, I probably would've helped out. I suppose it depends on the kid. Andy was amazingly self-reliant; he wouldn't've needed it. Jerry never really was."

The mention of Andy is so matter-of-fact, it seems natural to pursue the subject.

"Do you have any sense of what Andy would've wanted to do later on? Did he have any particular ambitions?"

"I don't think so." We're just past Gilroy, advertising itself as "the garlic capital of the world," and Boyd gazes out at the fragrant fields of garlic alongside the highway. "He was only in his freshman year of high school when he was killed."

"It must have been a horrible time."

"That it was." He hesitates. "He was the second child we'd lost." By then the Huffs had already survived the death of a week-old baby girl.

"Your daughter . . ."

"I never got a good explanation for that," he says, without evident emotion. "There'd been no problems at all with the pregnancy; we had a good doctor, a good hospital. But then there were these complications." He stops. "It was damn hard on Martha. On me, too, actually. I enjoyed the idea of having a little girl very much. I think I'd've been a wonderful father to a girl. But so be it. Anyway, the four of us were very happy down in Monterey."

We drive in silence for a good thirty seconds. "Then Andy. We were living on Laurel Drive then, a few houses down from the Coopers. My God, Martha just took an awful beating. What the hell do you do to comfort a mother that's just lost a son? She was home at the time; she heard the shot."

I knew only the general circumstances of that unspeakably horrible episode; a by-now familiar mix of kids—Andy and his best friend—and a loaded, too-readily-accessible gun. But in the early sixties, awareness of the harrowing possibilities was nothing like what it is today.

"It was my mistake, in a way," Boyd continues evenly. "The gun was in the cupboard, but it wasn't locked up. I never worried about it, because I'd given both Jerry and Andy such careful instruction. We'd gone hunting and taken a lot of hikes, and Andy, especially, handled a gun beautifully. But it was his friend, just hacking around . . ."

"Moe and Benny tell me Andy was a wonderful boy," I say, for both had described him as charming, bright, strikingly good looking. Later, Boyd will unearth a photo of Andy in a Boy Scout uniform, but there are apparently no existing photographs of all four Huffs together, since in her distress Martha destroyed the family albums.

"You know, we had dancing classes out there in Carmel Valley," recalls Huff now, "and when it came to the girls' dance cards, they'd all descend on Andy. And he was very popular at that high school—the whole school turned out for the rosary we had for him."

"Was he a ballplayer like his brother?"

"Oh, yes, he was developing into the most superb shortstop. The two of them were both such marvelous athletes. Not that you can ever predict how good he might've been."

"Of course."

"I'll never forget the first game I was coaching Andy in Little League. He was out in right field, and a little pop fly comes his way. He camps under it, then deftly steps aside." He laughs heartily. "He got over that pretty damn fast. I got him after the game and hit him pop ball after pop ball. I'm so sorry you never knew Andy; what a fine boy he was!"

Again he says nothing for a long time.

"And then, about a year after that, Jerry got sick. It was a real one-two punch."

"Think there might've been any connection?"

The subject is obviously a painful one. "Oh, you know, there are so many supposed causes; they can't put their finger on any one. Goddamn it, I got the best psychiatrists, the best doctors I could find. There was one guy—he later became director of the state hospital—God, he worked and worked with Jerry. If there is any great failure in this marvelous field of medical research, schizophrenia is it."

But Boyd is far too honest to leave it at that. "I'll bring up a subject that's pretty sensitive to me," he adds. "About eight years ago, the doctors up there asked me to visit them. The subject of the conversation was that I was the cause of his schizophrenia. The argument goes something like this: 'Well, you were a prominent academic, chairman of the history department down there at the Naval Postgraduate School, and Jerry's trying to compete with you.' They wanted Jerry to go on a regime where he only came home twice a year, Christmas and Easter. I don't buy it; I don't know where in hell we've been competitive; I look upon myself as supportive. But I told them I'd do anything to help. So that's how we do it now." He shakes his head. "It's all too Freudian for me."

We drive for a while. Off to the right, I spot an airfield, with the most enormous, dome-shaped hangars I've ever seen.

"What in the world is that?"

"Oh, Jesus Christ, we missed the exit! That's what happens when you get into these goddamn conversations!"

Only when he's gotten off at the next exit and we are back on the highway, heading south, retracing our steps, does he answer the question. "That was Moffett Field," he tells me, full of his old authority. "It's where they kept the dirigibles during the war to spot Japanese subs off the coast. Only, goddamn it, now we're gonna be late!"

✦ ✦ ✦

The state-run halfway house where Jerry Huff lives is in a largely Vietnamese neighborhood not far from the sprawling campus of San Jose State. Seconds after Boyd rings the bell, Jerry appears at the door.

Though it probably shouldn't be, the first sight of him is a shock. Nearly toothless, his sunken cheeks ill shaven, wearing baggy jeans, sneakers, and a faded San Jose State T-shirt, he could be a derelict.

"You were so late, Dad, I was worrying."

Whether as a result of his missing teeth or his heavy medication, he slurs his words; but there's no mistaking the depth of his anxiety.

"I goofed," says Huff. "We got to talking, and I drove right by the exit. We found ourselves up in the Peninsula someplace. This is Harry."

I'm roughly as knowledgeable about schizophrenia as most people, which is to say not very much at all. Most of what I think I know is from movies like *A Beautiful Mind,* plus some half-remembered documentaries and articles in newsmagazines. I vaguely understand that it can involve erratic behavior, an inability to concentrate, and/or multiple personalities. But based on his appearance, I'm far from sure the guy before me is even capable of normal conversation.

"Very nice to meet you, Jerry."

"It's good to meet you, too. I read one of your books."

"Really?" I say, surprised. "Thank you."

"The one about baseball. I don't remember the name."

"*Hoopla.* It was about the Black Sox scandal."

"Shoeless Joe Jackson and all of them."

It is quickly apparent that though Jerry's attention span is brief, he knows a great deal about a great many subjects; probably most of what he learned before the disease hit.

But what's most striking is his sweetness. There is not an iota of mean-spiritedness to Jerry. His childlike concern for his father is especially touching.

"I was worrying," he repeats, as we ride to lunch in the Daewoo. "I was hoping there was no accident. And I got my wish—no accident!" He turns to me in the backseat. "I worry about him."

"I can see that."

"What're you worried about me for?" booms Huff.

"I just do, Dad."

"Well, thank you, Jerry, I appreciate it." Huff glances back at me. "You'll enjoy this restaurant we're going to, Original Joe's, it's a very masculine place."

As soon as we step inside, I see what he means. Original Joe's seems out of the 1890s, with lots of burnished wood and a menu heavy on beef and steak. Once we're seated in a booth, Boyd orders his usual—bourbon and water—and Jerry asks for a coffee.

"I understand you were quite a pitcher," I say.

"I wanted to play sports." He gives an odd little chuckle—sort of "heh, heh, heh." "I knew I wasn't gonna make it, but I was gonna give it the old college try. Baseball, the all-American game."

"You had pretty good control?"

"Sporadic."

"Oh, no," says his father, "I think it was very good."

"What was your best pitch?"

"My curveball."

"How hard could you throw?"

"Oh, fifty."

"Christ, Jerry, it was more than that," says Boyd. "You reached ninety-one."

Abruptly, Jerry assumes a distant, disconnected look of almost infinite despair, and he begins rocking back and forth. I look to his father, but Boyd seems unfazed.

"So do you still enjoy reading?" I ask, changing the subject.

"Oh, yeah. Adventure stories. *Huckleberry Finn. Tom Sawyer.*" He looks at his dad. "I want to read *Khrushchev Remembers,* but I keep puttin' it off. I put readin' off; I put gettin' a job off . . ."

"That's all right, Jerry," reassures Huff, "you'll get around to it."

"So you love history like your dad . . ."

"I'm a history lover, yeah."

"Any particular period?"

"Oh, the Renaissance. And the Reformation. And ancient history, I really liked that a lot."

The waiter shows up with the food, and Jerry goes after his roast beef with ravenous zeal, as if he hasn't eaten in days.

"Dig in, Jerry," says Huff with a laugh.

We eat in silence for a couple of minutes, by which time Jerry's plate is nearly empty.

"You look like you're really enjoying that," I observe.

He looks up—"I can gum it all right"—then gives his laugh, "heh, heh, heh."

"They're still monkeying around with your teeth?" asks his father.

"Yeah." He suddenly looks stricken again. "I should go to the dentist and get my dentures."

He resumes his rocking.

"Jerry, I want to let you know how much I appreciate your talking to me," I tell him.

"Well, I saw the tape recorder; I had to keep my composure. It's not very easy to keep my composure."

"Don't worry, you're doing great."

"I'm more relaxed than I used to be."

Still, I can see that this business of socializing is quite an effort for him; that even now he's trying to mask painful feelings lurking just below the surface.

"Dad," he says suddenly, "could you see if I could come home for my birthday?"

Boyd seems momentarily taken back. "Well, we'd certainly like to have you home, you know that, Jerry." He hesitates. "As a rule, they like to hold it to twice a year."

"That's all right, Dad," he instantly retreats, "I'll make it Christmas and Easter."

"I think with a little pressure I could get 'em to make it three times a year."

Jerry makes no reply, just resumes his slow rocking.

In the lull that follows, I ask Jerry what he misses most about Monterey.

"The ocean. Cypress trees. They got a nice little library." He looks at his father, then asks, childlike, "Dad, could I have some cheesecake?"

"Why not? You see the waiter, track him down. By the way, Beverly sent some clothes for you—they're in the car; don't let me forget to give 'em to you."

"And can I have some money for cigarettes?"

"You can't smoke in here."

"I'll go outside."

Boyd hands him a ten, and Jerry stands up. "I'm gonna have to stop; I don't want that damn cancer bug. Right, Dad?"

"That's right, Jerry."

As we watch Jerry move toward the door, I observe, not just being polite, what a nice guy he is.

"Yeah, he is. Should've been a priest, I guess." Huff laughs, but his heart's not in it. "You know, he's deprecating himself regarding his baseball. I had some awful nice letters from his coach out in Arizona; he was really pleased with the way Jerry was shaping up." He sips his bourbon. "The thing is, you can't put any pressure on him. I have a couple of friends here on the faculty at San Jose State—or, Christ, I did have, both of them died recently—and they told me they loved having Jerry in their classes. But, goddammit, I can't get him to go back. Even to audit."

"It's clear he'd love to, if he could."

"Oh, yeah. Loves history, just like me. Moe has pointed out that schizophrenics traditionally choose to identify themselves as Napoleon—Alexander the Great's a far less common choice. I remind him that Jerry's a lot better read than most." He laughs. "I still bring him books, but he won't read 'em. His favorite present lately was a pair of fancy sneakers. You know, he goes walking at night through rough neighborhoods, and he gets chased by all these disreputable characters looking to roll him. And he has to outrun them. The thing is, he likes it."

What, I ask, could he possibly like about it?

"The challenge," Boyd responds quickly. "Same as when he was a kid playing baseball. When we got him the Air Jordans, his reaction was, 'Now I'll really be able to beat 'em.' Well, one day he came back with a black eye." Boyd offers a wan smile. "The nature of competition—win some, lose some."

"Would you say this visit is pretty much par for the course?"

"This is a good day. He's heavily medicated, and that lets him function reasonably well. There's nothing that'll cure Jerry, and nothing on the horizon. But at least with the drugs we have now, we can contain it to a certain extent."

Soon after the waiter brings his cheesecake, Jerry reappears at the table. "I see you guys are good friends," he tells me, as he digs into the dessert. "That's what my dad needs."

"That's one thing I don't think your dad lacks for."

"They got a real camaraderie over there," he agrees, still eating.

"How about you, Jerry, have you managed to make any friends up here?"

He looks up from his food and shakes his head. "Mostly they just want to sit; I want to get out. I want to walk maybe a mile or so, and see the trees and the architecture. At one time I wanted to be a landscape architect, but I only took two courses." He returns to his cheesecake, devouring the rest in seconds. "I kept waiting," he says to his father. "You were forty minutes late."

"That's all right, Jerry; no need to worry about us."

"Have you had your blood pressure taken?"

"Yeah, I had a physical exam just a few months ago. Healthy as a horse." Boyd laughs heartily and looks around for the waiter. Catching his eye, he signals for the check. "Well, I think it's just about time to push on."

We drive the mile or so back to the halfway house largely in silence.

"Okay, okay, that's good," says Jerry, when we get to the end of his block. "I can walk from here."

"That's all right, Jerry," says his father, continuing on. He eases to a stop before the facility.

"You got enough money, Jerry?"

"Could you give me an extra ten?" he replies guiltily.

"Sure."

As Boyd reaches for his wallet, Jerry turns to me. His eyes are indescribably sad. "Ain't I terrible?"

"Oh, I think it's okay."

"I know my dad needs the money. It's terrible, taking money."

Boyd hands it to him, smiling. "All in the family, Jerry."

"It's so good of you to have come," Huff says, as we drive through the Vietnamese neighborhood, heading back toward the freeway. "I've got friends that won't."

"You think it makes them uncomfortable?"

"Seems to."

"He seems incredibly devoted to you."

"Well, I'm very devoted to him."

"I notice he sometimes gets a look, almost like he's about to cry . . ."

"Yes. I don't know what weight you can give that. That's one of the great shortcomings of psychology—anyone with an active imagination can attribute a meaning that might not even be there." He pauses as he speeds down the freeway entrance and merges with traffic. "I had a long talk with a very perceptive woman psychiatrist after one of his breakdowns, telling her I thought he was terribly unhappy. She said, 'No, you can't judge him by our standards. Jerry is a very happy person. He lives in this world of past academic achievement and athletic triumphs.' " He stops. "Still, that doesn't really help you as a parent. Your concern is what the hell can you do to jar him out of that? And the answer is nothing! He lives in that world, and, goddamn it, there he sits!"

Boyd's outburst is really more of a release. After all, he is a man who instinctively responds to a crisis with decisive action; yet here, over the decades, there has been nothing to be done. More, he has been trapped in this world of psychiatry and "talk therapy," which for him, as for so many men of his generation, is so utterly alien.

"Oh, Christ!" he suddenly exclaims. "I forgot to give him the clothes Beverly had me haul up to him! She'll kill me."

Once again he has to get off the highway and turn the car around.

"It's this goddamn creeping old age," he mutters.

I expect to see him smile, but he doesn't. To the contrary, he looks genuinely stricken—and for the first time, nearly his age.

"You've been forgetting a lot lately?"

"Oh, you know how it is. I can remember things in the distant past, courses I took, names, details, every goddamn useless thing. But I'll be driving downtown, and suddenly I can't remember what street I'm on. It's so damn frustrating."

I tell him my memory's not what it used to be, either, and I'm more than thirty years his junior.

"Nice of you to say," he shrugs off my lame attempt at solicitude, but at least it makes him smile. "I won't say there aren't advantages. I can enjoy the same damn book over and over again."

Back at the halfway house, he hustles out of the car and leaves Beverly's package for Jerry at the front desk.

"There," he announces, upon climbing back into the driver's seat, "now she'll never have to know . . ."

"Boyd," I ask, more out of politeness than anything else, "would you like me to drive back?"

To my surprise, he replies, "Thank you, I would."

Once back on the highway, Boyd raises the question of Jerry's future.

"He's never had any money of his own, of course. But I've set aside a fairly nice sum, which builds up all the time. Beverly will be the chief administrator."

"That must be a comfort, knowing he's provided for."

"The greater comfort is knowing I'll be leaving behind someone who cares about him. Beverly gets out of sorts with Jerry from time to time, which I certainly understand, but she thinks the world of him. She wishes he'd do something about his roommates, and she's right about that, too. They steal him blind."

"I've heard some of these places are pretty violent."

"I daresay."

At which point Boyd closes his eyes. After a few minutes of silence, I figure he's fallen asleep.

"I tell you," he says abruptly, "before we married I was concerned about that—imposing a damaged son on a second wife. After all, she had three children and grandchildren she adores; it's a helluva burden. But I really lucked out with her." A look of incredible affection comes across his face. "They're my grandchildren now, too. Did I tell you the little boy is a fantastic baseball player? He pitches, plays shortstop, the outfield. All the potential in the world."

"Well, you deserved some good luck."

He laughs heartily, wide-awake. "I agree with you."

✦ CHAPTER 13 ✦

*You'll leave one helluva legacy, all that junk you've
picked up over the years.*

—BOYD HUFF

*My books'll be my best legacy. One of these days I'm really
gonna have to put 'em all in order.*

—MOE TURNER

THE TOP FLOOR OF MOE'S NOTORIOUS A-FRAME.

By now it comes as no surprise that the Girl Watchers will find the humor in just about anything. Still, I am a bit taken aback to discover that this includes the prospect of impending death.

As a matter of fact, it's a subject that comes up with some regularity. For instance, there's the day Earl shows up for a meeting with a hacking cough.

"Boy," says Harry, before his friend even sits down, "that doesn't sound so good."

"I shouldn't think so, it's the tail end of pneumonia."

"The old man's friend!" exclaims Moe. "Man, oh man, you're lucky to be alive."

"I am," Earl matter-of-factly agrees. "I was stupid. I kept thinking it was gonna get better, so I didn't do anything about it. When it got in my bronchial tubes, I knew I was in trouble."

"Do you start wheezing when you breathe?" wonders Cooper, with a mix of concern and clinical interest.

"More like rattling, actually. First time I fully understood the meaning of 'death rattle.' "

"Well," notes Harry, "before it's all over, you'll probably get to hear it again."

Everyone laughs, Earl as heartily as anyone.

Talk about a generational divide! Forget dying; mine is the generation determined to forestall aging entirely, the generation that turned Botox into a national craze and made cosmetic surgery and magazines about muscle and skin tone—hell, every kind of narcissism going—as acceptable for men as for women.

Indeed, observes the *New York Times,* a growing number of medical practitioners catering to this mentality "regard aging as a disease, as fierce as a malignant tumor, to be fought with any and all means, tested or not. . . . Dr. Ronald Klatz of Chicago, the founder and director of the Academy of Anti-Aging Medicine, says patients cannot wait for long-term studies, which are not even in the planning stages and would take years or decades to complete. 'We'd have to wait,' he said, 'until the baby boomers are dead and in the ground and worms' meat.' "

"I gotta tell you," I tell the Girl Watchers, "I'm really not used to hearing people talk so casually about life and death."

This is met with surprise.

"Well, I guess the war has something to do with it," says Walzer.

"Once you've encountered death on the battlefield, it definitely takes away the element of fear."

"It just doesn't seem like that big a deal," agrees Harry. "To me, death is like going to sleep and not waking up."

"Or maybe waking up someplace better," says Boyd, with a challenging smile. "Though I'd certainly never try to press my spiritual views on you nonbelievers."

"All right, then I'll ask you one." Moe, snatching at the bait, turns to Huff. "If you religious people say everyone's gonna resassemble after death, what age'll they be? When you get to the Pearly Gates, are your parents gonna be twenty-one, or fifteen, or what? Maybe they'll be infants, and you won't even be able to have a decent conversation with 'em!"

"No one knows, Turner; that's what makes it a goddamn mystery."

None of which is to say they're thrilled about the prospect of dying, just that they accept it with remarkable equanimity. All eat right and exercise; Moe takes a long walk down Jocelyn Canyon each day, rain or shine. Still, death is inevitable; it's no more worth getting excited about than the shifting tides in Monterey Bay.

I suppose the psychologically inclined might view this as "avoidance" behavior typical of so many men of this generation, part of a lifelong pattern of refusing to deal with especially painful realities—and in some cases they might even have a point. But an equally good case can be made that it is precisely their refusal to make a big deal about something they can't change that allows them to so enjoy the time they have left.

"Personally, I got a pretty good introduction to what death was all about when I was sixteen, working on the lifesaving corps on Galveston Beach," offers Cooper with characteristic mildness. Always the objective observer, he draws as many conclusions from his vast store of personal experience as from his work in the lab. "We had long ropes with weights and hooks, and every once in a while we'd have to haul in a body. Well, let me tell you, if you got a body that'd been under for twelve hours or so, man, the crabs would have had a field day. No muss, no fuss. It's pretty impressive how nature takes care of it."

"That's the key word," agrees Earl, "*nature*. When I was a kid in Nebraska, death was well understood to be just part of the life cycle. When someone died, it wasn't a big deal. For my father, they didn't even send him to a funeral home, they just buried him." He shakes his head. "These days every part of it is a big production. You can't even grieve the way you want; the government has regulations about what kind of casket you can use, how you get put in the ground, everything."

"Well, they do say a nice casket makes for a happy corpse," says Harry.

"I just want to get put in a doggone canvas bag," says Moe. "They can stick in a cannonball, row me out and drop me in the marine canyon down there, and let me go to the bottom."

"Christ, Turner, where the hell are they gonna come up with a cannonball?"

"A bowling ball, then. I'll pick one up at a yard sale."

"We can use my boat for the job, assuming I'm still around," offers Boyd. "You'll leave one helluva legacy, all that junk you've picked up over the years."

"My books'll be my best legacy. One of these days I'm gonna have to put 'em all in order."

"One thing going for you with this idea," Cooper throws in his practical two cents' worth, "is that you're plenty light enough to pick up and handle."

"Right!" says Moe. "That's just what I tell my kids!"

"Still, I really don't know if the family'll be up for it, Moe," says Walzer.

"You're right. I've already made my kids promise, but I'm not sure I can trust 'em."

"They really love you; what an awful shame."

"Didn't you come close to dying that one time?" I ask, referring to the infected gall bladder that led to the ill-advised "deathbed" letters to his superiors.

"I sure did!"

"They thought you were gone," recalls Cooper. "When you showed up at work that morning, you were completely out of it."

Harry leans close to me and whispers, "I lost money on that; I bet he wasn't gonna make it."

Still, unsentimental as they are about death, the possibility that the process of dying could be prolonged or painful—or, worse, that they might be a burden on their loved ones—is deeply unsettling to these men, and each has done what he can to prepare for those contingencies. Even Moe has taken what for him is an extraordinary step: he's consulted a lawyer (all right, it was Stuart, working gratis) and arranged for a living will stipulating that no heroic measures will be taken to keep him alive.

Moreover, despite the casual attitude they project when considering their own deaths, they suffer terribly watching their friends and loved ones go, something which is starting to happen with alarming regularity. Just in the time I've spent with them, almost all have lost close friends or relatives. Harry tells me he counts no fewer than twenty-six who have passed away this past year, including half a dozen he considered intimates. "It's gotten so every time I pick up the phone it's 'Who's next?' I suppose at this point you have to expect it, but this is getting ridiculous."

Then, too, there's another kind of death, in a way the most painful of all for those left behind: the kind where a friend fades away while still remaining physically present. Moe, for one, makes it clear that nothing terrifies him so much as the prospect of coming down with Alzheimer's. In fact, while he will periodically seek reassurance by demanding to know if he's "losing it," he otherwise resists thinking about the disease.

This is never more evident than the Saturday afternoon when the daughter of an old friend unexpectedly stops by the Turners' en route from L.A. to the Bay Area with her husband and kids.

Over the past decade or so Moe has seen a lot less than he used to of his friend, a fellow southerner and straight-talking iconoclast with the wonderful name Arley, for Arley has been living in the L.A. suburbs since his wife died. But he has maintained a tremendous regard for Arley, a once-gifted athlete who holds master's degrees in math, engineering, and physics, and still talks about the guy so often that even the Girl Watchers who have never met him feel they know him. They have heard, for instance, that "Arley Tripp used to be a heckuva amateur boxer, until he got in the ring at the nineteen thirty-four Chicago World's Fair with some muscle-bound guy offering five bucks to anyone who could last a round"; and that "when Arlie was fourteen, he went on a camping trip and he had to throw out some married guy that slipped into his tent with him"; and that it was Arlie who long ago taught young Moe, the "yellow-dog Democrat," an early lesson about diversity and tolerance. "Arley would go out of his way to help anyone," I've heard him exclaim more than once. "I can't believe the nicest person I know is a goddamn *Republican!*"

But one thing I've never heard Moe mention is that several years ago Arley was diagnosed with Alzheimer's.

The fact is, until today I'm not sure he himself has faced how far gone his friend is.

Arley's daughter, Jenny, is my wife's oldest friend, the one who as a kid dubbed Moe The Count, and she and her husband, Gerry, aren't at all reticent on the subject. To the contrary, finding themselves among old friends, they are clearly grateful for the emotional release. A wonderful writer, Gerry will soon write a moving piece about Arley's decline, comparing him with Marley's Ghost, "Moaning, groaning, rattling his chains, his breath loamy enough to make a pig blink. . . . He has to be directed each morning to the shower, encouraged to wash, shave, soak his dentures and put on fresh clothes. When he doesn't recognize me, he pretends to. He's good at pretending, as are most Alzheimer's patients; it's their camouflage on an unintelligible battlefield. Simple words often strike his ear like deranged notes on an accordion. He struggles with each one and reassembles them to make a clear meaning. Soon, we were advised, he will not be able to recognize his own face in the mirror."

But talking today, with us, there's mainly laughter.

Along with everything else, Jenny reports over coffee and cake, her father's hearing has started to go, making for some conversations right out of *The Twilight Zone*. "Tell what happened the other day, Ger."

"Well, you know," Gerry complies, "he's been living at a facility close to our house, which allows us to take him out a couple of times a week. The other day, when we got back to the place, a woman comes running up in a panic—her father, who's also a resident there, was missing. 'Do you know where he is, Mr. Tripp?' she asks Arley.

"It seems Arley's been having lunch with this guy every day, but he doesn't remember him, so he gives her the fish-eye, like she's trying to put something over on him. 'Who's that you're talking about . . . ?'

"'My dad!'

"At this, Arley glares at her and says"—here Gerry does a letter-perfect imitation of Arley's booming southern-accented voice—" 'Well, how old is he?'

" 'Eighty-four.'

" 'Eighty-four? Well, hell, don't look at me, he's probably out chasing some bitch!' "

"What?!" exclaims Moe.

Gerry holds up his hand and continues. "The woman is horrified, and she scurries away. At which point, Arley turns to me and says, 'What the hell's she thinking? An eighty-four-year-old DOG?!' "

Moe laughs along with everyone else but quickly notes, "Well, that doesn't mean he's losing his marbles, just that he didn't hear it right."

"Trust me," says Jenny, as good-humored and plainspoken as her father, "he's losing his hearing and his marbles."

"He thinks I'm a thief," says Gerry, and again makes like his father-in-law. " 'You sonovabitch, I'm watching you; I know you stole my pocket knife.' "

"Bless his heart; I love that man," says Benny sweetly.

"Grandpa doesn't think my mom and dad are married," notes Cordelia, Jenny and Gerry's sixteen-year-old daughter.

"I'm afraid that's true," agrees Jenny. "As a matter of fact, he's taken a rather disconcerting interest in me."

"Oh, God!" exclaims Moe.

"I can't even be flattered; he's completely indiscriminate. As soon as he meets almost any woman, he drapes himself over her. It's as if he's been stripped of everything else; he's down to the elemental core."

"Does he remember your mother at all?" Benny wonders.

"Oh, yes, of course he does."

"That's nice; I'm so glad of that."

"Doesn't stop him, though."

There's a moment of silence.

"He remember me?" asks Moe.

"Sure he does, Count," Jenny reassures him. "He asks me all the time, 'Is Moe still gettin' around?' "

Moe manages a laugh. "Well, tell him I say hello."

"I will. Any chance you'll get down and see him sometime?"

"Maybe," he says, though it's clear from his tone that it's never going to happen. "Man, he was such a sharp guy—he and I had so much in common."

"I'm sure he'd like to see you."

"Well, you know, I don't get around as much as I used to. But you tell him I was asking after him, will you?"

"I will; he'll like that."

"And that he's still one of the best friends I ever had."

There is a momentary silence.

"Hey, I got a joke for you," says Moe.

"Oh, Moe . . . ," implores Benny.

"Don't worry, it'll only take a second." He pauses. "This old guy goes to the doctor, and the doctor tells him, 'I've got some really bad news— you've got cancer and you've got Alzheimer's.' 'Well,' says the guy, 'thank God I don't have cancer!' "

CHAPTER 14

The Kitty Hawk was on a collision course with a Russian ship. He was heading north in the Tonkin Gulf with a whole load of trucks on board for the North Vietnamese, and we were heading south. . . . And I said, "Maybe we should offer to drop one five-hundred-pound bomb over the side for every truck they throw over."

—EARL GODFREY

GODFREY, CENTER, AS CAPTAIN OF THE
<u>KITTY HAWK</u>, 1971.

As it happens, during our luncheon following the one on 9/11, the Girl Watchers talk about the sixties.

Wait, that's not quite true. It didn't just happen; I set it up that way.

Why? Because it seems that in the aftermath of that terrible day we are at last emerging from a long period of national sleepwalking that began during that tumultuous, chaotic, epochal decade.

I understand why so many of my peers even now regard the sixties as the very best years of their lives, a magical moment of boundless creativity and seemingly limitless possibility; hey, I miss the Beatles, too. But the larger truth is that the multiple traumas of that era left much of our generation permanently dubious about the bedrock understanding that sustained our forebears: that for all its flaws, America is the greatest nation on earth.

I realize that to state it so nakedly will strike many as simplistic and naive. Yet that itself suggests how much our thinking was reshaped by the sixties. The truth is, coming of age with World War II movies and mythic tales of George Washington and Abraham Lincoln, we once fully embraced such an understanding ourselves. Indeed, an excellent case can be made that our vehement cynicism in the wake of Vietnam was in direct proportion to the strength of that lost belief.

Thus our generation's supposed best and brightest—a population that, talk about ironies, has enjoyed the fruits of America like none before—have gone on to systematically undermine faith in the idea of our nation's fundamental goodness and decency. From our elite universities down to the lowest elementary school grades, the stress is on our differences rather than on the remarkable heritage we share; with jackhammer subtlety, the history texts dwell on our flaws, past and present, rather than celebrate our remarkable capacity to face up to them. The cult of "multiculturalism" has made the merest suggestion that our values and traditions are superior to anyone else's a kind of secular sin.

Yet after the shock therapy of 9/11, all of that already seems to be changing. It is as if, in the very midst of unspeakable horror, a cloud is lifting, with tens of millions of Americans abruptly grasping that in vital ways the earlier generation had it right all along; and that their example of steadiness and perseverance—and, yes, good humor—might serve us admirably once again.

The first surprise, as I listen to the guys today, is that to a man they had nearly as many doubts about the war as my friends and I did, demonstrating in the streets and raising various degrees of havoc on our campuses.

"Man, Vietnam just really messed things up," says Cooper. "We never even knew what we were fighting for."

"Hell, before the whole thing blew up in our face, I'd taught the subject of Communist expansionism in Southeast Asia at the Navy School, and I thought that was a very legitimate concern," says Boyd Huff, who in his role as a diplomatic historian was sometimes called upon by the government to produce classified reports on policies under consideration. "But, Christ, it was the wrong war in the wrong place at the wrong time."

"Aside from that, it was fought the wrong way," adds Harry, who took a leave of absence from the Navy School to spend ten months in Vietnam running a study on how to protect the country's inland waterways. "You can't win a war run by politicians."

"The whole thing was corrupt from the start," agrees Godfrey, who served in Southeast Asia throughout much of the war. "Lyndon Johnson lied his way into it with that supposed North Vietnamese attack on our ships in the Tonkin Gulf, and Congress let him get away with it. That whole Tonkin Gulf thing was just a staged affair."

The reference, to an alleged attack in August 1964, led to congressional passage of the disastrous Tonkin Gulf Resolution, which gave the president open-ended war-making powers.

"Were you stationed out there at the time?" I ask Godfrey.

"I'd actually just left. But I know Jim Stockdale, who was on the flight searching for the North Vietnamese boats that were supposedly in the gulf, and he was convinced nothing occurred. He saw no boats at all. That's what he feels to this day, and I have no reason to doubt he's right."

"In other words," says Moe, "those people out there on the streets screaming that we had no business being over there had a point."

"They absolutely did," agrees Stuart.

Huff nods soberly. "No question, there was perfectly good reason to dislike the Vietnam war. What I could never understand was how so many young people could doubt the fundamental goodness of the country?"

He has it exactly right. Awful as it is to admit, a lot of us did turn not just against a specific set of policies, but against the country itself. Spoiled children that we were, when the Johnson and then the Nixon administration failed to heed increasingly widespread demands to end the war, we arrived at a point where pulling out was no longer enough. "Ho Ho Ho Chi Minh," went the fevered chant at every demonstration, "NLF is gonna win!" We wanted to see America humiliated; as common wisdom in our circles had it, Vietnam was less an aberration than a symptom of a *system* (one of our favorite words!) that by its very nature promoted aggressive and inhumane policies abroad, not to mention the exploitation of the powerless at home.

Yes, some of us actually talked that way.

"I tell you, the way things were, it was a very tough thing asking men to put their lives on the line," Earl understates it.

"Especially the way it was set up with guys going in knowing they're only going to serve there one year," says Harry. "It takes them three months to start figuring out what's going on, and the last three months they're just worried about saving their little behind. Which leaves six months of potentially effective soldiering. Can you imagine if they'd operated that way in World War II?"

"We'd all be speaking German," replies Huff, laughing.

"Exactly. We knew we were in it till the darn thing ended, so the point was to make sure it did."

"But that's another thing about Vietnam," points out Boyd, "if we'd been of age at the time, studious little boys that we were, chances are none of us would've gone at all. Because the goddamn truth is that anyone who wanted to dodge the draft could do so. There was just such a great unfairness to it all."

"You're right," says Moe adamantly. "Nearly all of us had kids the right age to fight in that war—my oldest son was right at the top of the list. But how many of them did?"

"What do you mean *kids?*" demands Earl. "I spent six years over there!"

"I'm talking about our children. We all know the people fighting that war were mainly blacks and poor kids; you didn't find hardly any college professors in our school that had kids over there."

As the sole beneficiary of this system at the table, I remain silent. It's not exactly that this is a sore point, but it's also far from a point of pride. Not long ago a kid the same age I was then, my daughter's boyfriend, asked me, given my revised take on the world, whether I'm sorry I acted as I did. Under the same circumstances would I do things differently? Would I be ready to go to any lengths—including, had it come to that, going to Canada—to avoid the war?

The honest answer is I don't know. It *was* a bad war. I won't for a moment say I regret opposing it. Another aspect of having grown up in the aftermath of World War II was the emphasis on individual conscience, the powerful sense that to have been a "good German" would not stand up as an excuse when it came time for moral reckoning.

On the other hand, all the antiwar rhetoric notwithstanding, the suggestion the behavior of the United States was remotely akin to that of Nazi Germany was a vile and appallingly irresponsible slander; we were a good and great nation pursuing a horribly mistaken policy. And, frankly, even now I have no idea of the right and proper course of action under such circumstances, or even if there is one.

Indeed, though knowing how it sounds, I would certainly never say it aloud, in some ways these guys had it easier. Theirs was the prototypical "good" war. Their only choices involved figuring out how to survive.

"In our day the army could be called plenty of things, including stupid," agrees Walzer now, "but undemocratic wasn't one of them."

"Jerry didn't try to get out of it," offers Huff. "He went down and volunteered, but the doctors got one look at him and sent him away."

"Well, I was proud of Larry also," says Moe. "He had a trick knee and he was really against that war, but he went up there for his physical and was ready to go. When they sent him back because of that knee, he went to a doctor to have it taken care of. Guess what the doctor told him? He said, 'I won't operate on it if it means you go to Vietnam.' "

"There were a lot of doctors like that," I point out. "In New York, where I took my physical, by the end they didn't even want people who were against the war because it was too much trouble. When I went for my physical, they were letting people out left and right."

"So what was your story?" wonders my father-in-law, at once vaguely accusatory and genuinely curious.

"Actually, I got a note from a psychiatrist—one of those antiwar guys like the one Larry saw. You went in, paid for one session, and left with a note."

"What did it say?"

"That I had trouble with authority, which was one of the standard lines. Not that, in my case, it wasn't true." I smile, but I'm certainly not comfortable.

The truth is, I was acutely aware at the time of the terrible inequity of the draft system; and, yes, of the manifold hypocrisies of kids like me that allowed it to go on. When I traveled from my suburban community of New Rochelle to Whitehall Street in lower Manhattan for my physical, every kid on that bus from the prosperous north end of town had a doctor's letter or an X-ray, but not one kid from the poorer parts of town had so much as a note from his mother. Attending journalism school at the time, I even wrote a piece about it to fulfill an assignment, describing how, to be on the safe side, one of my fellow travelers had actually brought along "two allergists' reports and notes from a doctor and a shrink"; while another, a tough Italian kid from the south end named John Larga, who had already been rejected twice because there was something in his urine, had dutifully returned when called back for yet another physical. John Larga wasn't sure whether a draftee was obligated to serve two years or three. He had not, I noted, "thought to bring a note."

I got a good grade on the piece, and when a friend of mine who went to Harvard had it published in that school's newspaper, I picked up a few more kudos for my thoughtfulness and humanity. In short, the episode was a fairly familiar one for those of my generation at that time. I got to feel noble without paying any kind of price.

"I'll bet it would've been good for you to go," says Moe now.

"It probably would have," I have to concede.

There is a momentary pause in the conversation—not, I think, an embarrassed one.

"Well, I sure as hell didn't want my kids to go," speaks up Walzer.

Godfrey looks at him. "Honestly? I didn't either."

"But one of your sons did serve in Vietnam, didn't he?" asks Moe.

"Yeah. At the very end."

"Well, of all our contemporaries, you might be the only one that can say that."

"My daughter's first husband went," notes Cooper. "But his mother called a senator. Know what duty they gave him? Lifeguard at the officer's pool."

The guys break up.

"Christ, they give him a battle star for dragging out someone's wife?"

"The guy she's married to now," continues Cooper, "my son-in-law, a very nice fella, he didn't go at all." A pregnant pause. "He has 'Fuck the Army' tattooed on his saluting arm."

Even more laughter.

"Earl, did you run across any opposition to the war among your men?" wonders Harry.

"Not so much. It wasn't quite the same problem in the navy as in the army. You didn't have guys going out on firefights, which made a huge difference. But if someone did have something to say, I'd encourage him to speak his piece in a bull session."

"May I presume you'd use the word *duty* in these conversations?" says Huff.

"Absolutely. Duty, honor, and country. That's the oath you take: to 'support and defend the Constitution of the United States against all enemies foreign and domestic.' Still, they knew as well as I did it was a war where we had no intention of doing what needed to be done to win." He pauses. "I remember one time the *Kitty Hawk* was on a collision course with a Russian ship. He was heading north in the Tonkin Gulf with a whole load of trucks on board for the North Vietnamese, and we were heading south. We came close enough that we actually had to maneuver to get out of the way. As this is happening, some of my people started saying, 'Wouldn't it be nice if we could eliminate some of those trucks?' And I said, 'Maybe we should offer to drop one five-hundred-pound bomb over the side for every truck they throw over.' Since it was a political war to start with, it seemed to me this might be a very nice way to conduct it."

"Was there ever any sentiment among the military over there to use nukes and get it over with?" I ask.

Earl looks taken aback by the question. "The very idea would've scared the heck out of me. I flew with nuclear warheads under my wings all through the Cold War, and, my goodness, the nightmares I'd have about some of those targets I was supposed to hit. And that was just training, not a shooting war."

"I'll never forget how they used to make us jump under our desks," I recall one of my generation's seminal memories, "and how silly it used to seem even to us kids. We knew nothing was going to save us if the bomb hit."

"You weren't scared?"

"Not till now—hearing how apprehensive *you* were. This sounds really naive, but the feeling was nothing's going to happen, they're grown-ups, they know what they're doing."

"As a grown-up, I'd say that's the *definition* of naive," laughs Walzer.

"But, no, I heard no talk in Vietnam like that, not at all." Earl returns to the question. "Almost all of those serving over there were honorable, decent, highly committed individuals. Yet here you had all these people saying they were war criminals."

Grinning, Moe jerks a finger my way. "You were probably one of them."

"I don't think I ever really went that far," I say lamely. "I never dissed a veteran."

"I'll bet you wanted to. Your wife, that daughter of mine, was up at Berkeley, and she wouldn't even look at any guy that was in the ROTC. There were a lot of nice guys in the ROTC, and, God, these women would treat them just like dirt."

"What I found so ironic was that our people often got treated better by civilians over in Vietnam than they did when they came home," says Harry. "I went into a lot of villages with the Special Forces, and I certainly never detected any antagonism on the part of the South Vietnamese. Quite the contrary. Yet at home, they'd get spat at, cursed at."

"I'll never forget when I was back home for a year, and we were living in Palo Alto," says Godfrey. "Going home one night from work with my uniform on, I turned into my place, and there was a load of kids, and, boy, did they start giving me the business! 'You sonovabitch, what the hell you think you're doing over there?' And, believe me, I'm cleaning up the language they used. It was an awful thing to see."

"Christ, we even had an incident over at the Navy School," says Huff. "Remember, some lunatic woman threw herself in front of a faculty member's car? They detested any goddamn thing that had to do with the military."

"Listen," says Earl, "we can't gloss things over; there were some terrible atrocities committed—My Lai was one. But by and large, our military performed very well under horrible circumstances."

"This is hard for some people to admit," observes Cooper, "but in wartime some of that is almost inevitable. Even in World War II our hands weren't completely clean."

"Wasn't there a time back in Korea when you refused to strafe civilians?" Moe asks Earl. "And didn't you get in trouble for it?"

"I didn't know I was going to get in trouble; I thought I was doing what I was supposed to be doing."

Earl pauses a moment. Even half a century later the memory is obviously unpleasant.

"What happened?" presses Stuart.

"We were flying the F-9F Panther off carriers, one of the first jet outfits in the navy, and I was on a road-wrecking flight. I failed to deliver my payload because I could see a lot people down there, going *south* from the line. But when I got back to the ship, I just caught hell. The admiral said, 'Your job is to clear that road; I don't care *what's* on it.' "

"You could tell they were civilians?" I ask.

"Looked like it to me—they had carts and so forth, but he said they were Chinese military who turned around when they saw me and pretended to be refugees."

"Well," notes Walzer evenly, "that was the first of our wars where nothing at all was really clear-cut."

"Who knows?" adds Earl. "It could well be he was right. I'll never know. But I'm also glad I don't have to stay up nights wondering about it."

Listening, I can't help feeling . . . *foolish* is far too mild a word. What jerks so many of us were! To think how casually during the sixties we impugned the morality of men like this! How callously indifferent we were to what they and theirs had to endure!

But what's worse is knowing how much the attitudes of that era continue to inform the thinking of so many supposedly enlightened people even today.

✦ ✦ ✦

"What really got me about those Vietnam protesters is they weren't even consistent," picks up Moe. "With all their complaining about what us Americans were doing, they let the real bad guys off scot-free. The way the North Vietnamese treated our POWs, *they* were the real war criminals!"

"Didn't you know some of the guys in the Hanoi Hilton, Earl?" asks Harry.

"Very well. Jim Stockdale, for one. If you want to talk about heroes, he's always been one to me. To him every day was a triumph—just withstanding the beatings and the business where they'd pull ropes taut to strain the joints to dislocate the arms. He survived that by sheer force of will. And afterward he never tried to make more of his imprisonment than it was."

"I read not long ago that Jane Fonda got selected as one of the top hundred women of the twentieth century by some magazine," adds Earl. "Remember how when she visited the Hanoi Hilton, the prisoners tried to slip her notes as she shook hands with them—and when she got to the end of the line, she turned the notes over to the guard? I'm a forgiving guy, but something like that isn't easy to forget."

"What a stinker!" exclaims Moe. "I tell you, though, when she was young she had quite a good body."

The pity, of course, is that many of us know Stockdale only as Ross Perot's inept vice presidential running mate, brilliantly parodied by Phil Hartman on *Saturday Night Live* as an inarticulate boob. Of course, he *was* out of his depth, and should never have put himself in that position; yet it is also the case—and further evidence both of the man's character and that he did not belong in the political arena—that he steadfastly refused to exploit his heroic past during the campaign.

I ask: "Knowing Stockdale beforehand, could you have guessed how he would act in that kind of situation?" I know I often wonder that about myself; but maybe that's just what happens when you've never been tested.

Earl shakes his head no. "It's impossible to know. I certainly don't know how I would."

"Boy, I do! I wouldn't last one day. One day, and I'd be gone."

"You flatter yourself, Moe," says Harry mildly, "more like one hour."

"Right, more like an hour," he readily agrees. "Boy, Earl, it must've been something when you were skippering the *Kitty Hawk*, watching those planes leaving the flight deck knowing they might not return."

"Well, you know, we were in contact with them, so you knew they were in trouble as it was happening. You could hear it like you were there: the missiles being fired at them, someone saying, 'Missile at six o'clock, break right,' every bit of it.' "

"Would there be any panic in their voices?" I ask.

"Oh, no. The volume might get a little higher if someone was getting shot up or if the flaps stopped working, or the landing signal officer might get a little tension in his voice, especially if it's a friend up there. But basically this is what people were trained for."

"My God, that war just had corrosive moral effects in so many ways," interjects Cooper. "Just look at the problems it created raising kids. I'd have to say it was as rough out here as anywhere in the country."

Walzer feigns surprise. "Here? In this lovely little piece of paradise?"

"Carmel was the absolute extreme, every bad thing you can think of. And I'm not just talking about the drugs. What I could never abide was how so many young people sneered at our values. It may have started with the war, but it ended up being contempt for the whole way we lived our lives."

"That's the word for it, all right," murmurs Huff, "*contempt*."

"Kids really were convinced they shouldn't *have* to work."

"Maybe they didn't have time," muses Harry. "Remember, they were getting a lot more sex than we were."

But the unflappable Cooper is as exercised as I've ever seen him. You can just picture him back then, watching in stultified disbelief as his kids' generation casually belittled so much he and his generation had worked and fought for and believed in. The arrogance, the smug self-certainty of it all. The presumption that we, their children, understood the world—the very meaning of decency and morality—as they never could.

The fact is, for some of these guys, the most memorable war stories of the sixties have nothing to do with jungles or rice paddies, but with their own children.

"They thought those of us who believed the easy road won't take you anywhere were fools. My God, the trouble it took to convince a kid to work or put serious effort into education!"

"Remember that time when Susan tried to sneak off and you caught her, Turner?" recalls Boyd with a chuckle. "Around when was that?"

The reference is to a notorious family episode featuring his second daughter, my wife's younger sister. I've already heard about it—but only from Priscilla's perspective, which is probably not the fairest one; as an older sibling, she enjoyed the hell out of it.

Moe glances around the table—the story is a new one for most of the guys. "It must've been around 'sixty-seven or 'sixty-eight," he replies, "'cause Sue was around fifteen. We'd given her and some of her friends permission to sleep in a tent in the front yard, and around about midnight, I went out to check on them. They were gone! Well, since there was a pretty big hippie scene around here, I had a pretty good idea where they might be, so I got right in the car and headed downtown. It didn't take me long to find them—I spotted her through the window of one of these light show places they used to have, sitting at a table with these other girls, laughing it up. Man, was I so mad I couldn't see straight! The guy at the door told me I had to pay to get in, but I said, 'The hell I do!' and walked right past. Before she even knows I'm there, I grab her right across the table. The table goes over, and everyone's horrified, and Sue starts crying and carrying on. But I drag her outside and spank her right there, in front of all her friends. When we got home. Benny was real upset; she kept saying, 'She's gonna run away; she's gonna run away.' " Moe shakes his head. "Well, I tell you what, the next day Sue was just as good as gold. She got right up and, without a word about it, went off with me to some garage sales."

"Your greatest moment," observes Huff. "Unconditional surrender. How often could you say that?"

"Not too often."

"Man, those were rough times," repeats Cooper. "But you're right; tough as it was, sometimes you had to lay down the law."

"Even if the kids couldn't stand you for it," adds Godfrey meaningfully. "That's how you showed your love, by *not* letting them get away with that stuff."

"Well, I showed her plenty of love that night. She knew it was my way or the highway. She's fifty years old, and I'll bet she still hasn't forgotten it."

Even as he says it, I am keenly aware that all these years later such a tale, far from eliciting praise, will upset a lot of people. In some localities it might even be grounds for prosecution. Of all the many changes in American attitudes from that time to this, those having to do with child rearing may be the most sweeping. The general sense today, at least in enlightened circles, is that as good parents we relate to our kids and communicate with them, that we always be seen as understanding rather than as bullies and enforcers.

Yet here's the part we almost never hear about: such old-fashioned, no-nonsense parenting, when leavened with love, generally *works;* especially compared to the relentlessly permissive, my-child-is-my-best-friend, let's-not-be-overly-parental parenting style that started in the sixties and still flourishes today.

"It was such a crazy time," says Cooper, "especially out in this part of the world."

"God, there was so much awful stuff going on!" Moe looks at me. "Did your wife ever tell you she took LSD?"

"Just once," I say, "it scared the hell out of her—she said she thought about jumping out a window." I look at the others and feel obliged to explain. "This was years before I knew her."

In fact, like me, Priscilla was a relative straight arrow. But try to convince her father of that.

"She was smart enough not to tell me till years later," he adds with consternation. "How about you? Were you also a druggie?"

"Moe, neither of us was a druggie. Sure, I used to smoke a little marijuana. I was in college then; everyone did. But all in all I was considered pretty straight, and so was Priscilla."

"It's amazing how little you can know your own kids," he replies, not buying it. "And I always watched mine pretty closely. A lot of people I knew didn't."

"Amazing, wasn't it?" says Cooper. "In some ways kids come preprogrammed, and there's not a whole lot you can do about it. But one thing you can always do is ruin 'em. My God, drugs messed up so many kids' lives out here, and a lot of parents didn't even seem to care."

"Well, you know, it was an artists' colony, full of wild and independent spirits," offers Harry with a smile. Pausing, he retrieves a phrase from the mists of time. "Responsibility wasn't their 'bag.' "

"Of course," agrees Stuart, "they wanted to 'do their own thing.' "

"Christ," exclaims Boyd, "half the time they were sharing the drugs with them!"

"And meanwhile they were cheating left and right on their spouses," says Cooper. "Out here, the lunatics truly took over the asylum. Almost every one of my daughter Jeannie's friends was from a broken-up family. *We* were the ones out of step for staying together."

"Kind of a preview of what was coming with the explosion of divorces," observes Earl. "This part of the world was almost a laboratory for what would happen in the rest of the country. Because I think it was a result of these attitudes that came out of the sixties—this idea that responsibility was a negative thing, and that if things get tough, it's okay to walk away. People started thinking of that as freedom instead of what it really was: narcissism and selfishness. So of course children paid the price; they always do."

On the face of it, one might think such a topic is a bit dicey. After all, Stuart Walzer was for decades a prominent divorce attorney. But Stuart seconds the proposition immediately. "No question, as divorce became easier, kids paid the steepest price. In the worst cases, where the fights really got nasty, homes became chaotic, parental authority disappeared. I can't tell you how many angry, neglected, troubled kids I saw over the years."

"My goodness," exclaims Earl, "you really have to wonder if people who'd put their kids through that ever think about the definition of a successful life."

"Well, some of the people I dealt with—let's just say introspection tended not to be their strong suit."

"You just look at the results of all those kids raised without any structure," says Moe. "One of Sue's friends, girl from a good family, she went on drugs and ended up a hooker in Seaside."

"Seaside?" exclaims Stuart. The community is the least affluent on the Monterey Peninsula. "Doesn't sound like she had a good head for business."

"Stuart," says Handler, "I wouldn't touch that 'good head' reference with a ten-foot pole."

"Well, the state she was in, I don't think she much cared where she was. It was pretty awful. But here's what I'm getting to: she used to come over to our house because there were grown-ups who imposed some rules. A bunch of kids did."

"What kind of rules?"

"That they had to be back at a certain time, things like that. They had their own parents running so scared, they'd be afraid to tell them anything. These kids liked playing at being grown up, but inside they knew damn well they were still kids."

"Could've set up a business there, Turner, ask for a percentage of that young lady's profits."

"Actually, she ended up okay. Straightened herself out and went into the decorating business. Plenty of them didn't."

The exchange reminds me of a kid back home in my own little suburban community, the daughter of a very nice guy I've gotten to know. As my friend acknowledges himself, he and his wife were classic sixties types, big into alcohol and drugs and light on structure; and only too late did they come to realize that in one's role as a parent, that adds up not to coolness or enlightenment but to abdication. Their eighteen-year-old daughter, herself a chronic substance abuser, dropped out of high school and is living on New York's Lower East Side, doing God knows what. "The hope," the guy's wife is quoted, bravely, in a *New York Times* article on such messed-up suburban kids of baby-boomer parents, "is to keep her alive until she realizes what she's doing and makes the changes."

It's a terrible lament, and it's impossible not to feel for such parents. But it also seems painfully obvious that, now as during the turmoil of the sixties, it is the children of parents who refuse to surrender to the laxness of the times, continuing to impose limits and set standards, who give their children the best shot at emerging themselves as thoughtful and responsible adults.

"I had one of my sons who participated in some pretty bad behavior," acknowledges Godfrey. "Anger, drugs, bad grades, all of it. He went to high school right in downtown San Francisco. One time he and a friend decided to have a sit-in out at the navy housing where we lived."

"What the hell for?" asks Huff.

"Fifteen years old—they didn't know why, just to go against the grain. But they sat there, right in the middle of the street. It wasn't an easy situation. For a while there, he all but stopped going to school."

"How'd you deal with it?"

"I kept bailing him out—sent him to summer school, spent big bucks to see to it he passed this or that . . ."

"We had one like that also," says Stuart, "and that was always our impulse, too. It's hard not to."

"Not that you ever got much gratitude," says Earl. "We argued all the time; it became part of our way of life. Any position I'd take, he'd take the opposite one. Being in the military, I had certain standards I tried to live by, but of course he didn't want any part of that. Long hair, messy clothes, everything he could do not to be anything like me."

"That must've been pretty difficult for you," says Harry.

"Well, I didn't see that I had any choice but to accept it and keep plugging away. What are you gonna do—put him in a chair and have a barber cut off all his hair?"

"Plenty of people did just that."

"That's true—but I really can't say that it ever worked."

"You try spanking him?" asks Moe.

"I didn't, but I could hold onto his arm pretty darn tight."

"Well, let me ask you something," Moe puts it to Godfrey. "Our kids did all sorts of things we didn't approve of, right? They lived with people they weren't married to, didn't they?"

"That's true."

"And we disapproved of that thoroughly—you even more than me. But did we do anything about it?"

"I didn't say that—I know I made them feel they were doing wrong. But, no, I was not willing to disavow them."

"I'm just saying we've got very strong beliefs on this, and yet we sat here and watched our kids do what we didn't believe in. In the old days, that would never have happened."

"That's so, and maybe we can be criticized for that. I certainly can be. But to me, that's my main responsibility in life, caring for my children. It's the only reason I'm here."

"I'm agreeing with you," says Moe. "We'd rather keep their love for us than—"

"It's not their love for us," cuts in Earl. "It's our love for them. And I think it's the only way to ride out the rough times. My son who rebelled is now completely the opposite. It took till he was in his thirties, but now he has a master's degree in geology. Just a complete flip."

"It was the same thing with my oldest son," notes Stuart. "He took acid, smoked pot; today he's Mr. Straight-arrow—a quasi vegetarian and a lawyer."

Godfrey nods meaningfully. "All those teachings took, even though we didn't know it at the time."

"I think that's right," agrees Cooper. "You look around today, and the kids raised in that period with love and some discipline generally ended up okay. It just came a little later. Take my son-in-law. He started out so wild; now he's a highly successful business person and just a great guy. He and my daughter couldn't be more solicitous of us. They've even made clear that if something should happen to one of us, they have a building on their property that will be available for the other." He smiles. "He still does have that tattoo on his arm, though."

"No question, that's when it all pays off, all right," says Moe, "when you're too decrepit to look after yourself."

"Good old Moe," says Harry, laughing, "such a sentimental fellow."

"Well," says Moe, "we all know Sue turned out just fine, too. She's a teacher now with two teenage girls of her own. Now it's her turn to worry about them."

In fact, my father-in-law is more sentimental than he likes to admit—and a lot more softhearted. When I later ask Sue about that long-ago evening Moe dragged her from the club—the most excruciatingly humiliating event of her adolescence—she remembers it even more clearly than he does. Among the additional details she provides are the name of the long-defunct place, East-West; the identities of her friends (including the future hooker); and that as he stalked over to confront her, he tripped over an electric cord, cutting off the club's booming sound system, a comic detail that surely undercuts Moe's fondly remembered show of fatherly authority. "Oh," she adds, "something else he probably didn't mention. As he was spanking me, I saw I wasn't the only one who was crying."

✦ CHAPTER 15 ✦

*We've gotten pretty detached from the natural order of
things. Some people have this idea that dying is just another
problem that can be licked. They'll all find out otherwise.*

— GENE COOPER

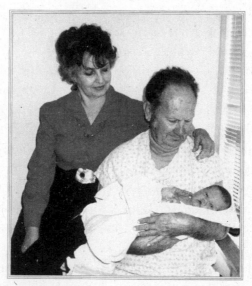

JODY AND GENE COOPER WITH THEIR
GRANDSON, AUGIE.

Several weeks after this session, I'm back home in New York when
Moe calls with the news. There's no beating around the bush: "Cooper's
got cancer."

"Oh, my God! What kind?"

"I don't know," he says mournfully, "he didn't say."

"He didn't say?"

"I didn't ask. But it sounds pretty bad. Give him a call."

I'm a bit hesitant, as one tends to be in such situations. You don't want to bother the guy; it feels intrusive. There's no telling what he's feeling.

But when I reach him, Cooper is as matter-of-fact as ever. He tells me that one morning he noticed a swollen lymph node in his neck. "I had a hunch what was going on, so I went in, and they did a biopsy, and of course it came back positive. What that means is that the disease has spread into the lymph system—and once that happens, essentially it goes everywhere."

"How are you feeling now?"

"Oh, fine. Pretty much the same as always."

"Have you started any kind of treatment?"

"It's early; I'm still exploring my options." He pauses. "You know, I'm nearly eighty-six. I've got no complaints. I'm just hoping I can get another year or so."

When I return to Monterey a couple of weeks later, I'm surprised by Cooper's appearance: he looks better than when I last saw him. The few pounds he has lost have restored angles to his face that actually make him seem younger. Nor is there anything in his manner to suggest ill health.

Still, Cooper is nothing if not completely candid about where things stand. Tests confirmed that the disease is a result of the melanoma he had removed several years ago—" All those years as a beach boy catching up with me," he offers with an easy smile—and the prognosis is not good.

Despite Gene's straightforward approach to his diagnosis, his search for a suitable treatment plan has been disheartening. "I started with the bunch up at Stanford; only they let you know right off you don't mean a damn thing to them. They'll be all around, pushing and pulling at you, but they only talk to each other, never to you, even if you ask them questions. Basically you're a human guinea pig; they don't even have the good grace to disguise it."

If such an experience is always humiliating, in the case of Gene Cooper, who has long had an interest in medicine and had researched all aspects of the disease with characteristic thoroughness, it was particularly so.

That is not to say he took it personally. Having been around scientists all his life, he is all too familiar with the type. "Let's face it," he understates, "there's a certain amount of arrogance among specialists in this area. They are very driven individuals, engaged in a cutthroat competition. At a research center like this, their aim is not to cure particular patients but to cure cancer itself. Every one of these big cancer centers is chasing a rabbit—the treatment that will be a breakthrough. So you walk in with cancer, and essentially what they want to know is what *you* can do for *them*." There is only the faintest trace of annoyance in this; Cooper is nothing if not a realist. "Well, let's face it, the answer in my case is not all that much. Once they find out you're more than eighty-five years old, that pretty much ends the conversation right there. They're interested in compiling good data, and the data on someone my age isn't the kind they want. They know, going in, I probably won't be able to take the treatment physically, which would mess up their results. So I wouldn't be a *good* guinea pig."

Eventually, he says, he decided to go with a woman oncologist at nearby Salinas Memorial Hospital, where until recently his daughter worked as supervisor of nursing. "Not only was there the personal connection, but this doctor was pretty straightforward, which I appreciate. I told her I didn't expect to be cured—something's gonna kill me sooner or later—but it would be nice if we could stretch things out a little bit. So she's worked out a program that's not too rough; not a new therapy, it's been around a little while, but maybe it'll kind of hold things off. At least with her I feel I'm more than just an inconvenient data point."

One side effect of the medication, which he has been taking orally at home, is that it leaves him with a continuous, dull headache. "When it first showed up, it just felt like you had a tight hat on, and then gradually the pressure got worse. Nothing seems to affect it—not that I want to try too much; I'm taking too damn many pills as it is. Among other things, I take two thalidomide."

"Thalidomide?" I exclaim.

Though I was only a kid forty years ago when thalidomide, widely prescribed at the time to help ease the discomfort of pregnancy, provoked headlines and launched innumerable lawsuits, the very word still evokes horror. The photos of all those limbless infants are beyond forgetting. "You mean the same stuff that—"

"Yep," he cuts me off, "the same stuff."

"My God, I didn't even know that was still legal."

"Well, they're really careful with it; you actually have to sign an affidavit before they'll give it to you. They want to know if you're sexually active and might cause a pregnancy." He laughs. "And, man, do they soak you for that stuff! It was a cheap drug at one point, but now two weeks of it runs you about five hundred fifty dollars—twenty bucks a pill. I figure they're doing it to pay off all the liability suits."

"Doesn't taking it give you pause?"

"Oh, no, why would it? The thing is, like a lot of medications, including aspirin, physiologically speaking they really don't even know exactly what it does. I poked around on the Internet trying to find out a little more about what they use it for these days, and it turns out one of the things they treat with it is Hansen's disease, as they now call it."

"Which is what?"

He smiles. "Leprosy."

"So how's Jody dealing with this?" I ask.

"Oh, you know, she's a pretty strong gal; she takes things pretty much in stride." He anticipates the next question. "So do my friends. They're a pretty solid bunch, not inclined to fight nature. When you come out of engineering and the physical sciences, it's hard not to be aware of the natural progression of things. After all, looking at it honestly, I've already smashed the actuarial tables."

Not for the first time, I find myself marveling at Cooper's reserves of calm. He is not a religious man, not like Earl Godfrey or Boyd Huff, yet the understanding of what is coming, not just death itself but the likelihood that it will be difficult and painful, seems not to have thrown him off his game even a little. If it would be imprecise to say he is wholly objective about his condition, he clearly regards it, and even himself as he grapples with it, with a certain detachment. It seems even what he's going through now is something to study and learn from.

"That attitude's at odds with a lot of the thinking in today's culture, don't you think? A lot of people I know seem to think they can stay young and healthy forever."

"Oh, well, you know, we've gotten pretty detached from the natural order of things. Some people have this idea that dying is just another problem that can be licked. They'll all find out otherwise." He smiles. "Maybe people have wised up a little bit in that regard since nine-eleven."

"Has nine-eleven affected you very much? Has it changed your view of things?"

"I'd say more like confirmed it," he says with a smile. "If you didn't already know all the most important things about humanity after living through World War II, you were probably never going to learn them. I remember the explosions down in Texas City during the war—the closest thing that ever happened in this country to the A-bomb. Ammonium nitrate improperly stored on two ships in Galveston Bay. It leveled all the oil refineries and blew a tremendous hole in the harbor, practically wiped out the entire fire department of Texas City. But those fellows ran right in, same as these guys."

In response, I remark on a moving article I recently read by the classical historian Victor Davis Hanson about the police and firefighters who survived the ordeal of the World Trade Center that terrible morning. Hanson discussed the factors, from family background to deeply ingrained values, that enable such men to perform as they do. What I don't say is that I've jotted down some of Hanson's words because they very much seemed to apply to the Girl Watchers also: "Their voices remain calm, never frightened. . . . They talk—often incisively—of a slow, growing and enduring response that accords with their own very American sense of fairness, righteous indignation and humanity. . . . I would not wish to meet people such as this in battle."

"I think it's important to feel that you've lived your life reasonably well," Cooper picks up after a moment, and I'm not immediately clear if he's talking about the Texas City firefighters in 1946, or those who died on 9/11, or he himself, sitting here in this room; then it hits me he's talking about all three. "That makes dying easier. If you don't feel that way, I'm sure it's a lot harder."

"You think that's why so many people are so terrified of death?"

He nods. "My whole life I've known people whose egos were big as a house, and most of them are pretty much incapable of finding any kind of peace. They're constantly worried about the next achievement, the next word of praise, looking over their shoulders to see what the other guy might be doing to get ahead of them. That's the nature of the driven personality type, and there are a whole lot of them out there. I've always been very lucky that way. I've had a wonderful wife and children. And I had my teaching, so the outside engineering I did was just fun—and I had a lot of fun." He smiles again. "All in all, it's probably not a bad time to be checking out. Frankly, there are aspects of today's world—and not only in the professional area—that if I were a young man, would probably scare the dickens out of me."

"How do you mean?"

"Oh, the extent to which people are desensitized. Technology is moving so fast right now, human beings can't properly adapt to it; things like the Walkman and cellular phones are no longer aids to human connection—just the opposite, they shut people off from one another. You watch people walking down the street these days, and they're completely lost in their own private worlds. It's not healthy for them or for society.

"I also worry quite a bit about overpopulation. It's basic mathematics; if we continue to multiply at this tremendous rate, it is seriously up for grabs whether we'll make it or not. Theoretically, we might one day place colonies on one of the moons of Jupiter, but in this solar system that's about it."

"Have you been thinking more about all this since your illness?"

"Oh, maybe just a bit. Maybe those of us who've spent our lives around the physical sciences appreciate more than most people how finite life really is—how rare and delicate the conditions are that must come together to produce it. It really is nothing short of a miracle, and we so take it for granted."

He falls silent a moment.

"Of course, I've been thinking a lot about Augie, my grandson. Have you ever read Robert Roark?"

"I know the name, but, no, I've never read his work."

"I enjoy his writing very much. He once wrote a series for one of the sports magazines—*Sports Afield,* I think—called 'The Old Man and the Boy.' It was about all the time he spent with his grandfather, mainly hunting and fishing together in North Carolina. The grandfather was a pretty wise old guy, very knowledgeable about the ways of nature, and they're wonderful stories. Well, in one of them, toward the end, the old man develops cancer, and the two of them drive up together to Johns Hopkins Medical Center in Baltimore. After they run an examination on the old man, he comes out and gives the boy the bad news. Of course the boy's pretty shaken, and he asks. 'Isn't there anything we can do about it?' And the grandfather answers, 'No, there ain't nothing we can do about it. If there was, I'd've heard of it.' "

Cooper gazes at me evenly. "Like the boy's grandfather, I'm fairly knowledgeable about these things, and also pretty realistic. It would be interesting to live another fifty years and see how things work out. On the other hand, all things considered, maybe it's not a bad time to bail."

I had suggested earlier that at some point we could take a break and I would buy him lunch. He's looking a bit weary, so I suggest this might be a good time.

"Actually," he says, "I'm afraid I haven't had much of an appetite. That's another consequence of this thing."

"Well, look, I've probably kept you more than enough . . ."

He doesn't object, and when I stand, he follows, rising slowly from his deep, comfortable chair to lead me outside.

We linger in the driveway, where the Coopers' two white Lexuses sit beneath the carport Gene put up when they moved to this house a half century ago.

"So," I ask, since he is, after all, reputed to be the last word in automotive expertise, "would you say Lexus is the best car around these days?"

"Oh, I don't know, there are an awful lot of good cars out there, most of them foreign. It's been a long time since we had anything like a monopoly on top-drawer engineering." He pauses. "I was reading just the other day that in Australia they're developing a very light, slightly elastic bodysuit, tight enough you can hardly realize you're wearing it. Full protection, head to foot. Pretty soon people'll be able to spend as much time as they want on the beach and not even worry about the sun."

"That's fantastic."

"Guess I was born just a little bit too soon. We sure did have our fun on the beach, though."

I walk to the car I drove over, Moe's Ford Explorer, its back loaded with books, old tools, and miscellaneous junk.

"Thanks so much, Gene," I say, opening the door. "I guess I'll see you at the next lunch."

"Think nothing of it." He stops, suddenly catching sight of one of the Explorer's front tires. "Oh, my, will you look at that? That thing's nearly bald."

He kneels down for a closer look. "You know, when I recommended to Moe that he get this thing, it was in tip-top shape. Look at it now."

"I know. The shocks are going, too."

He shakes his head, moving to the back of the car. Same story with the rear tires. "Basically, his attitude about cars is drive 'em till something bad happens. I don't understand it. A tire blows at the wrong time, and, man, that can be it!" He shakes his head sorrowfully. "It really amazes me how people can be so irrational. I guess there's no sense trying to convince Moe to get a new set on this thing, is there?"

"Probably not."

But now, catching himself, he breaks out in a grin. "Then, again, talk about a bad data sample; look who I'm using to make a point about rational behavior! You can't draw a single conclusion about anything based on Moe."

✦ CHAPTER 16 ✦

If you can justify cheating in school, you'll cheat at cards,

and chances are good you'll cheat in your marriage. . . . If

you cut corners in one area of your life, it very easily

becomes a habit.

—HARRY HANDLER

MOE AND HARRY; THEIR REGULAR
FRIDAY GIN GAME.

"*Say, Boyd,*" says Moe, taking the seat alongside Huff at the start of another meeting, "did you see in the papers where they're teaching a course up at Berkeley in screwing? Man, oh man, we sure went there at the wrong time."

"What the hell are you talking about, Turner?"

"That's what it said, they're doing sex right in the class!"

"Hold on, Moe," I jump in, for I'm the one who pointed the article out to him in yesterday's *San Jose Mercury*. "It was a class on 'male sexuality'; it said some of the students had sex at a party afterward."

"Close enough! It also said that sometimes the teacher does sex right in the classroom!"

Handler chuckles. "Isn't that what a good instructor is *supposed* to do, demonstrate core principles?"

"Wonder what you have to do in that class to get an A," muses Boyd.

"And to whom?" Walzer follows up.

"Probably just show up," says Moe. "In college these days that's usually all it takes."

This is how we have arrived today at one of their favorite topics, the lamentable decline in educational standards. Though the sentiment is partly a result of so many of the guys having been educators themselves, even those who weren't share the feeling. After all, everyone reads the papers; it's no big secret that reading and math scores are in the toilet—and that's before we have even gotten to the emphasis on "politically correct history," let alone the discipline problems in so many of today's schools. Once this train gets rolling, it can be hard to slow down.

"Man, have things ever changed in this world!" continues Moe. "Just look at the grades they hand out these days. They say ninety percent of the class graduates with honors at Harvard."

"This grade inflation stuff is awful," agrees the professor formerly known as Hatchet Harry. "In my classes, a guy knew if he didn't work, he'd get a low grade, and if he didn't appreciate it at the time, he did later, when he ran into hard reality."

Now, the door behind him opens, and Gene Cooper walks in, the last to arrive.

"Well, I'm here—more or less."

The others laugh.

"Well, being here is ninety percent of the battle," offers Stuart.

"Today has not been a good day for me. I just had chemo, so I'm a little woozy."

"I think we're all a little woozy at this stage."

"Keep it quiet, Harry, keep it quiet," Huff stage-whispers.

Cooper chuckles softly. "I always suspected the objective of chemo was to sort of marginally kill you. So what've you gents been discussing?"

"We've been bemoaning the fate of modern education."

"Count me in," says Cooper, taking a seat, "that's one of my personal bugaboos. I was raised with the certain knowledge that if you want to amount to anything, it's proportional to the effort you put in, and that no longer seems to apply."

"I'll tell you," says Moe, "when I was at the engineering school at the University of Arkansas, I was top man in my class, and I had a low B-plus average. My first day there, the dean of the school told us, 'Look at the student on either side of you; only one in four of you is going to graduate.' "

"Last time you told that story, Moe, it was one in three," notes Harry dryly.

"All I can tell you is the engineer's exam used be to tougher than the bar," Moe presses on, oblivious. "I had to guess my way through it. I put down a bunch of equations and drew a circle around the answers."

"I assume educated guesses . . . ," says Stuart.

"Like they'd ask, 'What's the rate of climb of an airplane?' Well, I hadn't the slightest idea. But I knew propellers were noisy, so they're probably about eighty-some-odd-percent efficient; and wings are quiet, so they're maybe ninety-five percent efficient; and I knew the power of the motor, so I figured out if I had an elevator with that motor, how fast could I lift it; then I put in a bunch of coefficients, wrote out a bunch of aeronautical equations, and put down the answer."

"It impresses me, Moe, but I'm only a lawyer."

"I tell you, it wasn't like today—back then people really knew how to work."

It strikes me that as complaints about the shortcomings of subsequent generations go, this last is shakier than most. If there is one thing that can be said about baby boomers with absolute certainty, it's that a lot of us work damn hard. In fact, if anything, too many of us, men and women both, are obsessed with career virtually to the exclusion of all else; including, too often, spouses and kids. Indeed, if you want to start poking around for the causes of the divorce epidemic among careerist baby boomers—which is something else the Girl Watchers remark on with some frequency—that's not a bad place to start.

But Cooper makes the point before I do. "I wouldn't generalize that way, Moe. There'll always be people with lots of drive. I think the big difference is in the way we *approached* work." He pauses, glancing my way. "Remember we were talking the other day about Moe's bald tires . . . ?"

"Oh, those tires aren't so bad," protests Moe.

"Well," continues Cooper, ignoring this, "I got to thinking about a fellow I knew in the early forties when I was teaching at Southern Louisiana State. He'd come down there from Clemson, where the War Department was underwriting a research program to extract latex from goldenrod. At the time it was tough to get new tires because of the war, so when his tires started getting threadbare, he wrote back to Clemson and they sent him down two carloads of goldenrod." He chuckles. "My friend put his whole senior class to work extracting the latex. It was a real Rube Goldberg operation, a massive effort with miniscule return, but everyone got completely into it. He ended up with what must have been the most expensive set of tires in history!"

"These days it might get them in the *Guinness Book of Records*."

"My point is it wasn't a bottom-line thing; the enjoyment was in the effort itself. Once they decided to do it, come hell or high water they were going to do it right—it was a matter of pride."

"Naturally."

"There's still some of that attitude around today, I suppose, but I don't think it's nearly as much the norm. Back then you just assumed people would approach things that way. I understand part of it was economic—times were more demanding; you could get fired pretty quick if you were half-assed about things. But hard times also made for character."

"I think a lot more people are content to ask less of themselves in general," agrees Earl. "Fifty years ago you never saw the kinds of allowances made for personal shortcomings that you do today."

It hardly needs to be said that for those of my generation, this sort of good-old-days talk by our elders is generally derided as nostalgic hooey. Who can forget Dana Carvey's hilarious old codger character on *Saturday Night Live*, a feisty malcontent so bristling with contempt for everything new and modern that he fondly recalls even those parts of the past that were clearly horrific? ("We walked to school eight miles in the snow—barefoot!—and *we loved it!*")

There does seem to be something genetically encoded into the aging process that makes the past look better than the present. Who knows? Forty years from now—better make that twenty-five; time's galloping up on us—my peers and I could be comparing Keith Richards to some degenerate musician our grandkids are listening to and recalling him as the very essence of propriety.

I've been meaning to put the question to the group for a while—and now seems as good an opportunity as any. "Isn't it possible you guys have a tendency to romanticize the past?"

There is a momentary pause; less, I think, of confusion than a kind of bafflement. After all, as they see it, they're just telling how it *was*.

"Listen," Stuart speaks up, on everyone's behalf, "that's probably a human tendency, not particular to any generation. I mean, I'm sure we all recognize the important ways things were a lot worse then."

"Healthwise they certainly were," allows Moe. "My sister had diphtheria, which is unheard of today."

"Polio, tuberculosis, all the way down the line," says Cooper. "Before penicillin, the slightest infection could kill you. If you stepped on a rusty nail, that was pretty much it."

"I'm not sure toilet paper was quite as soft, either," adds Moe.

Harry smiles. "A small thing, but life is composed of small things."

"And of course everything was far worse for minorities," says Stuart. "And for women."

"No question about that," agrees Moe. "It's amazing to think how bad things were just in our lifetime. When I was growing up down in Arkansas, you never even thought about segregation, that's how ingrained it was."

"It was the same down in Texas," says Cooper.

"I mean, even the words we used. The black part of town was called 'Niggertown'; in the theaters they used to call the balcony 'nigger heaven.' I'll never forget that, because when I was little and went to the pictures with my mother, she'd refuse to use that word. She was an extremely high-minded person, not like my father, who was a bigot to the core."

I've heard secondhand about Moe's deep ambivalence toward his father, and powerful admiration of his mother, from Priscilla, but this is the first time I've ever heard anything about it from him. I do know that, having grown up in the Deep South, he has always been acutely aware of the race issue. He has never had any use for the Trent Lotts of the world, that sorry species of individual who wouldn't know a moral principle if it hit him in the face. Moe was thirty that presidential year of 1948 when, according to Lott, we would all have been better off had the Dixiecrat Strom Thurmond won, and he voted for Harry Truman.

"No one's nostalgic for any of that!" says Huff, the historian. "Of course not. What we're talking about is a certain kind of honesty and integrity, which are the foundations of a decent society. Young people today hear about all the bad in our past, but what they don't hear enough about are the qualities that have made us face up to our problems. Goddammit, as long as we're on the subject of schools, *that's* something they should be taught."

"America and its traditions," concurs Cooper. "By the way, we'd also be wise to make sure immigrants learn not only the language but something of our history, so they'll understand what makes this country unique and special. That's how we used to do it."

"Amen to that."

"This hyphenated-American stuff is just fragmenting the culture. You go to certain parts of California today, and you may as well be in Mexico. I have a guy that does some yard work for me, twenty-five or -six years old, and he absolutely will not speak a word of English. It's almost a point of pride with him."

"It's been made a point of pride," says Godfrey, "and it's just wrong. Things have gotten all turned around. It's not the celebration of diversity that's made this country so strong, but the toleration of difference."

"We have to respect other cultures," cautions Stuart.

"Of course. But when people start identifying themselves mainly as Mexican-Americans or African-Americans or Arab-Americans instead of just plain Americans, it inevitably leads to conflict. We're so concerned with respecting other cultures, we undermine our own."

Moe turns to Huff. "How come no one ever calls us British-Americans? That's what we are."

"No, we get called 'angry white men.'" Boyd laughs. "I'd love to meet the idiot that came up with that one."

"We're so concerned with fairness," adds Cooper, "that sometimes we push the idea of fairness right into unfairness."

"Like with Al Sharpton and this reparations stuff," says Moe acidly. "That's the goofiest thing going. My mother had two uncles killed fighting as Union soldiers to free the slaves. Why doesn't our family deserve something?"

"Al Sharpton, the black Elmer Gantry," muses Harry. "They say he's running for president."

"Boy," observes Earl, "I really hope he gets the Democratic nomination."

Walzer, the liberal Democrat, laughs with him. "You want to ruin the Democrats but good, don't you?"

"I sure do."

Earl looks meaningfully around the table. "The bottom line is this victim mentality isn't good for anyone. It says you're helpless when you're not; it says you can't fend for yourself so someone else has to do it for you. That isn't good for the individuals involved, and it isn't good for the country. What we've got to get back to is that it doesn't matter what your background is: you can make what you choose of your own life."

It strikes me that this is the root source of their . . . *nostalgia* isn't even the right word. It's more like an abiding appreciation for the lost standards of the America in which they grew up. Yes, in many ways, some of incalculable importance, life in this country was far worse then. But in this vital way it was better: people didn't look for excuses and certainly weren't offered any; they expected a lot more of themselves.

That idea is timeless, and it is not for nothing that so many of us decades younger today feel the same yearning. I'm just barely old enough to remember when the quiz show scandals hit, and it made a tremendous impression on me when the brilliant Charles Van Doren was forced in disgrace from public life for having cheated. It seemed so sad, such a terrible waste of a promising life—yet also completely appropriate and just. As in the fairy tales of my youth, and the heroes of the Silhouette biographies I used to love, rotten behavior—lies, duplicity, backstabbing—had to be punished. That's what it meant for the good guys to win.

That's so long ago that among today's young the very idea of an unambiguous "good guy" is suspect. Not long ago I heard Gary Cooper's daughter Maria on a radio show, and she told of attending a college film class where *High Noon,* her father's classic tale of good confronting absolute evil, was being discussed. "It was really distressing to me how many of the young people didn't get the moral message," she said. "Their position was it was selfish of you to ask me for help when it's so dangerous to do so."

These kids were raised in a time of rampant relativism, a time when to presume to pass moral judgment on someone else—unless that person is guilty of racism, sexism, or homophobia—is a kind of secular sin. As small children, they were far more likely to have been exposed to bland, let's-make-nice fare like *Sesame Street* than to the sometimes harrowing fairy tales on which prior generations were raised; since these had been decreed scary and upsetting by educators and therapists (never mind that the very point was to imprint messages about goodness and evil so strongly, they would last a lifetime).

The message kids have picked up is that there is little percentage in noble and principled behavior. How could it be otherwise when, a blink of an historical eye after Van Doren slinked from the scene in disgrace, we are awash in a celebrity culture where far worse transgressions are instantly forgiven via a sit-down with Barbara Walters or a few weeks in rehab. "Everyone does it," once a powerful incentive toward honorable behavior, is now completely the opposite. As one recent survey has it, fully 74 percent of high school students acknowledge cheating as a matter of course—without evident embarrassment, let alone fear of serious retribution.

"What we just don't hear about enough these days is a stress on personal honor," says Earl now. "But without it, nothing else in life will really work. This is something many people never learn, even though it's proven every day."

"If you can justify cheating in school, you'll cheat at cards," agrees Harry, "and chances are good you'll cheat in your marriage. All these things are interrelated. If you cut corners in one area of your life, it very easily becomes a habit."

"I think, again, you have to look at the effect of the sixties on all this," says Cooper. "Look what was happening at the universities. At the universities, the places where society's standards had traditionally been upheld, almost no one was held to account for misbehavior because the administrators were sympathetic to the antiwar movement. There were no consequences to some of the most awful behavior."

"Horrible!" says Moe. "Even after that big disruption at Columbia, where the kids did all that damage, they let them off scott-free! Boy, what a message *that* sent. If I'd been running that place, I'd have kicked every one of them out of that school right on the spot!"

As someone once threatened with expulsion himself (along with two hundred or so others, after we had disrupted an air force recruiting session on our campus), I can tell you they have it exactly right. When the administration gave us "suspended suspensions" instead, we may have been relieved, but we were also even more deeply contemptuous of authority than when we had started out.

"There just can't be any give when it comes to accountability," says Huff. "Of course cheating is rampant these days; people know they can get away with it. The surrender of the universities to the forces of political correctness has done more damage than you can possibly calculate."

"Did you see much cheating at the Navy School?" I ask—though given the character of the place, I assume not.

"Definitely," replies Harry immediately. "Very much so."

Cooper spots my surprise. "The Navy School draws young officers from almost every part of the world, you know. People may react against this idea of ethnic stereotypes—that's part of this whole p.c. business—but certain attitudes and behavioral tendencies really are a result of cultural background."

"And not all of those tendencies reflected very well on the cultures involved," observes Huff. "I'm especially thinking about some of the students from the Islamic world."

"They had a tremendous degree of comfort, shall we say, with dishonesty," notes Harry. "They cheated an enormous amount. Actually, this might have some application to what we're seeing in the world today. Because you really had to watch some of those students very closely."

"My Iranian students cheated like crazy," adds Moe. "And the Turks. There was always a tremendous contrast with the Israelis—those guys were top of the line, just tremendous officers."

"They had to be. Lose one war, and that's it." Cooper pauses. "But some of these others, they actually had the attitude that they had a responsibility to cheat, and it was your responsibility to prevent them from doing it. As I say, it was cultural; they really and truly did not feel they were doing anything wrong."

"What's amazing is that these were military officers, responsible for defending their countries," says Harry. "It sometimes got so bad I'd tell my section leader to seat U.S. officers between the foreign students."

"What about the American officers?" I ask. "Did you ever have any trouble with them?"

Handler doesn't even have to think about it. "Our military has generally held to a pretty high set of standards, and these people were the cream of the crop. In my thirty years, there were only two U.S. officers I even suspected."

"What were the circumstances?"

"I got two exam papers with the same mistakes. I told the men involved I suspected collusion and offered them an oral exam—which was declined." He pauses; it is clearly an extremely unpleasant memory. "But that's why they stand out, because they were so far from the norm."

"Exactly," says Earl, the veteran of almost four decades in the navy. "Our tradition stresses integrity. And especially when it comes to the military, there's still plenty of that left." He gently taps the table with his knuckles.

"Those two American officers I mentioned? I reported them, and it went into their records."

Everyone here knows full well what that must have done to their careers. In the silence that follows, Huff gets slowly to his feet and goes to the sideboard for some coffee. "Good man, Harry," he says, "I agree with that very strongly."

"I really hated to do it, but, by God, how could you ever trust any officer who'd cheated with the lives of our sons?"

✦ CHAPTER 17 ✦

I looked upon America

as a beacon of hope—really, the only hope.

—GEORGE HAHN

GEORGE HAHN'S PASSPORT PHOTO, 1939.

"*If you want* to talk to someone who has real interesting things to say about being an immigrant in America," Moe out of the blue picks up one of the group's themes several hours later, "you oughta go see George Hahn. He's a guy who came over here and started a whole new life."

Moe regularly pushes those in the larger circle of Girl Watchers for inclusion in the book, and this is the fourth or fifth time he has mentioned Hahn. The truth is I don't really need to be convinced. A refugee from Nazism who in many ways succeeded in reinventing himself on these shores, George comes with a pretty remarkable story; one at once harrowingly familiar and chillingly unique in its details. His outsider/insider perspective on American life might well have added much to the group discussions.

In fact, the only reason George hadn't been part of our little group is that he is often out of the area these days, either visiting one of his grown children or at the family's vacation home in Central America.

"I thought you said George was out of town," I say to Moe.

"I just talked to him; he and his wife got back from Guatemala a couple of days ago. Real neat guy, very tall for a Jew."

"You think he'd have some interesting insights on this?"

"Of course! You want his number or don't you?"

At seventy-six, tall, thin, and lightly bearded, with lilting Austrian-accented speech, Hahn is an updated version of old-world charm; but, since he is dressed in jeans and sneakers, and possesses a quick, understated wit, it is with a distinctly California twist. Having done well in the stock market—gauging the price of certain high-techs to be remarkably out of proportion to their actual worth, and then getting out three months before the bubble burst—he appears to be about as worry-free as a man can get.

"It's a funny business, not needing money," he offers, as we relax in an open-air restaurant not far from his home in the Carmel Highlands, the waves crashing down on a pristine beach a quarter mile below. "My wife and I grew up poor, so we both still have our habits of frugality, going to Safeway and shopping for bargains. Otherwise I've found it's quite easy to get used to."

I have met George a couple of times before and am familiar with the broad outlines of his early years. He was twelve in 1938 when Nazi Germany annexed his Austrian homeland and his comfortable upper-middle-class boyhood was turned upside down. Friends and neighbors turned into enthusiastic Nazis. In school he was suddenly a pariah. His father was picked up on the street and sent to Dachau. Soon sent for his protection to Holland with a trainload of other Jewish children—none of the rest of whom would survive the war—he and the rest of his family actually escaped the continent three months *after* the outbreak of hostilities, and then only through a bureaucratic quirk so improbably miraculous it would never pass as fiction.

But the next part of his life was in its way every bit as compelling. After a brief stay with relatives in New York, the Hahns relocated to, of all places, Sacramento, where young serious-minded George, devastated by the knowledge of what was happening to the friends and family he had left behind, was cast into an utterly alien world: the complacent adolescent pre–Pearl Harbor America of hot rods and sock hops. Then, after several more years, he was back in Europe, this time in an American army uniform and—talk about divine justice!—charged with interrogating ex-SS men.

Now, in the restaurant overlooking the Pacific, George tells me he wrote a novel, *Black Milk,* in which the main characters are three SS men. "It explores how a normal person turns into a monster—which is a more complex thing than most people realize. Yes, some of these people were pure evil. But some just joined because girls liked the uniform."

Indeed, while in those early years he was an eyewitness to humanity as its cruelest and most base, he also, at least occasionally, saw glimmers of unexpected decency. "Some of the boys who'd been my closest friends became Nazis—it took a very strong person not to. But I also got a letter from one boy right after my father was arrested. He sent me back some stamps he had stolen, and apologized, and said he wanted me to know his family had nothing to do with this sort of thing." In school, while now forced to sit in the back, forbidden to join in games at recess, and abused by formerly congenial teachers, he also "had a math teacher who was an old Nazi who didn't change at all. He'd been fair before, and he continued being fair. At the end of the year he asked me, with a big smile on his face, whether I wanted to receive an A or a B, but if I wanted the A, he'd slap my face. I said an A, he slapped my face, and that was that. But he would have done it anyway—I used to talk too much in class. Yet there were other teachers who were just the opposite: before the Nazis, they'd always been perfectly friendly and reasonable, but now, to prove their bona fides, they became especially cruel and vicious."

The most memorable episode of this part of his life involves the day in October 1938 when he was alone in the family flat, his mother having journeyed to Berlin to plead his father's case, and found himself in the midst of the murderous, anti-Semitic pogrom history would come to know as Kristalnacht. He survived by his wits and good luck, dressing in his best clothes, hurriedly gift wrapping a book so it would look like a present, then riding the streetcars all day, pretending he was going to a party.

Seven years later, in an American uniform and suddenly in a position of authority over those who would have murdered him and his family without a second thought, he concedes he sometimes found his own morality tested in unexpected ways. "Part of our job was to try and reconstruct the SS hierarchy, to get names or to confirm information we already had, but it was infuriating; some of these bastards would absolutely clam up. I'd feel like taking their balls and squeezing. But, of course, that was the difference between us and them; I'd only imagine doing it."

Indeed, he says the most effective torture the Americans used was psychological, grounded in their reading of the Nazi psyche; using to advantage not only their profound race hatred but their conviction that given the power, others would be no less indecent than they were. "The interrogation room was in the basement, with a furnace going, and it was hot as hell, and we'd make them think we were gonna beat the shit out of them. We'd have two huge GIs in there with their shirts off holding baseball bats—usually one was black—and, oh, boy, would they suddenly be cooperative."

In fact, prior to the novel Hahn wrote another book, this one nonfiction, dealing with that period through the eyes of the child and the young man he once was. Titled *The Lottery*—an allusion to the incredible odds his family overcame in escaping the Holocaust—in considerable part it is a paean to America, the land that took them in and restored their faith in humankind. As Moe suggests, the contrast between George's attitude and those immigrants who resist embracing our American history and culture could hardly be greater.

Yet reading the manuscript George gives me, I also find myself caught up in the intensity of young George's relationship with the story's most poignant character, his father.

In its way, this too harkens back to some of my conversations with the Girl Watchers. For while it is a given—make that a cliché—that the father-son bond is the most complex and ambivalent of all male relationships, I had always more or less assumed, without really giving the matter much thought, that such feelings come with a statute of limitations. But already my exchanges with a number of the Girl Watchers had convinced me otherwise; for whether their relationships with their fathers were strong (as in the cases of Huff and Cooper) or troubled (Moe's and Walzer's), they had made clear that the example of their fathers had profoundly shaped their own behavior even into old age, influencing the choices they make, the values they live by, perhaps most of all, the kinds of fathers they have been themselves.

By the standards of men of his generation, Hahn is unusually self-aware, and he leaves no doubt that while the old hurts and misunderstandings may have dimmed, they will never be forgotten; and, far more significant, they stand as a permanent object lesson on how to do it better.

As he tells it, his father was one of those proud Viennese Jews who simply could not fathom, even after the evidence was before his eyes, that his countrymen might ever regard him and his family as anything but 100 percent Austrian. After all, he had been an officer in the Great War; he was fully assimilated, a respected businessman, not in the least religious. Thus it was that he made no effort to get out until it was way too late. In the end his family was saved only because years before, shortly after Hitler came to power in neighboring Germany, a foreign-born Jewish employee in his radio importing business, far less confident about the future than Herr Hahn, happened to have put the Hahns—George, his older sister, and their parents—on a list at the U.S. embassy while applying for his own visa. Before learning this, with war already declared and all escape routes closed, he had been told that their application would not even come up for consideration until 1948.

By the time the family arrived in Sacramento, aided by a Jewish refugee agency, they were almost penniless. "My father, who had been a big shot back home, became a gardener, working for himself. People would hire him because they could pay him less than anyone else." George pauses. "I never thought at the time how incredibly hard it must have been for him. All he'd say was, 'It's much better than a concentration camp.' "

Otherwise his father didn't talk much about the camps. It was from his mother, with whom he had always been closer, that George heard some of the details. His father had been arrested with his best friend, and—this being the prewar period when such things were still possible—they were to be released at the same time. "When the other man's wife showed up, they handed her a box. It was full of ashes, and they told her, 'Here's your husband.' "

George found this new life in California a confusion of contradictions. On the one hand, after all he had endured, the place was literally almost unbelievably welcoming. "The very first time I went to school, wearing my knickers and knee socks, people looked at me like I was an animal coming out of the zoo—but not at all in an antagonistic way. People here truly didn't give a damn whether you were a Jew or not, which was unique in my experience."

Indeed, he adds, "like other refugees from Hitlerism, I quickly became an American chauvinist. Abraham Lincoln had always been my hero, since I was a six-year-old back in Austria. But now, upset as I was by what was happening to the Jews in Europe, I looked upon America as a beacon of hope—really, the only hope."

On the other hand, for that very reason, he soon found himself wholly out of sync with his peers, caught up as they were in the rites of American adolescence. "I was a real outsider," he says. "I couldn't identify a Chevy or a Ford; I wasn't interested in dancing or football. And I was extremely interested, in a way few of them could understand, in the larger world. People would say to me, 'Your father was arrested? What did he do?' It made no sense to them—because of course it *didn't* make any sense."

Soon deeply bored by a curriculum that after Austrian and Dutch schools was the opposite of challenging, he began regularly cutting school, often to indulge an obsession with pinball machines.

After everything he had been through the previous couple of years, most American parents even then would probably have identified this as a fairly harmless case, as modern psychobabble has it, of "acting out." But to his classically stiff-necked European father, Hahn "was a juvenile delinquent. He wanted to send me to reform school and was offended that he couldn't do it, since it was the police and the courts that made that decision, and my crimes were considered insufficient." He smiles wistfully. "There was very little communication between us. My father had always been difficult to speak to, and I'd been on my own all that time in Holland, so I wasn't going to be the compliant little kid I'd been before they took him away. One time he beat me, and I told him if he ever did that again I'd leave and he'd never see me again. So he stopped."

Even as his truancy caused his grades to plummet, Hahn remained a voracious reader, reading "just about every book in the Sacramento library"; by his senior year in high school, despite simultaneously working the four-to-eight shift as a crane operator at the Southern Pacific rail yards, he was once again soaring academically.

Soon after graduating, he was in the army, assigned to counterintelligence. Among other things, he was charged with grilling GIs during the Battle of the Bulge, to make sure they weren't Germans. "It was absurd. Here I was, an eighteen-year-old kid, asking these people questions about baseball, which I knew nothing about. If they'd been interrogating *me,* I'd have been at least arrested, maybe shot."

(An intriguing point of information: while they of course wouldn't bother asking suspected German infiltrators something so obvious as the name of the American president, they tripped up quite a few by asking the name of the vice president, Henry Wallace.)

It was during the two years after the war's end that, first in Heidelberg, later in Berlin and Bremen, Hahn faced the long succession of ex-SS men. It is an experience that, for all it taught him about the depths of human depravity, he talks about with curious detachment. "They all claimed to have been in the motor pool," he sums it up with a cool smile. "If you believed them, the entire SS consisted of guys in the motor pool."

He was still only twenty-one at the end of 1947 when he made it back to the States. As eager as the others to get on with his real life, in rapid succession he got his undergraduate and master's degrees from Berkeley in physics, married, and started a family (all the while driving a cab nights to support them).

Hahn is too modest to say it, but since I hang out with Moe, he doesn't have to: according to my father-in-law, he was as gifted an engineer as they come, right up there with Cooper.

In fact, in those early years his career trajectory was similar to Gene's. He was involved in the development of a broad range of innovative gear for both civilian and military uses—most notably, something called the coherent radar system, which revolutionized airborne ground mapping—before joining the faculty of the Navy School. Even then, he continued to augment his teaching salary by working as a consultant for, among others, General Electric.

Before today, this was pretty much all I knew of George's story—the nightmare of his early years having given way to a Technicolor, all-American happy ending.

But it was a lot more complicated than that. The part of the story I didn't know began in 1961 when one of his children got lymphoma.

Hahn was thirty-five at the time, secure in his position at the Navy School, and David, the second of George and his wife Joyce's four kids, was twelve. "He was an amazing boy," recalls his father now, "the body of an eleven-year-old, the mind of a sixteen-year-old, wonderfully sensitive, extremely gifted in math and physics.

"We were a very close family. I had decided long ago I wasn't going to be like my father. Of course, that's hard—even when you're conscious of those patterns, your tendency *is* to be like your own father. You know you should do things differently, but you can't, not completely."

In his case, he says, he tried hard not to impose his expectations on the children or hold them to his own demanding standards. "But they were there, and obviously they knew."

Still, in this moment of crisis, he responded in a way that would have been inconceivable for his father. He dropped everything, arranging for a year's leave of absence from the Navy School to be close at hand while David was being treated at Stanford.

And that eventually led to an entirely new professional life. "This guy who was treating David and I just hit it off very well," explains Hahn, "so I asked if he could use someone in the lab for a year. He encouraged me strongly and felt my background would make me useful in this field. At the same time, I got a National Science Foundation fellowship to take courses at Stanford."

Financially, the family was taking a major hit—Hahn was making barely a third of what he had—but that didn't even register as a consideration. "My initial impetus, and of course I knew it was romantic, just a dream, was to cure him."

The boy had initially been given no more than a 20 percent chance of making it, and his odds fell sharply when the primary treatment at the time, radiation, failed to slow the cancer's spread.

"Did David realize how bad things were?" I ask.

"We never kidded him. We never used the word *cancer;* we said, 'You have a tumor. But one day early on we found him with the encyclopedia, looking up *lymphoma.* I don't know if he fully digested what he read, but I suspect so."

Hahn pauses. "Just an extraordinary child. When he died, he was listening to his favorite piece of music, which was the 'St. Matthew Passion.' " He stops again. "You don't get over it. I still cry about it."

But he also knew there was now much other work that needed to be done. Devastated as they were, he and his wife were keenly aware the other three children were suffering also and so required even more than the normal degree of support and love. Back in Austria, his own parents had been so casually oblivious that when twelve-year-old George joined an illegal socialist youth group and distributed subversive literature, under the Nazis a potentially suicidal act, his mother and father thought he was out with a Boy Scout troop. All these years later, a father himself and in the midst of this wholly different crisis, he was wise enough to know that if he and his wife were not attentive to their kids in the fullest sense, the consequences could have been devastating. "It was just a horrible time," he recalls, "very difficult. And we had some setbacks. David's older brother suffered the most—they were a year apart and very close. But eventually we made it." He pauses. "It was probably harder on my wife. I was lucky. A good part of my own quote-unquote salvation"—he makes the marks with his fingers—"was being able to do this work."

Hahn ended up with a Stanford Ph.D. in biophysics, going through the program faster than anyone ever had and afterward remaining on the faculty to devote himself to cellular research on cancer. "Always, in my work, I had been a problem solver, which I enjoyed, but I'd never really been all that excited about the work itself. But this I loved; what we were doing was really new."

His focus, in lay terms, was on inhibiting the ability of cancer cells to repair themselves. "When you damaged them with radiation, very quickly the DNA would recover and they'd go on like nothing had happened and continue replicating themselves. Over time, we tried all kinds of chemical techniques to affect this process, which generally weren't very effective. Then I tried cold—exposing the cells to extremely low temperatures. This inhibited repair, all right, but when the cells returned to normal temperature, they started dividing again. So eventually we turned to heat—which had a much more lasting effect on inhibiting repair. Under proper conditions, it increased the effectiveness of radiation astonishingly. We looked into why this happened and began to draw some fascinating conclusions."

In the end, Hahn's work was key to the development of a therapy which, while not widely used in this country, has taken hold in Europe and the Far East, proving especially useful against soft tissue cancers. A recent joint trial by Dutch and British researchers gauging the impact of hyperthermic treatment on recurrent breast cancer yielded particularly dramatic results.

Over the course of this second career, Hahn has been much honored, and it has, he says, been an extremely satisfying existence. "When someone thanks you for saving his life," he understates, "it is a very nice thing to hear."

But the curious thing—or maybe not so curious, because it's a pattern I'm already getting used to—is that when we talk about his work we end up talking mainly about family. Indeed, my visit here has been yet more confirmation of what might be called the Tsongas Dictum, after the late Massachusetts senator who reputedly uttered the words during a respite in his own long and ultimately losing battle against cancer: "No one ever said on his deathbed he regretted spending too little time at the office."

"Might David have been treated with your therapy?" I ask.

Hahn hesitates. "I've certainly asked myself that many times. Many times. I don't know; it might have helped a little."

But of course he realizes it's foolish to waste time wondering. "There are some things I do regret in my life. Primarily my relationship with my father. It was always strained; we never really got past that. It's an incredibly horrible thing he went through—besides what he experienced personally, he had six sisters, all of whom died in the camps—and I never had enough sympathy for that, at least not for the first twenty-five years of my life. After that, I suppose it was too late.

"Not that he was an easy man to get close to, ever. I remember an incident right after we got back from France, where I'd been for a year working at a cancer center outside Paris. The Jewish community of Sacramento was putting on a dinner for him—he'd become very active in Zionist activities, raised a lot of money—and I showed up with my tie in my pocket. I hadn't seen him in a year, and the first thing he said to me was 'Where's your tie?' After a year's absence, not the least sign of affection."

Nor, though he doesn't say this, of respect, notwithstanding all his son had accomplished.

I ask if his father ever got close to his own children.

He smiles and shakes his head. "He was fine with my sister's children. She had two before we had any; that was enough for him." But Hahn is a fair man and so quickly adds, "He was very good when David became ill. He came to the funeral and was extremely sympathetic. He actually stepped forward, and he prayed for peace. But that was the only time."

Once again, the contrast with how he has done it with his own children and grandchildren could hardly be more striking. All three of his children ended up in fields not far from his own; one son does research in cellular radiation on the East Coast; his daughter, a veterinarian, researches Lyme disease; his younger son is a computer engineer for a medical software company specializing in oncology. Between them, they have produced four grandchildren, all boys, to whom he is fiercely devoted. The home in Guatemala is a refuge for the entire clan.

"I probably shouldn't even go on about my father," he concludes. "All things considered, it's rather foolish to have those sorts of regrets. After all, he actually taught me a great deal"—he smiles—"even if a lot of it was inadvertent."

✦ CHAPTER 18 ✦

I'm goofy as a toad, I know that. I don't have to pay

someone to tell me. What is it they charge, forty dollars

an hour or something? Just for talking? For whining about

your mother and father and grandfather?

—MOE TURNER

THE TURNER CLAN, CIRCA 1910, MARSHFIELD, MISSOURI. ROBERT
NEWTON TURNER, MOE'S GRANDFATHER, IS AT CENTER.

"*Buckle up, Turner,*" commands Huff, as we set out one Saturday morning in May for a new round of garage sales. "It wouldn't be a pretty picture to see you launched through that windshield."

Moe glances at me in my usual spot in back. "See how Boyd and I look out for each other?"

"The cops'll stop you and see if you have it on. They're vigilant, trying to get rid of us old drivers. They got me just the other day."

"You probably went through a red light or something. Were you wearing your glasses?"

"Goddamn it, Turner, don't start micromanaging my driving!" He pauses, "You look at the paper this morning? I figure we'll go first to the sale at the Elks Lodge."

"Good, they usually have good books at the Elks sale."

Huff starts the Daewoo down the hill. "Did I tell you I caught Beverly the other day boxing up some of the books in my library to sell? I had to bar her from the library."

Moe shakes his head in commiseration. "Benny's the same way; she'd rather have all those sheds empty than have 'em full of my books. I don't understand the way my wife thinks."

"Beverly doesn't understand the great pleasure it gives me to just go in there and just handle 'em. That may be a little harder for women to appreciate."

"But I remember your telling me how much your own mother loved history," I say.

"She did, but it still wasn't the same as my father. It's a whole different feeling. My mother used to try and talk to me about things, but I didn't trust her as much."

"Why didn't you trust her?"

"Oh, hell, she was always disciplining me about some supposed transgression or other. But I trusted my father—he was my buddy. We used to play a lot of ball together, toss footballs around, hunted together."

"Huff was just a daddy's boy."

His friend doesn't bother even pretending to take offense. "Christ, I could talk to him about anything. But only if I needed to. I remember when I got to the age when I was going out with girls, my mother was always after him, saying, 'Wayne, you must tell Boyd about the facts of life.' And he'd say, 'Don't worry, let him pick it up on the street.' Which of course I did. We were very streetwise indeed. In my high school period, we were completely fascinated with aphrodisiacs—Spanish fly and all that. We used to read up on 'em."

"You dirty boy," says Moe. "Bet you didn't talk to him about that."

"Dammit, Turner, that's the point—he respected it; it was the male code." He laughs. "I remember during the Depression, the town had an abandoned brewery where they put in bunk beds, washing machines, and cooking facilities for the transients. My father and the mayor used to sit in the living room, smoke cigars, and talk about it. My mother would pipe up, 'You've got to get rid of those houses of prostitution down there on Main Street,' and they'd say, 'Dolly, we can't do that with all these unmarried men around here.' "

"And no one ever accused 'em of being male chauvinist pigs for it, either, I bet."

"Christ, no, it was a different world. Back then there were all these wonderful male bastions. My father would never shave at home; he'd go down to Charlie's Barber Shop over by his office and pay two bits. I used to go there too for my haircuts, read *Field and Stream* or *Popular Mechanics* while I waited. It was an institution. Men would get in there and conduct business. It was the same with hardware stores. And saloons. Guys'd go into a saloon and settle all the business of the world."

"That's all gone," notes Moe.

"Barbershops became 'hair salons.' About the only place maybe still left are golf clubs. And look what's happening to them."

Suddenly Moe demands, "You know where you're going?"

"The Elks Club, goddamn it. Seat of the exalted ruler!" He points vaguely to his right. "It's up over there."

"Long as you know. So, did your wife get her mind straightened out? That psychiatrist get her all squared away?"

"Oh, Christ." Huff chuckles. "I told her to fire that psychiatrist."

"Beverly sees a psychiatrist?" I ask. "How often?"

"Once a year," he replies matter-of-factly.

"Once a year?"

"She's with Kaiser. Up in Gilroy."

"One hour every year?" I press.

"About that."

"That's the strangest psychiatric treatment I ever heard of."

Huff laughs. "She's a friend of hers. Beverly's got friends all over the place."

Apparently, this is as close to an explanation as will come. In any case, it has opened up an intriguing line of conversation. "You ever think of seeing a psychiatrist, Moe?"

He turns back to look at me and replies in a voice heavy with contempt. "No."

"Why not?"

"Yes," Boyd readily agrees, egging his friend on, "why not?"

"I'm goofy as a toad, I know that. I don't have to pay someone to tell me. What is it they charge, forty dollars an hour or something? Just for talking? For whining about your mother and father and grandfather?"

"More like a hundred and forty."

"My God, now that is crazy!"

"But if you know you're nuts, didn't you ever want to address that?"

"Why should I?"

"You're saying you don't believe in psychiatry?"

He shakes his head. "Not a bit. I think it's a lot of baloney."

"You know, Moe, there are those who might say that's a defensive posture."

Boyd laughs, enjoying this. "He's afraid to have himself opened up to that kind of scrutiny. All the classic symptoms, Turner."

"I don't even associate with people that go to psychiatrists," he proclaims. "It's all talk, no action."

Needless to say, this is a position that enjoys a lot less favor than it once did. In an America conditioned by TV therapists to think almost every personal difficulty or shortcoming, from anger to obesity, is rooted in the psyche, Moe's disdain for the whole business leaves him an even odder man out than usual.

I, on the other hand, am far from averse to pop psychologizing, especially when it comes to a subject as irresistible as my father-in-law; and the more time I spend around Moe, the more I want answers. How can a man so inherently decent, and so deeply averse himself to pain, often behave with such seeming insensitivity? How, for all the depth of love for his family, could he have sometimes been so amazingly oblivious even with them? I recall my wife's youngest brother, Whitney, who has only partial use of one arm due to a birth injury, saying it was pointless expecting sympathy from his father when his condition made the usual hellish trials of adolescence even more excruciating. "Don't be such a prima donna," Moe would snap, when Whitney came home after being unmercifully teased for his inability to catch a football or do chin-ups in gym. "Look at Ronnie down the street; she has polio!"

Yet at the same time, Whit has long since come to treasure some of the ways his quirky and erratic father shaped his own outlook and perspective. Today a teacher himself, in his low-key way he is as ethically demanding as was Moe, and as a recent father, he is just as intent on imparting life lessons about right and wrong. The difference is he goes about all of it with eyes wide-open. "We place all this emphasis today on introspection," Whitney observes, "but he didn't have the time or the tools for that. It was a luxury, as it was for a lot of these guys. You have to look at where my dad came from and how far he went. Really, in a way, that very lack of introspection was part of his strength—it's what enabled him to accomplish so much."

"You know." I say now, "a couple of your kids are great believers in therapy."

"That's okay; they can believe what they want. My wife believes in God; doesn't mean I have to." He points. "It's over this way, Huff, bear right. You know where you're going?"

"Focus on the issue at hand, Turner."

"Have you ever talked about it with them?"

"No, they know how I feel. You have to indulge people a little, you know."

"I'm pretty sure Walzer believes in it also," I point out. "And George Hahn, too."

"Well, they're from a different background than me."

"You mean they're Jewish . . ."

"You said it, not me."

Let's not kid ourselves here; there's more than a little to that. Though Stuart and George were born an ocean and half a continent apart in Chicago and Vienna, speaking different languages, both were part of a larger culture nearly as alien to Moe's as that of the Aborigines; one that always placed great stock in introspection and what my peers would come to call, as it became generational gospel, letting it all hang out.

"What do you make of it?" he asks.

"Therapy?" I hesitate a moment for, in fact, my feelings are some-what ambivalent. "Well, I think you're partly right. For a lot of people it is an indulgence; they'll go on forever talking about themselves. But there are other people who'll go through life refusing to look closely at themselves at all."

"That's me right there." He pauses. "Tell me this: what about these psychiatrists who come in there and brainwash people and make 'em say they were abused by their fathers and mothers?"

"This 'recovered memory' stuff—I agree, it's a lot of hogwash."

"And those poor people in those day-care centers, like that place down in L.A., who got put away for years because the therapists got these little kids to say they'd done these awful things! It was just like the witchcraft trials; there was no truth to any of it. And the ones that did it never even apologized for it. Not the therapists, or the prosecutors, or the journalists, or anyone. It's like Al Sharpton and those guys with the Tawana Brawley case. They never admitted it was a fraud, even after they lost the legal case."

"You're right, Turner, that was an absolute travesty."

"Of course it was." I agree. "So you're saying you never thought it could do you any good?"

"Course not. Did you?"

"As a matter of fact, I did," I say, surprised by the question. "Didn't you know I was seeing a therapist when Priscilla and I got married?"

"You're kidding! I knew you'd be goofy enough to do something like that!"

"It was because before I met your daughter, I was going out with another woman who really put me through the wringer."

"Good for her."

"She was one of these women who, when things were going well, would deliberately create problems just to keep herself interested. And when things started going really well, she dumped me. Then she'd want to get back together. I mean, she just thrived on emotional instability. And I finally thought, 'Why the hell am I attracted to this woman? What is wrong with *me* that I want to be with her?' "

"I was about to raise that question," says Huff.

"You were nuts," observes Moe helpfully.

"I was nuts, okay. But she was also really sexy, which was part of it. And there is a phenomenon known as 'make-up sex.' Anyway, I started seeing this therapist, who was very helpful, and while I was still seeing her I met Priscilla."

"Did Priscilla know all this?"

"Of course. In fact, she saw the therapist once also. After we got engaged."

"She did? Why?"

"Because she's your daughter—and there were all these things I wanted to talk about and she'd never want to. So finally she agreed to come with me to see this woman."

"What happened?" he asks, fascinated.

"It was great; we had a wonderful conversation—she was very open, talked about all kinds of things she'd avoided before. And as we're standing by the elevator afterward, she turns to me and says, 'Don't you ever talk about me that way to a stranger again!' "

Moe cackles delightedly. "That's my girl."

A couple of minutes later, we pull into the lot outside the Monterey Elks Lodge, the conversation at an end. Moe gets out first and, as always, moves briskly ahead of us toward the entrance.

As we start to follow, Huff suddenly says, "I've been to one once."

"Really?"

"In the hospital in Paris, when I was recuperating from my POW experience, I had about a half-hour talk with this guy."

"He was concerned you'd been traumatized by everything you'd been through?" I surmise.

"I don't know what it was. I mean, I was all right. Half starved—I weighed eighty-eight pounds." He shrugs. "The guys they really worried about were the ones that lost a leg or something like that. They're the ones that needed talking to." He chuckles. "And maybe Turner, of course."

Later that afternoon, back at the Turners, I wander into the greenhouse, where Moe is rereading Lawrence of Arabia's autobiography while Mahler's Fourth plays in the background. "Got some time?" I ask. "I'd love to hear a little more about your family."

"Can't you see I'm busy?"

"That's what you said last time I asked, and the time before that."

"Well, I'm saying it again."

"C'mon, Moe, give me an hour or so. You've hardly ever said anything about when you were a kid."

In fact, reflecting on this morning's conversation, it's occurred to me that at this point I probably know less about my father-in-law's past than that of any of the other Girl Watchers. Or, more precisely, what I do know is mainly ancient history, gleaned from what my wife calls Moe's "ancestor worship." I've heard him say that he is distantly related to the Boones of Kentucky, and the James brothers of Missouri; as well as to the McKinneys, who lent their name both to a Texas town and, as a middle name, to my son, Charlie. He talks even more readily about Benny's forebears who came over on the *Mayflower* and fought with distinction in the Revolution.

"I don't remember my childhood at all," he protests. "Huff and Cooper remember theirs like it was yesterday. Talk to them."

"I have already. Tell me a little more about your father. You said he was a real bigot . . . ?"

"I don't know why Cooper's bothering with all that chemo," he says. "What a terrible thing to go through just for a few more months."

"Can we please stay on the subject for once?"

He sighs and lays aside the book. "The plain fact is, my parents should never have married; they were just about as different as two people could get."

"Different how?"

"My mother, first of all, she was a northerner, and an intellectual, real quiet and reserved. And my father . . . I mean, he was the sort of bigot you can't even think about being today."

"So how did they end up together?"

"Hold on. If you want me to tell it, I'll do it my way." He looks at me severely, then, satisfied, continues. "I'll start with my great-grandfather, my mother's grandfather. He was a master stonecutter in Indiana, and he married this gal named McKinney, a real redheaded demon, who was a real pill. But since they didn't have divorce in those days, the only way to get out from under was to kill himself, which he did."

"Wait a minute," I say, almost losing this last in the rush of words. "You say he killed himself? Your great-grandfather?"

"You wanted to get to my parents; this is the way I'm doing it," he replies evenly. "See, my mother was born in eighteen eighty-three, the brainiest member of a brainy family. My mother taught herself to read at three, and by five they had her figuring out how much feed her father should buy for his farm. Anyhow, when she was just a tiny girl, Mother read in the family Bible about her grandfather killing himself, and she got so upset, she burned it."

"How horrible!"

"But that wasn't the end of it. Twelve or thirteen years later, her own father—my grandfather—did the same thing. He'd lost his farm and couldn't get it back. By now my mother was in college, the Normal School in Muncie, and she came home one day and found her father had committed suicide."

"My God!"

"I don't know how he did it; I think he might've cut his throat or something. She'd never really talk about it."

Fleetingly, I'm reminded of something my wife once told me: that one of the reasons he married Benny was in the hope she would bring more stable genes to the family.

"What kind of effect did all this have on her?"

"How should I know? I told you she wouldn't talk about it. Anyhow, with her father gone, she had to make a living to help support the family, so she ended up getting a teaching credential. But since they were the only Democratic family in the county, she couldn't get a job. So she took a business course, and learned to type a hundred and twenty words a minutes, and ended up being the private secretary to Allison of Allison Speedway. Then she decided she'd go out to Hollywood and be a screenwriter. This was nineteen twelve, nineteen thirteen, something like that."

"This is around where your father comes in?" I had a vague recollection they married shortly before World War I.

"That's right. My father met her on her way out West, so she never made it. She was thirty-one when they got married, and he was thirty-six."

"Pretty old for that time."

"My father wasn't in a hurry. He was a real charmer, from a long line of charmers. His grandfather—my great-grandfather on that side—was from Tennessee, the black sheep of a wealthy slave-owning family, and at some point he left one step ahead of an irate husband. He hid up in the Ozark Hills, with his silk shirts and stuff, and married a girl up there, and they settled in Marshfield, Missouri. Hubble—the Hubble Telescope guy—was born there a few years later, and also that gal who wrote *The Little House on the Prairie*. What was her name?"

"Laura Ingalls Wilder."

"Her. Anyhow, they had ten children, five of each, and one of them was my father."

"So he would have been born—when?—around eighteen eighty?"

"Something like that. The Civil War was still a big deal at the time, and on this side they naturally were all Southern sympathizers. When my grandfather was twelve years old, the Union army came marching through Springfield, and he stood on the roof shouting, 'Hooray for Jefferson Davis!' They say one of the soldiers was just aiming his rifle to shoot him down when an officer told him, 'Put it down; he's just a kid.' "

"Quite a story."

"Lucky for your kids that officer was around," he tells me.

"Lucky for you, too."

"True enough." He smiles. "Funny how things work out, though—about fifty years later my grandfather was shingling a roof and fell off, and that's how he died."

"So," I ask, "was the Civil War—all the feelings that went with that—an issue between your parents?"

"Well, like I say, my mother's family were Yankees—her mother had three brothers fighting for the North—two were killed in the same battle, and the other was wounded. The one that was wounded would never cash his pension check; he said he didn't need to get paid to fight for his country. Quite different from people nowadays."

"So did your parents ever discuss these things . . . ?"

"Not really. They didn't discuss much of anything. Back then the man pretty much ruled the roost, and that was it."

"Even though your mother was a well-educated woman . . ."

"Their dispositions were just too different, My father always took a dim view of my mother's whole family; he used to say he never heard a Stoner whistle." He stops. "I don't know if he married her 'cause she had a little money or what. But they got married. Six or seven months later, my sister Dorothy was born. Later on, Dorothy saw her birth certificate, and she was horrified."

"So obviously that's *why* they got married."

He actually looks offended. "There was no way in the world; my mother was much too straitlaced! When Dorothy came to her with this birth certificate, my mother laughed, 'cause when she was born, she only weighed three pounds; she was very premature. My father used to stay up all night with this little baby; they say they could put her in a shoebox."

"What was Dorothy like?"

"She was a strawberry blonde, nice-looking girl, but very bossy. Died very young, at twenty-nine, of Bright's disease. I couldn't stand her." He pauses. "Anyway, now we get to me. I was born during the flu epidemic of nineteen eighteen. My mother had the flu—she was the only woman around who survived both the flu and childbirth. After that, I had a pretty normal childhood. That's about it."

"Were you close to your mother?"

"You know, she wasn't very warm. She really didn't know how to mother. Probably, if she was around today, she'd have continued on to Hollywood and made a big success of it, and that would be that."

I recall what Benny told me about how Dorothy used to ache for their mother's touch.

"I do remember she had long auburn hair," continues Moe. "As a little boy she used to let me comb and braid it for her. But she never said 'I love you' or anything like that."

"Did that bother you?"

"What kind of a screwy question is that? We just knew she wasn't really all that impressed with her own children, not after coming from such a smart family herself. As a matter of fact, she wasn't very impressed by the whole human race. She thought mankind was foolish"—he laughs—"and she was right."

"I can't count the times I have heard you say the same thing."

"And I'm right every time. We almost done?"

"Just a little while more. So your mother was pretty cynical."

"But she was also very kind, she had a very soft heart, and she treated everyone the same, no matter their background. I remember one night a tramp came around. Daddy wasn't there, so she told me to be polite while she went in and made sandwiches for him. Next morning, I saw he'd thrown the sandwiches away, he hadn't even touched them, and that got me furious. But in this very gentle voice, she told me, 'No, John. I'd rather that happened a dozen times than let one of them go hungry.' That really stayed with me. Even in her old age, when she was in a retirement home, she used to take care of children. She was just a very high-minded person."

"In contrast to your father?"

"You don't understand a thing about it!" he replies with sudden, surprising vehemence. "These things are complicated. Bigot that he was, my daddy got along with everyone, blacks included. But it only went so far. He always taught us to be polite, to say 'Sir' and 'M'am,' but one time he heard me say 'Sir' to a black guy and he gave me holy hell. Then, again, he gave me holy hell a lot."

"For what kinds of things?"

"I was the sort of kid who always had a smart remark to make, which he didn't go for at all. If I made a smart remark at the table, he'd slap me right there. I remember my very first day at school the teacher asked if anyone knew any poetry. Well, my sister had taught me a little poem, so I stood up and said: 'Yankee Doodle went to town / Found a load of switches / Every time he turned a corner / Down came his britches.' " He laughs. "I caught holy hell for that one."

"So in your case, the poem proved prophetic."

"Oh, he made me cut switches all the time, or he'd use a razor strop." He pauses. "I was a dreamer in school, which he didn't like too well. When I was seven or eight, my daddy used to punish me by making me wear a dress—that was a pretty standard punishment back then in our part of the country. I'd take it off when he left for work and put it back on before he got home. But my sisters squealed on me, so I'd get a spanking anyhow. He just didn't get along with me at all."

"What kind of work did your father do?"

"Maybe that was another part of the problem. When he met my mother he was working as a carpenter. That's what his father, the black sheep guy, was also. Later on my father became a salesman, which he was tremendous at on account of his charm. He could sell anything to anyone. But what he should have been was an inventor."

"Really?" Moe's often said the same thing about himself.

He nods. "One time he invented a quick starter for gasoline engines. See, this was back when you still needed a crank to start your car. This invention of his worked like a charm. Unfortunately, the same year he got his patent, the electric starter came out."

"So your father was a pretty bright guy."

"Oh, yes. But, see, he was also highly dyslexic, same as me. And back then if you were dyslexic, a lot of people considered you just half a step above retarded."

"How about later on? Did your relationship with him ever improve?"

"Not really that much. There was one time—Hoover was running, so it must've been thirty-two and I was fourteen—I made some remark that I kind've liked Hoover, 'cause he was an engineer. I'll never forget, my daddy looked at me like I was a speck of dirt and said, "When you were a baby in that crib, I thought maybe you'd grow up to be a murderer or a thief. But I never thought you'd grow up to be a goddamn Republican!" He laughs.

"So what do you think of your father now?" I ask.

"What do you mean? That's what I'm telling you." He pauses. "He had plenty up top; I'll give him that. I remember when he died, at the funeral I asked Mother if she thought Daddy was smart. I was already grown up by then, but she said, "He was a lot smarter than you."

Though on the page all this perhaps registers as something out of Dickens or, times being what they are, Jerry Springer, what's striking is that he said it without so much as a hint of bitterness. Later, when I mention the conversation to my wife, she is reminded of something her aunt Roberta, another of Moe's sisters, told her long ago: that as a small child, bookish and unathletic, a complete mystery to his father, Moe used to have a special corner where he would retreat and lose himself in his books. It was his refuge and his salvation.

"I don't know," he concludes now, reflecting on his mother's assessment of his father and himself, "maybe he was smarter."

"Maybe that's what made him so angry—that he didn't do more with it. Maybe that's why he used to beat you up."

"What do you mean 'Beat me up'?" he says with real scorn. "When I did something wrong, he spanked me. I didn't like it, but I deserved it." He reaches over to turn on his radio. "I don't know why any of this matters, anyway."

"It's very interesting. It explains a lot about you."

He looks at me blankly. "Glad I could help. Okay, I'm gonna get back to my book now."

✦ CHAPTER 19 ✦

No one ever gets off scot-free for anything. No parole,
no good behavior, no nothing. Plus, every year we should
go to the prisons, skim off the worst ten percent,
and deep-six 'em.

—MOE TURNER

INDEPENDENCE DAY, 1918. BOYD HUFF IS AT
LEFT, IN A COWBOY COSTUME.

"*I knew a kid* once that grew up to be a killer," says Cooper. "Went to grade school with him."

Moe lights up, as the Girl Watchers' back-and-forth about a true-crime show on TV last night abruptly takes a personal turn. "Who?"

"John Beeler was his name. Went to school with him."

"Who'd he kill?"

"Two people, actually. He got off on the first one—self-defense, I think—but the second one they gave him the chair. They did it fast in those years, no beating around the bush."

"So this killer was a friend of yours, was he?" asks Moe, delighted.

"Not exactly. But I knew him from the earliest age. Even then he was meaner than a hornet, just delighted in hurting people. Way back around second or third grade someone walked by his desk, and for no reason at all Beeler stuck a little knife two or three inches long in his thigh."

"Man, oh, man!"

"Right there you could tell he was on his way to the chair."

And so begins a conversation on the subject of crime and punishment, as well as the larger philosophical questions linked to the subject. What makes seemingly decent people go bad? How far does society have a right to go to protect itself from them? Or, to put it another way (and since Moe is involved), is it best to merely kill someone, or do you provide a more effective example by torturing him first?

"What do you think made him that way?" wonders Harry.

"In most cases it's a combination of bad genetics and bad background. But some people are just *born* bad. The last time I saw him, I guess I was in my late teens, I was working in an ice cream parlor—he came in and was actually friendly. He'd just gotten out of the penitentiary, and I asked him what he was planning to do."

"Murder someone."

"That turned out to be about the size of it. He was just a lost cause from the word *go*. I've known only two or three really bad people in my life, but he was one."

"In fact, I don't think you ran into nearly as much nastiness in general back then," says Earl. "It seemed like a less angry time."

Obviously, it is possible to make the case to the contrary. In addition to horrific accounts of racial violence, one will find in the history books episodes of casual barbarity scarcely imaginable today. In Cooper's hometown of Galveston, as one such account has it, in the aftermath of the devastating 1900 storm that left more than 1,600 people dead, 125 men were shot to death for robbing the dead, and one of these men was found to have twenty-three human fingers bearing rings in his pocket.

But of course they are talking about something else entirely: what it *felt* like to be alive in those years, the sum total of one's small daily interactions as one moved through life.

"I think that's true," agrees Harry. "You'd actually be surprised at bad behavior. I remember what a terrible shock it was when someone swiped gas out of my car. Things like that just didn't happen; it really ate away at my faith in humanity."

"Harry . . ."

Handler looks Boyd's way.

"It was me."

"I wouldn't be a bit surprised."

"I had a Model-A Ford I bought for twenty-five dollars, and I used to siphon the gas out of neighbors' cars. Sorry. I didn't realize it would still be an issue sixty years later."

"But today, almost nothing shocks us. Look at my friend Dick Wilson. Have you been reading about this in the *Herald?*"

Of course they have. A local attorney, Wilson has been accused of looting the estate of an elderly Chinese-born couple he was representing of a million dollars.

Continues Harry: "Seems like the nicest guy you'd ever want to meet, fair-minded, friendly, competent. He handled my mother's estate and did a very nice job. He served on the Carmel School Board." He pauses. "Did you hear his lawyer's explanation for his behavior? That the Chinese couple had left it to a hospital in Communist China, so what did it matter? It was perfectly all right to steal—because they weren't American, they'd have no record of it!"

"He also claimed Wilson didn't really steal a million," notes Stuart, "just five hundred thousand."

"Half a million here, half a million there, it can start to add up to real money."

"Again, I think we have to look back to the sixties," says Earl.

Harry, beside me, gives me a gentle elbow in the ribs. "We can blame the sixties for everything."

Harry is being facetious, but for me the comment hits home. Over the first twenty years of my life, I never swiped so much as a pack of baseball cards; over the next seven or eight, I shoplifted regularly. In my circle lots of people did. After all, as the thinking went, when you took a steak from a supermarket or an album from a record store, you were *ripping off the system.* Then one afternoon the owner of a stationery store caught me swiping a magazine and, sick to death of arrogant young jerks like me, dragged me off to the local police precinct. If the tongue-lashing I got from that young no-nonsense cop didn't exactly scare me straight, it started my retreat from the ethic of the times and back to my senses.

"No question, it wasn't the most morally rigorous period," I say.

"When we were young, no one even put it in terms of morality," says Earl. "People just understood the difference between right and wrong. It would never occur to anyone to *explain* wrong or try to understand it."

"The problem then was a bad economy," Huff readily agrees, "not a lack of character. With all that poverty, there was so much less crime. People weren't just more innocent, they were *nicer.* In Spokane, where I was, there'd be all these big, tough-looking strangers looking for work: displaced miners and guys laid off from the lumber mills, and the workers from the great wheat fields in the Big Bend. Yet no one was scared in the least."

"Same thing in Galveston," says Cooper. "We'd have a big influx of hoboes every winter, a lot of them eating canned heat—jellied alcohol. But we never had any thievery at all. We never locked the house, and neither did anyone else."

"Same with us in Nebraska," agrees Earl, "and people were hurting in ways we can hardly even imagine today. No one's saying poverty is good—"

"Let's hope we all agree there," says Harry, laughing.

"—But it sure can help teach you what's really valuable in life."

Walzer has been quietly listening to all this. "I'll tell you," he interjects now, "I wouldn't go too far with this glorification-of-poverty business. Being poor can also make people pretty mean and vicious. Look what happened in Germany."

"We're not Germany," counters Huff, the historian. "We have a completely different history, a different tradition."

"That's true. But we had our share of vicious bigots in that period too, like Father Coughlin and Huey Long. And there were also plenty of run-of-the-mill nasty, tough sons of bitches out there."

"That's life; there'll always be some of those."

"I bring it up because I had some personal experience in that regard. You might say it was when I lost my innocence." Stuart gazes around the table. "It was just after I turned seventeen and was hitchhiking across the country. Down around Amarillo, Texas, I fell in with a bunch of hoboes. Confused adolescent that I was, I started shooting my mouth off, telling them about my middle-class Chicago background. Along the way, I let it drop I had a wallet with about thirty-five dollars in it."

"Oh, man!" exclaims Earl.

"Lucky you're alive," says Cooper.

"That finally dawned on me, because I noticed they were getting just a little bit too interested. I'd been planning sleep out there with them, but around nine o'clock, I excused myself to pee and just took off. I swear, I *ran* all night."

"Your first mature decision, right there," says Harry, laughing.

"Course, you wouldn't want to do that today; you might get accused of stereotyping them, which is something else you don't want to get accused of."

"It's considered wise to wait till you get your head bashed in before making such a judgment," notes Huff.

But Cooper wants to get back to the larger point. "The fact there was less thievery is just the tip of the iceberg. What we're really talking about is civility. In those days most people just seemed to treat each other with more courtesy than they do now."

"Tell me about it," says Harry. "Just yesterday I was driving near our house and a woman made a California stop—sort of slowing down—and I damn near broadsided her. I saw she had this little kid in the car, taking her to school, so I followed her all the way there. I got out and said, 'Excuse me, Ma'am, you nearly caused an accident back there." He pauses. "I will not repeat the language she used, but it was not very polite and she used it in front of her child. Can you even imagine something like that happening fifty years ago?"

"Or a kid not standing for a pregnant woman?" asks Cooper. "When I was growing up, if a pregnant woman got on a streetcar and a young person didn't give her a seat, people would murder him." He chuckles. "Enforced civility."

"Today if someone gave a kid a hard time not giving up his seat, people would probably come down on that guy instead," says Huff. "Christ, look at all the ruckuses these days at Little League games—among parents! And how do they propose to deal with it? By passing some goddamn piece of legislation! What used to be basic courtesy, they now have to make a matter of law!"

"It's really just a few parents who are out of control," I observe, with the authority of a recent Little League coach, "but that's really all it takes."

"I just worry all the time about this next generation of kids," says Moe now. "I got robbed blind by a boy right up the street here, ten or eleven years old. I'd been real nice to him, too; he used to come around and borrow my tools."

"What did he take?"

"I had a set of nice old silver dollars, and one day I heard this kid was going around selling silver dollars for a dollar and a dime. That's what he was getting, a dime profit!"

"Not much of a businessman!"

"Turned out he was on dope. But what burned me just as bad was when I found out a neighbor was buying them. I went right over there and said, 'Didn't you realize there was something wrong?' He said, 'Oh, no.' Just a total lack of shame."

"Were the kid's parents divorced?" Huff wants to know, "That's the question you always have to ask these days."

"His mother was raising him. He didn't have a father, never had one as far as I know."

Earl shakes his head. "My goodness, of all the things that have changed for the worse, that might be the worst of all. All these divorces, and so many people are willing to overlook the consequences. Not having a father has such a terrible impact on a child—a boy in particular. So often he'll be angry, violent, totally lack direction."

I glance at Stuart, the divorce lawyer, wondering how he will react.

Then, again, he is also the father of four sons. "That's all true," he says simply.

"But I shouldn't even be complaining," says Moe, turning to Cooper. "You got robbed a lot worse than me. How much did they get from you?"

"Oh, we probably lost twenty-five thousand dollars' worth of stuff. Mainly photographic equipment."

"My God!"

"Houses get robbed; that's life. What's worse is what happened afterward. The insurance man tells me to go over to Brooks Cameras in San Francisco, and the insurance company will pay for replacement equipment. So I go up there, and while the man is getting replacement cameras, I strike up a conversation with his secretary. She's kind of a cute little gal, and I tell her what happened. She says, 'Sounds like a pretty good assortment of material you had. My boyfriend's in the business.' I said, 'You mean he replaces cameras?' 'Oh, no', she says, 'he steals them.' "

There is a burst of astonished laughter.

"You end up getting your own camera back?" asks Harry.

"No. But this attitude of hers just floored me! Her thinking was, 'We make money on the replacement, the insurance company makes money, the manufacturer makes money, the thief makes money—what's the problem?'"

"And more jails get built," points out Walzer, "don't forget that. Creates lots of jobs."

"This is what I truly find horrifying, the total lack of embarrassment. So many people have no trouble at all letting themselves off the hook for their own rotten behavior. It's the same attitude we see now with these CEOs; there's no thought whatever to the human part of the equation." Cooper pauses. "I lost two things in that thievery that just broke my heart. One was my father's pocket watch, which he left to me. Before that it had been his father's. Just a beautiful thing, in wonderful condition."

"Oh, my!" exclaims Earl.

"The other item was an old Winchester saddle gun a great uncle of mine gave to my son."

"Octagon barreled?" asks Huff. "Those things are hard to come by."

"That's right. The insurance company threw a few bucks our way, and, you know, they gave me another pocket watch. But a part of you is gone forever."

"We also have to focus on the other part of the change," says Earl. "There's a lot of lip service these days to the concept of personal responsibility, but we have to get back to meaning it."

"What a crazy idea," says Harry, smiling.

"Because right now, no matter what you do—whether you do drugs, whatever—the feeling is, 'Don't worry. Someone'll clean up the mess; someone'll take care of you.' And the first part of that is bringing back the idea of stigma—saying these are things that are not good for society and following up with real consequences."

"I'm with you," says Moe. "In the old days if you did something bad, you knew it wasn't going to be pleasant. If you murdered someone"—he snaps his fingers—"two, three weeks and you're gone. Before the damn lawyers messed it up."

"But, Moe, that's our *job*," protests Stuart.

Since I'm already familiar with a couple of my father-in-law's theories on criminology, I'm only mildly surprised by what comes next. "First off," he declares, "no one ever gets off scot-free for anything. No parole, no good behavior, no nothing. Plus, every year we should go to the prisons, skim off the worst ten percent, and deep-six 'em. We can start with some of those CEOs, just to discourage the others."

"Moe," observes Stuart reasonably, as if he's speaking to another wholly rational soul, "haven't you heard of the constitutional provision against cruel and unusual punishment?"

"Well," Moe presses on, "they say they're running out of money to run the prisons. Would you rather turn loose all these horrible criminals or put them to sleep? I swear, we're so goofy about death in this country; we'll save some murderer and let innocent people die. Look at that guy who killed that Polly Klaas gal. He was one of the most evil people I ever heard of, and that guy's still alive, and I'll bet you several lawyers have made a fortune off him."

Stuart smiles and allows him to continue.

"And another thing—if you're gonna have capital punishment, make it drastic and quick, not wait around till they die of old age. Two weeks and, bingo, like they did with Cooper's guy."

"I believe you also highly approve of the routine in the Arab countries, chopping off hands and all that, don't you, Moe?" asks Cooper.

"I do! The way I look at it, we got too many people in this world anyhow; why not get rid of the bad ones?" He pauses. "I have got a couple of other ideas I could tell you. Only these you might think are a little rough."

"Your ideas?" Harry laughs. "Why would we ever think that?"

"Let's hear them, Moe," says Stuart, genuinely intrigued.

"Well, I'll tell you about the Dispose-u-all, which I think would straighten things out quite a bit—put the fear of God in anyone who did a crime. Here's the deal: Anything that gets you convicted in court—drunken driving, bank robbery, shoplifting, anything—and your name gets put in a central computer. And once you're there, you're in it for life. And, see, there's a jitter factor—"

"What's a jitter?"

"A random motion indicator," explains Cooper.

"—which is the most important part. See, every so often, the machine will spit out a name, and that guy'll immediately get executed."

"So you could theoretically be executed for shoplifting?" asks Stuart, caught somewhere between amusement and horror.

"Well, of course the odds change according to the crime. If you drive drunk twice, the jitter goes up twice as much, and on and on." He pauses triumphantly and repeats, "The Dispose-u-all would put the fear of God in 'em all. Even if you don't do a capital crime, sooner or later the jitter could get you."

"What about all the people who were later shown to be innocent," cautions Harry, "some of them convicted of murder?"

Moe brushes this away. "Listen, they got DNA now, so a lot of the time there's no doubt. Anyway, this idea of worrying about one innocent person is crazy! For every guilty person you get, you're saving a dozen innocent people!"

"You might have a few problems with civil libertarians there, Moe," notes Cooper dryly.

"Execute some of them, while you're at it!" He grins, making it clear even he recognizes how all this sounds. "Listen, it's no crazier than the way we do it now. Look at how we're dealing with the drug problem. The solution's not going over to Colombia and places like that; you can close 'em down, and thirty other places will do it. Instead, you find a dealer at a certain level and you execute him—and the lawyers who help those guys, while you're at it, execute *them*."

"There's another solution, Moe," says Earl, who has a powerful libertarian bent, "give 'em all the drugs they want. Decriminalize the whole thing. Because you're right, the current policy is absolutely disastrous."

"Of course, the argument against that is you'll have people lolling around in the streets, drugged out and all," points out Stuart, "which aside from everything else is a terrible example for young people."

"I hate to say it, but the way we're going, that may be something we just have to live with."

To nobody's surprise, Moe jumps back in. "I'll tell you the solution to the drug problem; it's very straightforward. We got these remarkable genetics-based medicines—right?—so we develop something where, anyone who takes drugs, it makes 'em deathly ill. You just inoculate all these drug takers with this stuff, and that's pretty much the end of it. They can surely find something like that if they put their hearts to it, and, by God, it'll stop the drug problem just like that."

"You know, Moe," offers Cooper, "you might actually make a little bit of money with that one."

"I just come up with these ideas; someone else has to do 'em. As for the drug dealers, if they traffic above a certain amount, just take 'em out and shoot 'em. In the long run, you'll be a lot better off."

"Wasn't that Milosevic's policy in Serbia?" says Stuart.

"He did it because of race; I'm doing it because of actions! One other idea: outlaw smoking in prison. In fact, that's the first thing I'd do, because so many of these types enjoy it so much. It would stop a lot of people from committing crimes in the first place."

After a startled pause, the others erupt in laughter.

"Let me get this straight," says Walzer. "A guy's about to hold up a liquor store and he says, 'Wait a minute, I'd better not do this cause there's no smokes in prison.' "

"Right."

"So you want to keep them from anything that might ever make them feel good."

"Right. Or else maybe *make* 'em smoke; that's another alternative." He chuckles, already warming to the idea. "Capital punishment by small degrees."

"Moe," notes Handler with mock sorrow, "I'm afraid this is one of your poorer theories."

"Well, you know, we've actually been having this argument since way back when I was in law school," observes Stuart, "although generally

with a little more, shall we say, subtlety. Is it society's role to seek reha-
bilitation or revenge?"

"Don't lump me in with Moe here," says Earl, "but I don't think of
severe punishment as revenge. It is society saying we have fixed standards and we will not overlook it when they are violated. The alternative
is to make those standards meaningless, which is pretty much what
we've done."

"And you can blame the lawyers for that," repeats Moe.

"But I also don't think you walk away from people," says Stuart. "How
about trying to give someone in prison a skill, especially if he's young?
The truth of it is, when you've got a lot of people and not enough for
them to do, a lot of them will turn to crime."

"Then what do you say to all those people who live under the same
terrible disadvantages and act well," counters Earl, "because that's the
great majority?"

"That's true," Stuart readily agrees. "I'm saying sometimes harshness
isn't the best answer. But that doesn't mean I don't understand the frustration people feel with talk of 'root causes.' Some crimes absolutely are
so heinous we should never try to understand them. A couple of years
ago, at a seniors group I'm involved with, I met a woman who lived in
the Salinas Hills, like you, Boyd, and one night a bunch of kids got into
the house. They shot and killed her husband; then they made her
teenage daughter strip and violated her with the gun."

There is a collective gasp.

"They didn't shoot, but the daughter has been absolutely out of her
mind ever since. Well, this woman now goes around speaking about this
crime. They've got the bastards locked up, probably for life, but she will
never begin to forgive them, and how could she?" He pauses. "If it were
up to me, I might even hand them over to Moe."

"Well, you know, I've got one more idea," Moe picks up his cue. "You
take people like that, the worst of the worst, and let 'em loose in some
wild wilderness area, far from any civilization. Then you'd get these
really rich gun-nut types and sell 'em hunting licenses at about a hun-

dred thousand dollars apiece and let 'em go into these areas with all the high-tech stuff they want to hunt 'em down. Get rid of 'em and help the economy at the same time."

There is an instant of stupefied silence.

"Maybe you could throw in a couple of those Enron guys, too," adds Moe, giving the idea a little more luster.

"What if one of the killers escapes?" asks Harry.

"Well, see, you'd have some kind of electronic sensor on them. If worst came to worst, you could bring in a copter and get 'em with rockets."

"There's another one you're going to have trouble getting through," says Walzer. "You might even get pretty roundly criticized for it."

"I know it," he indignantly agrees, "that's the problem, right there; they discourage both creative thinking and honest talk. It's like Galileo and the Dark Ages; there are certain truths you just can't say." He looks at me. "You're gonna put all this in the book, I hope. Because I think I'm just gonna have to start speaking up a little more with these ideas."

Harry can't help laughing. "Please don't; I really want to continue playing gin rummy with him."

"Can't you see it," asks Huff, nodding toward the window, "hundreds of them out there in the yard, picketing Turner?"

"I can see him getting shot," offers Cooper. "In fact, come to think of it, I don't know why he hasn't been shot already."

Moe thinks that over for a second. "Well, that's another idea, right there. I'm gonna die one of these days, anyhow—might as well be a martyr to a good cause."

CHAPTER 20

There are many people, especially in a place like L.A., who consider their lives meaningful only if they're constantly around others who they regard as successful and important. It's self-worth by association.

—STUART WALZER

STUART WALZER AND CLIMBING
BANKSIA ROSE.

For all the flak the other Girl Watchers give Stuart on the subject of the divorce explosion and his alleged role in it, it's also hard not to note that the ribbing comes with a heavy dose of respect. While Stuart's profession may give some of them the creeps, especially since he practiced in a town they regard as maybe the worst place on earth, he somehow escaped after four decades with values largely identical to their own.

Indeed, his status as a refugee from that mysterious and alien world sometimes allows for the sort of dialogue that challenges long-held views, casting them in an entirely new light.

One afternoon Moe offers the familiar lament, "Lots of people get married these days almost expecting they'll get divorced; no one'll hang on to a wife if he thinks there's something better out there." He turns to Walzer and adds pleasantly, "Well, at least all those bad marriages down there in L.A. kept you divorce lawyers happy."

"They kept us busy," responds Stuart in kind. "Happiness is a metaphysical question."

"You had some famous clients, didn't you?"

"Oh, yes. And some were very talented. Others, their only real talent was making themselves rich."

He launches into a story about one client, the youngish wife of a famous Hollywood writer, who by the time she hired Walzer was working on her third divorce and her umpteenth million.

"There used to be a name for a woman like that," observes Huff dryly. "An entrepreneur."

"What do you suppose she had that all these guys went for?"

Stuart doesn't even have to think about it. "She'd been a cheerleader in high school; I think she held on to the costume."

The guys erupt in laughter.

"Divorce law is a fascinating field for a voyeur," he adds. "You'd love it, Moe."

"I bet I would."

"The trouble is, you really do begin to see everything in terms of pathology. Everyone you run into seems to have marriage trouble."

"Well, down there in Los Angeles . . . ," observes Cooper.

"The fact is, these days it's not so different anymore here or anywhere else," says Earl.

Moe shakes his head. "Pretty pathetic, isn't it? When I was growing up, nobody in my town ever got divorced. I mean, an aunt of mine got divorced after she found out her husband was cheating on her, and it was still a great scandal."

"But maybe that's why you can't be quite so black-and-white on this," says Walzer, "because that kind of discontent is also part of the human condition. There were always lots of unhappy marriages."

"I gotta say," Moe acknowledges, "my own parents' marriage was far from happy. They were really ill suited for each other."

"I had a grandfather and a grandmother who didn't speak to each other for ten years," says Earl. "They were civil to each other, but they never exchanged a word."

"How in the world did it come to that?" asks Harry.

"As far as I know, it was all because she was going to take a ride on a wagon or something into town—some very minor thing."

"There must've been a lot of that going around. Benny's great-grandfather, when he was dying, his wife came in there to see him. He opened his eyes and said, 'Get that woman out of here!' " Moe cackles. "They say those were his last words!"

"Fitting and proper ones," says Huff, above the general laughter.

"Well, that's my point," notes Stuart. "You see people like that all the time today—sitting in a restaurant, not a word to say to each other the whole meal. The difference now is they probably get divorced, where before . . ."

"They endured," says Earl. "And frankly I think there's a lot to be said for that, especially where children are concerned."

"I agree that makes sense if the hostility isn't crippling and the man and woman are both willing to look at the problems," says Stuart. "But do you really think people who hate each other should be forced to stay married?"

"Of course not forced," says Earl, "but they shouldn't be allowed to pretend there aren't serious consequences."

Moe grins. "See how this clever lawyer twists everything his way?"

The day after this exchange, I stop by Stuart Walzer's home in Carmel, wanting to hear more about his days as a big-time divorce attorney in the Sodom to the south.

How, I want to know, did it happen? How, doing what he did, in a culture that so reveres status and celebrity, was he able to maintain a clear a sense of what really matters in life and what is ultimately hollow, then walk away from a prominent career without evident qualm?

I find Stuart in the place where he can be found several hours each day and which, in fact, itself begins to suggest the answer. In his garden.

Many people leading stress-filled lives in highly competitive fields claim to long for the day when they'll be able to stop and smell the roses. Walzer literally has. Also salvias and marigolds and amaryllis and literally hundreds of other plants and flowers of every size and color, representing species from all over the world, each carefully tended and scrupulously tagged, comprising a veritable mini–botanical garden so impressive that passing cars regularly stop for a closer look.

"You've done all this yourself?" I ask, as we pause on a slight rise that allows a view of much of the front yard.

"That's the fun of it—not just the digging and the planting, but lifting things, hauling out the garbage, raking the leaves, all of it." Stuart gazes around, surveying his domain as Jefferson must once have gazed upon Monticello. He indicates a relatively spare patch of ground. "I'm still mulling over what to put in that corner up there to complement those maple trees. It's a constant challenge."

"What's that one there?" I ask, pointing to a particularly interesting-looking flower.

"A protea. It comes from South Africa; it's known as 'the fiery duchess.' See how it's just beginning to open—that bloom's going to be pink-gold."

"So for you this is a lot more than a hobby."

"Well, I suppose that depends on your definition of 'hobby.' " He smiles. "There's a guy who says to his friend, 'I've got a new hobby; I collect bees.' And he holds up a jar. 'But there's no holes in the jar,' says the friend, 'and, wait a minute, all those bees are . . . dead.' 'Well,' says the guy, 'its *only* a hobby.' "

We laugh, and he asks, "Do you do any gardening?"

"Not really. When we moved to the suburbs, we did try growing watermelon and got exactly one fruit. When it got a wormhole, we put Scotch tape over it."

"Worth a shot. I always encourage innovation."

"It worked; we actually ate the watermelon."

"And if you ate the worm, you got a little extra protein."

"Did you keep a garden down in L.A.?" I ask as we head toward the house.

"I did. But that was put in by a landscaper, and we had regular gardeners. It wasn't the same. I had more limited goals then—for the garden, I mean."

"What are your goals now?"

He stops and looks over the garden. "Well, I suppose my goal would be having the tour buses stop." He laughs. "But actually, the day when I'm completely satisfied will never come. And I wouldn't want it to— that would defeat the whole purpose."

By nature philosophical and bookish, Walzer says he has always struggled to hang on to a measure of perspective. Even when he was among the hottest divorce lawyers in the acknowledged capital of marital instability, he taught largely blue-collar night-students at L.A.'s Southwestern Law School; and he launched the Lawyer's Literary Society, a book club more devoted to the classics than the works of Scott Turow or John Grisham.

Which is to say, he can now look back on his old life and the man he was then with candor and few regrets.

"A lot of people down there thought I was crazy to give it up," he admits a few minutes later, as we settle into his comfortable, sunny living room. "Occasionally, even now, I'll see one of those guys. He'll say, 'How can you live this way?'—by which he of course means how could I possibly turn my back on this glamorous, important life. I mean, truly, there are many people, especially in a place like L.A., who consider their lives meaningful only if they're constantly around others who they regard as successful and important. It's self-worth by association."

"They had no idea how easy leaving was," says his British-born wife, Paula, laughing, from across the room.

Paula, who shares her husband's values and then some, clearly had a lot to do with what made it so easy. An artist and print maker whose work has won wide praise, she is in an essentially solitary profession, its satisfactions often understated and internal; which is to say, in style and temperament, not to mention intellect, she is the opposite of the women, so dominant in the L.A. social scene, who measure their own worth by their husbands' status. Like her husband at the front, as a teen in Britain, she also endured character-enhancing trials during the war, including prolonged separation from her family and close brushes with V1 and V2 rockets. The two of them met on a blind date—July 3, 1951—and, as Paula says, "we started talking the moment we met and never stopped."

"Paula and I were talking just the other day about our life in Beverly Hills," Walzer tells me.

"I was saying we lived all those years in Beverly Hills, but we were really never *of* it," she notes.

"And I think that's true." Stuart pauses a beat, too honest to leave it at that. "But I also have to say that that kind of life can be awfully seductive."

Indeed, through the seventies and eighties, as Walzer's career took off, he regularly found himself on lists of the best lawyers in America. In

1981, in what surely must be close to the profession's supreme accolade, an article in the *L.A. Law Journal* actually called him the town's "dean of divorce."

"The problem," he adds now, "is that once you get used to being treated like a big-time player, you'll do whatever it takes to stay one. You start going to all the right parties, and giving to all the right causes . . ."

"God, some of those parties!" moans Paula.

"And I became a total print hound—always looking to use the press to raise my profile, playing up to reporters."

"Don't be so hard on yourself, Stuart. You were never nearly as bad as most."

He nods in acknowledgment. "Well, part of it was, unlike a lot of others, I didn't start out with this ambition. I fell into the law almost by accident. I actually went to business school before trying my hand at law."

"I didn't know that."

"A total waste of time. Today UCLA's business school is a big prominent place, but back then it was absolutely inane. For a course on business management they gave us a book full of pictures of adding machines and desks and chairs. I couldn't figure out what was supposed to be important, so I underlined everything in the book."

I laugh. "So you moved on to law school?"

"Actually, from there I went to work as an 'executive trainee' for Lerner shops, the women's clothing chain. They put me down in the basement, hanging up clothes. I was down there with a bunch of gays, and I just didn't get it. Since I'm dyslexic, I hung all the hangers backward. If I could hang those hangers straight, you could be looking at a retired women's wear executive right now."

Only when an aptitude test showed potential in the law, as well as teaching, did he decide to send out applications, and he was more than a little surprised to find himself accepted by Harvard Law.

Coming to specialize in divorce law was equally a matter of chance. Having returned to L.A. after Harvard for a sensible reason—"I'd gotten my heels frozen in the war and wanted a warm climate"—for a time he practiced general interest law, first on his own, then in a small firm. When he got involved in a complicated divorce case, he totally screwed up. "I ended up drafting a settlement agreement all wrong, so that our client could never get her alimony raised or altered, and the other side rammed it down my throat. Almost in contrition, I wrote a long essay on how *not* to make that mistake and got it published." In short order, he was writing regularly in the field, which in turn started to bring in a lot of divorce work; one of his partners eventually suggested he might consider doing divorce full-time. "I was so insulted, I could've hit him," recalls Walzer. "I mean, it took a while to get used to."

To be sure, his decision to follow his associate's advice was partly a matter of knowing the field was potentially lucrative. But, oddly enough, it also reflected Walzer's instinctive idealism. He saw divorce law, as then constituted, as profoundly unfair and in need of dramatic overhaul—and already he was formulating ways to bring that change about. The most glaring problem, he felt, the cause of endless hypocrisies and injustices, was that it had to be shown that a failed marriage was the fault of one of the parties. "As a result, you'd get into these huge, pointless fights about fault, and all the horrible things the other person had supposedly done. Even in a friendly divorce, one that didn't involve adultery or abuse, you'd have to prove something. So you'd have to have your client claim that the other party didn't do the dishes or had insulted your friends. I mean, it was all so demeaning. And what's worse is that it often made things a lot harder afterward, especially if people had to cooperate on raising children."

Moreover, he says, the division of assets was often profoundly unfair, especially to women. "A lot of people were just getting the raw end of the stick, and it stuck in my craw."

Walzer's writing on fault, including a book on the subject, made him an expert in the field, eventually leading to his appointment to Governor Pat Brown's Commission for the Family, which in 1970 redrafted state law, eliminating fault in divorce. Since California is on the leading edge of social change, the statute would soon serve as a model for similar statutes in the rest of the country.

Not that Walzer kids himself. Though the changes achieved their baseline objectives—there is clearly less overt hypocrisy these days, and a good deal more equality in the law—he finds the social landscape as disheartening as the other Girl Watchers do. Not only is divorce more prevalent than ever, but its collateral damage, measured in lives derailed and distorted, is even more apparent. "People now fight over money and the children as bitterly as they used to fight over who was the wrongdoer, and with just as little understanding of the consequences. That's what really disappoints me, that what we did failed to make life any better for children. In some ways, it probably made it worse."

"Did you ever talk to clients about that aspect of it—what they might be putting their kids through?"

Stuart shakes his head no. "They don't want to hear that. They say, 'I've got a psychiatrist.' A lot of people don't see the impact on the children or won't let themselves see. Maybe if I were doing it again, I might try, at least in situations where it's obvious they're screwing up their kids. But the truth is, when you're supporting a large family, you watch your step. I mean, people change lawyers like they change their socks."

He points out that over the years clients have gotten increasingly cold-blooded and hard-hearted, even if their kids suffer as a result. Never mind Mother Teresa; some of these people have values more akin to Ma Barker's. "More and more, the first question became, 'Are you tough enough?' They'd hire you to be a killer, their instrument of vengeance. Which really wasn't my style; I worked hard to establish a reputation as a nice lawyer, someone who tried to help the parties reach an amicable understanding. But as time went by, that became increasingly counterproductive."

It goes without saying that many other divorce lawyers had less trouble meeting the new standard, fashioning themselves as ever more efficient killers and as especially frightening instruments of vengeance.

"Wouldn't you say that was the biggest change from when you started, Stuart?" observes Paula. "At the beginning even most of the toughest divorce lawyers were human beings?"

He smiles at his wife. "Well, at least they pretended to be. The truth is, even at the best of times so much that passes for camaraderie in those circles is really an ongoing roast. Supposedly you're kidding and he's kidding, but you're both putting each other down as hard as you can."

"Would you say you had many lawyer friends?"

The question gives Walzer momentary pause. "I was certainly friendly with a number of lawyers. Only the thing is, for most lawyers, anything that doesn't involve getting or doing the work isn't productive time; every relationship has to be professionally useful, or what's the point? And I always had trouble looking at it that way."

"Of course, it's complicated in L.A. by the movie business," Paula says.

"Oh, you bet. Lawyers are basically just ordinary folks, but down there they all want to be rich and famous like their clients. So you can hardly go to a party without some lawyer dropping the names of his celebrity clients. Somebody'll ask about the details of the case, and the lawyer, very self-importantly, will say, 'I'm sorry, I can't do that'— because of course it's a fundamental canon of ethics that lawyers are forbidden to talk about their clients. But then, sure enough, after a few minutes he's spilling his clients' every innermost secret. The stories almost never even have a point, other than 'I represented so-and-so, and he's worth four hundred million dollars.' The rest of it, the intricacies of the case, make your eyes glaze over."

"Did you talk much with your colleagues down there about the war? Did many of them share that background?"

"Not really. But it's an interesting question. Because, in a way, all the bragging and bullshitting about important clients by lawyers serves in the place of war stories. Except they're the opposite of genuine war stories, where you're tested in a real and meaningful way. Peculiarly enough, living through a battle can be a very elevating experience— living through these other experiences is debasing.

"But, again, I can't say I was much better. I did it along with everyone else—and I'd hate myself in the morning. The cliché is accurate; you really do forget what you set out to do, which was help people. So you play the game. There was a woman from the *New York Times* with whom I kept in especially close touch, always letting her know about articles I'd written. Even then, I knew how terribly wearying and artificial it all was, but it was hard to give up."

Still, as time went on, it got harder and harder. "I mean, not long ago I read an article by a guy I know bragging that every lawyer in his firm had been divorced. To him and his colleagues this was great advertising: the idea is they can be more effective because they've experienced all the bitterness and anger personally, not to mention the abandoned and troubled kids." He glances his wife's way. "Who knows? Maybe they've got a point. But that's not me. Actually, the work ended up giving me a very useful sense of perspective; I'd seen enough that I never had any illusion about there being a perfect life waiting for me, if only I could find someone better than the one I was married to. I always knew I was married to the best woman possible."

"Nice of you to say, Stuart."

"Easy for me to say."

Then, too, he adds, all the while he was getting older, nearly as fatal a disease for divorce lawyers in Los Angeles as for movie stars.

"One day I looked around and found myself surrounded by all these young sharks, circling, waiting to take a bite out of me," he says. "And frankly I realized I *was* starting to miss a few beats. I'd be sitting in the courtroom, and yawn, and have trouble following some of the intricacies of the proceedings.

"Plus, now there are all these women in the game—fifty percent of the divorce bar—and some of them are more manipulative and vicious than the men could ever be. They bring to it—how shall I put this?—a particular sensitivity to the psychological aspects. They'll pick out a sore point and drive it straight home. They'll out-macho the guys.

"One of the objects these days is to humiliate the other lawyer in front of his client, so the client will say, 'You looked like a fool; I shouldn't have to pay you.' "

When I ask if that ever happened to him, there is a long pause. "It's too painful," he says finally. "Listen, it's a personal choice. I have friends still practicing in their seventies. One went right up till eighty. But he was very slow and deliberate, and you could see the other lawyers were laughing at him. Who wants to do that if you don't have to? How much money is enough?" He shakes his head. "I was seventy years old; I'd practiced for forty-two years. Enough already."

True to form, Walzer admits that even now, fleetingly, he misses it. "I still sometimes have a little twinge; that mentality isn't easy to shake even when you know the value system behind it is completely empty." He stops and considers. "What can I tell you? The truth is, that sense of competition is built in. On some level we never stop being fourteen years old, and it's always the first year of high school. Everybody else is bigger and smarter and knows more than we do. And we spend our lives looking for someone who has the answers. But here's the big secret: Nobody has them. Every human being, even the most successful, is basically flying by the seat of his pants."

Indeed, the keen awareness of what he was leaving behind made the transition to this new life far less traumatic than it was liberating. Walzer is easily the most active of the Girl Watchers, his days and evenings given over to a dizzying array of intellectual and physical pursuits. He goes to the gym daily, usually after his work in the garden, practicing a vigorous regime of aerobics, yoga, pilates, and what he calls "bodybuilding for old folks." He takes classes at both Monterey Peninsula College and UC Monterey Bay. Together, he and Paula run a reading group called the Literary Circle at the Monterey Library, and not long ago they won the Carmel Foundation Spelling Bee. (Winning word: "*Googol.* G-o-o-g-O-L. Not g-o-o-g-L-E, which is the search engine. It means an infinite number.") In addition to other civic-minded activities, he keeps a hand in the law by serving on the board of Legal Services for Seniors, which offers free legal advice to indigent older people.

And, of course, there's his new, quite unexpected group of friends.

Speaking of the whirlwind that is his daily life, I recall Moe's bemused observation one afternoon, when Stuart rushed from lunch to head to some other activity, that "all this running around won't help; you're still gonna die."

"Well, you know Moe," he says now, "he throws out his little remarks to stir things up. But he's actually a wonderfully softhearted guy. Moe's the opposite of most people: he loves individuals and hates humanity."

"Harry Handler was saying the other day he's always a little shocked to open the *Herald* to the obituary page and find your picture—before he realizes its just the ad for Legal Services for Seniors."

Stuart laughs. "Well, to paraphrase Shakespeare. 'I die a thousand deaths, other men die but once.' "

"Do you find it odd that for all the obvious differences between you, you guys seem to have so much in common?"

"I just find the group tremendously satisfying. And comforting. And relaxing. There's a straight talk among these men, and a real kindness, that is so different from what I came from. There's never that undercurrent of 'I'm smarter' or 'I make more money'—we've all very happily opted out of that kind of competition."

We are silent a long moment, Stuart glancing out the window toward his glorious front yard. "I know there are people who could never understand that. They'll look at us and say, 'They're nothing but a bunch of old men waiting to die.' Well, I got news for them: at some point, if they're lucky, that'll be them. We're all gonna be old and waiting to die. It's just a matter of what you do with it."

✦ CHAPTER 21 ✦

*Moe's problem is he always thinks the world ought to adjust
to him instead of the other way around, and it seldom works
out. The world's stubborn that way.*

—GENE COOPER

COOPER IN HIS ELEMENT, THE EARLY FIFTIES.

Whenever you ask Gene Cooper these days how he is feeling, you're
pretty sure to get a variation on the same answer: a very pleasant, "Just
taking it day to day, day to day." Nor does this seem to be just pro forma.
Judging by appearances, his condition in fact does seem variable on a
nearly daily basis—frail and exhausted one day, he will be very nearly
his old self the next.

When he unexpectedly drops by Moe's one afternoon, he looks positively robust.

"I was just running a few errands," he announces, taking his familiar spot at the kitchen table, "so I figured I'd drop by."

Moe couldn't be more delighted. The fact is, he sometimes seems more alarmed by his friend's illness than Cooper himself. He brings up Gene and his cancer at least four or five times a day. Sometimes, to be sure, it is only to grumble about the stupidity of his friend's decision to undergo a painful treatment that stands merely to postpone the inevitable, but even then it is with an undercurrent of anxiety and sorrow, as if the straightforward talk will keep the harsh reality of the situation at bay. Cooper has always been a pillar of strength for Moe; he has relied on His Omniscience for emotional support almost as much as for practical advice.

"Want a little ice cream, Gene?" he offers now. "It'll do you good."

"Sounds pretty good."

Moe takes out a couple of bowls and heads for the refrigerator. "I'll put some chocolate sauce on it—shoot the works."

But even as he is scooping it out, he has something else in mind: he needs Cooper, his consigliore in all matters electronic, to show him how to work the inexpensive digital camera he got Benny for Christmas, which was almost six months ago. Since then the camera has sat in the closet, and Moe has made no effort to operate it himself.

Indeed, it's hard not to get the idea that by now the matter has taken on a symbolic importance far beyond whether or not any pictures ever get taken. Just last week, the previous time Gene was here for a gathering of the guys, as things were breaking up Moe grabbed the camera and hustled out after Cooper, following him to his car. But that was one of Cooper's not-so-good days, and, politely pleading fatigue, he made his getaway.

"Say, Gene, think maybe you'd like to take a look at that digital camera I got?"

"Oh, I suppose I will. Let's just give it a few minutes."

"Maybe he ought to take a look at Benny's car instead," I suggest, referring to the decade-year-old Caddy Cooper referred him to seven or eight years ago when he was in the market for a used car. "I drove it the other day, and it stalled out a couple of times. I'm not sure it's safe."

"Oh, that's all right," says Moe.

"Moe's problem is he always thinks the world ought to adjust to him instead of the other way around, and it seldom works out." Cooper chuckles. "The world is stubborn that way."

"That just about says it all," Moe readily agrees. "My God, you always think Cooper's going to be so gentle, but his remarks are sharp as nails."

"It just might be about time to replace that thing," suggests Cooper.

"Why should I? We're probably only going to live another year or two."

Cooper looks momentarily startled. "That's a strange philosophy."

"Well, that's my philosophy. I'll get her a bicycle; that's what I'll do. Your wife's stopped driving, hasn't she?"

"She gave it up—as a matter of fact, I'm driving her around today. But she's going to have to start again. My condition right now is fine, but you gotta face the facts, something could happen any day."

Moe nods. "Let me ask you something, Gene, what kind of resolution can you get with these digital cameras? What's the highest number of lines per inch they give you?"

The shift back to the camera is unsubtle even by my father-in-law's famous nonstandards, and Cooper can't help but smile. "Well, Moe, how deep is your pocketbook? You can get a camera that'll get fantastic resolution; it'll go up to ten megabits. That's over a thousand lines per inch."

"You're kidding! So you can't hardly tell the difference from a regular camera."

"The only obstacle is money. Of course, the printer's as big as this table, and that alone runs about twenty-five thousand dollars. But you can get a home printer for about a hundred and forty dollars that'll do a nice job. For the camera itself, you can spend anything from seventy to seven thousand dollars."

"I got mine for about a hundred."

"What make is it?"

"Hold on." In an instant, Moe is on his feet and hurrying into the back bedroom.

Cooper turns to me and shakes his head, grinning. "Another day with Moe."

"I can't believe he's gotten you to do this. It can take months and months, but finally it happens."

"He does wear you down."

"Micronta," calls out Moe, heading back with the camera.

"That's Radio Shack, their trade name." Cooper takes it from Moe and studies it a moment. "Basically a pretty simple camera."

"I think it's got batteries in it. You want to shoot something and see?"

"Moe, you don't start just pushing buttons; you read the manual first."

Moe has also brought that, and he tosses it on the table before Cooper. "I just don't have the patience to read those little magazines. What's that little screen back there for?"

"You haven't ever even looked at this thing?"

"No. And I hope you're not gonna force me to do it."

Cooper sighs in mock exasperation. "The digital camera I've got, it took three weeks of study before I even took a picture with it. Though, I tell you, my grandson looked at it, and in ten minutes he was already beyond me, without even picking up the manual."

"You were the same way once yourself, Gene."

Cooper nods. "I guess that's true."

"You think Augie'll be an engineer?"

"I don't know. He's interested in just about everything and good at all of it. But he's really an engineer at heart."

Cooper flips open the manual. " 'Getting Started,' " he reads. " 'Turning the Camera On and Off.' You know how to do that, don't you?"

"I forgot my glasses."

Cooper laughs and hands back the camera. "Press the power but-ton, Moe."

Moe does so. "Nothing. There's nothing on the screen."

"You should hear two beeps. Looks to me like someone's left this thing on and the battery's dead."

"Hold on, I'll get my battery tester." Moe is on his feet again, charg-ing from the room.

"You know," observes Cooper dryly, "it can keep you busy, looking after all these things that don't work."

In half a minute Moe is back with the machine, along with a handful of used batteries. "I'll measure 'em and see if they're dead." He tries the first one from the camera, then the other—"point three, deader than a doornail and . . . point seven." Moe tries one from his other batch. "One point forty-four. Is that good?"

"Marginal." Cooper slowly rises from the table. "Just a minute. Let me check something in the car."

He returns with a set of fresh batteries, which, installed in the cam-era, instantly bring its display to life. "Now, basically, you aim and shoot."

"Gene is a fountainhead of knowledge," says Moe admiringly. "When they bury him, it's gonna be a great loss to the world."

Cooper chuckles. "Now, I hope you know how to download the pic-tures on the computer, Moe, 'cause I've got to hit the road."

"That reminds me, Cooper, why don't you come back and look at Benny's computer a minute? Because actually we've been having a little trouble with the printer."

The trouble, to be more precise, is with the ink cartridges, since rather than spring for a new one, Moe bought a syringe and has been trying to inject ink into a used one—so far without success."

"Can't right now, Moe. I've gotta take Jody to the beauty shop."

"Well, just give it a quick look."

Unbelievably, a moment later we're all standing behind Benny, who is sitting at the computer, trying to get the printer to print.

"I just don't get it," says Moe. "You think maybe we clogged up the ink jets?"

"That could be it. We'd have to take that thing apart to tell."

"That's not much; it opens right up."

"Oh, Moe, leave him alone," pleads Benny.

Moe nudges me and offers, as if neither were here, "If Benny had married Cooper, they'd both be dead now—they'd have killed each other with kindness."

"Well, Moe," concludes Cooper, "I'm sorry, but I've really got to be running along. You got a manual for this thing?"

"Somewhere around here."

"Good. Maybe I'll look it over next time. Nice seeing everybody."

"Bye, Gene," says Benny.

He turns and starts out. A moment later, Moe follows.

"How about the flash on the camera, Gene, does that work automatically?"

"It's supposed to."

"Well, it doesn't."

By now Cooper is already out the door. "Read the book, Moe," he calls back, heading for his car, "read the book."

✦ CHAPTER 22 ✦

Lauren tells Earl stuff she can't tell anyone else; her

illness made them even closer. . . . She and her mother can

shout at each other all they want, but Lauren knows

she always has Earl.

—GERRY GODFREY

GERRY GODFREY AND GRANDDAUGHTER LAUREN.

As I sit with Earl and Gerry Godfrey in the living room of their condo in the Monterey Hills, it occurs to me that this is the first time I've actually seen the truism in practice: these two really do finish each other's sentences. Maybe it's because they have known each other forever, having first met when they were sixteen and thirteen and he was earning college money scrubbing pans in a hotel kitchen in her hometown of Kearney, Nebraska. Or maybe it's just more that way than usual when they talk about what I've come to discuss today: what they've been through as the grandparents of a pair of kids going through the ordeal of their young lives.

It's been nearly a year since Earl first told me of his seventeen-year-old granddaughter's need for a kidney transplant, and that her brother, three years older, would be the donor, but since then the topic has hardly come up at all. It's not that the ever-straightforward Godfrey was avoiding it, just that there wasn't much to say. Lauren's kidneys were failing rapidly; they would do what had to be done.

The surgery finally took place about ten weeks ago in Los Angeles, near the kids' home. Afterward, for Lauren, there have been some serious complications, but her recovery now seems to be on track.

"She's feeling a whole lot better now," reports her grandfather. "They did a plasma pheresis first, involving a stent . . ."

"And a port," adds Gerry, a lifelong military wife who is as quietly rock solid as her husband.

"To get into the artery, you know."

"We had to learn all the terminology. It involved replacement of the plasma . . ."

"So your own blood isn't running through the kidney," says Earl. It was just last Friday she got that port removed—thank God."

If it is an obvious truism that grandparents have always doted on grandchildren, that makes it no less touching to see men of the World War II generation soften at the very mention of theirs'. These are people for whom too readily giving in to emotion was often construed as weakness, frowned upon by one's peers; everywhere from the ball fields of childhood, to the battlefields of young manhood, to the nation's executive suites it could actually get in the way, an impediment to clear thought and decisive action. But having slowed down to a figurative crawl, the once-consuming obsession with making up for lost time far in the past, the sixties battles with their now-middle-aged children generally no more than the stuff of anecdote, they embrace their grandkids with an eagerness and zeal that would surely have stunned their younger, more stoic selves. I've seen this behavior with several of the Girl Watchers. In these children they have invested not only bottomless reservoirs of love but their hopes for the continuance of the best in themselves.

Lauren's condition, the cause of which is unknown, was first diagnosed when she was nine, and if there's no such a thing as a good time to be hammered by such news, it's hard to imagine a worse one. Her father, Earl's son-in-law Barry, was dying of cancer.

In response, the family did what healthy families do: they found ways of handling it. After Barry died, their daughter, Julie, changed jobs to be able to work at home, and everyone else pitched in.

"Have you two spent much time down South over these last years?" I ask.

They exchange a quick look.

"All we can," says Earl simply.

"Jared has a very close group of friends; they call us Nana and Baba. And with Barry being gone, Lauren particularly leans on Earl. Lauren tells Earl stuff she can't tell anyone else; her illness made them even closer. They're on the computer every day. She and her mother can shout at each other all they want, but Lauren knows she always has Earl."

"Well . . ." Earl hesitates, there's no one worse with praise. "Like I say, awful as it is, this whole thing has been wonderful for her character."

Earl and Gerry were at the meeting at Children's Hospital in Hollywood, midway through Lauren's junior year in high school, when the decision on the surgery was finalized. Kidney deterioration is measured by the level of something called creatinine, and when, as Earl puts it, "the number hits five, basically the kidneys are gone." Doctors hoped to get her through the school year and operate before the reading reached 4.5.

After the meeting, says Earl, "Lauren went right to the Internet, downloading everything she could find. It was too much information—she started to get paranoid. She kept saying, 'I don't want school to end,' as if then she wouldn't have to have this done."

Meanwhile, her brother, Jared, had to endure months of tests. A preliminary operation to decide which of his kidneys to take determined that during the main event they would have to remove part of a rib, making the aftermath even more painful than he had bargained for.

By the time of the surgery in late June, Lauren's creatinine was so high—6.5!—the doctor had trouble believing she was still able to function. But both kids were ready.

"Jared's not real churchy," says Gerry, who is, "but when the hospital minister came by and offered to say a prayer, he went for it." She laughs. "He wasn't taking any chances."

By then, too, the Godfrey family support system was in full swing. A couple of days before the surgery, Lauren's Aunt Wendy, Earl and Gerry's younger daughter, took her camping at Big Sur, long one of Lauren's ambitions; then afterward, when complications left the girl terrified and weak, Wendy again assumed responsibility for Lauren's morale, good-humoredly needling her so continuously that, says Gerry, "she got so annoyed she started to feel normal again." Jared, meanwhile, was the particular responsibility of his uncle Allen, his mother's older brother, who, says Earl, "came and stayed. And I mean *stayed*. He was in the room with him, out in the hall with him, with him wherever he went.

"Of course, their mother, Julie, was back and forth between them. I don't think she got ten hours' sleep that week—and that was on the floor of one or the other of their rooms. It was pretty hard on her."

"How about on you two?"

Earl hesitates before answering—and when he does, it's not precisely to the question I asked. "The problem was they'd overloaded her with a brand-new antirejection medication, and she had a bad reaction—it was damaging her other organs. Then they discovered she was draining fluid into her stomach cavity, and she had to go back to surgery for that."

"Something didn't get hooked up right," explains Gerry. "It caused her tremendous pain. Potentially, it was life threatening. Afterward one of the doctors told her, 'My vows say my first responsibility is to do no harm. Well, I just about poisoned you.' "

Godfrey turns to his wife and says with deep feeling. "I will never forget that. Now, that's an honorable man! With so many people in this day and age ready to sue at the drop of a hat, how many doctors would ever admit that kind of mistake?"

We're interrupted by a phone call. Gerry gets up to take it in another room.

"So," I say to Earl, "after all this, how would you characterize the difference between being a parent and a grandparent?"

I suppose I'm expecting what has become the standard response: that compared to the endless tribulations of parenthood, grandparenting is an absolute pleasure because, bottom line, there's someone else bearing the brunt of the responsibility.

Instead, Earl ponders the question a long moment. "Frankly, I can't answer that. Because to me they're the same."

"You mean, because of all you've been through with Lauren and Jared?"

"Not only that. My older son Allen got divorced in the late eighties, and for a while each of his two girls lived with us. I mean, obviously it has to do with family circumstances. If it's a stable family and the parents are the kind the children need them to be, you're more out of it. That's the way it is with our other son and his wife and their children, and we play a more traditional role there. But, no, otherwise you have to be available, and you *want* to be. I wouldn't trade what we have with Lauren and Jared for anything in the world."

"It sounds like things are okay with Lauren now."

"Oh, yes. Though of course there's still always a twenty-five percent chance the body will reject the new organ."

"Even now?"

"Even eight years from now. Forever. But otherwise we're pretty much back to normal. As a matter of fact, we had our fantasy football draft the other day."

"You and Lauren have a team together?"

"We each have a team—so do six other members of the family. Some of us are pretty far apart, but it keeps us in close touch. I'm the commissioner and secretary; Lauren's the assistant commissioner."

"What a great idea."

"We take it pretty seriously. For now, we're only using offensive stats. We were thinking about adding defense this year but got preoccupied with these other things."

I have to laugh. "You mean the operation actually interfered with fantasy football?"

Earl grins. "Isn't that a shame?"

When Gerry reappears after the call with slices of coffee cake, I ask how much they think their military background had to do with how calmly they seem to handle this kind of crisis.

Earl looks momentarily baffled. "I don't think much at all. It's just if there's a challenge, you face up to it. It was actually fairly routine."

"But that's what I'm talking about. Trust me, not everyone would take it that way."

Me, for example.

"Well, you do wring your hands a little," offers Gerry, trying to be helpful.

"That's true," says Earl, who then repeats, "but the fact is, there isn't anything you can do about it. What's the sense in worrying about things you can't do anything about?"

"Lots of people do," I point out. "'Woe is me; the world's not fair'— that's the attitude of a lot of people in this country these days."

This draws a chuckle from Gerry. "In *parts* of this country, maybe. I certainly don't think 'woe is me' is the attitude in Nebraska."

I nod. "Earl was telling me things are getting back to normal with the kids."

"I'd say so. Julie was just saying on the phone that Lauren was shocked when she saw the cost of the medication that came in the mail: three thousand dollars for a month's supply. She said, 'That's thirty-six thousand a year! I could go to NYU for that!' I love it that she's thinking that way, about her future instead of the disease."

"She's really thinking of going to college in New York?" Somehow the idea of so close a relative of the rock-ribbed traditionalist Godfrey choosing to live in my hometown doesn't quite compute.

"Oh, I'm opposed to it. But I'm not the one with final say."

Having recently gone through the college process with both my kids, I never hesitate to claim some expertise on the subject. "Well, if nothing else, she'll get a great personal essay out of this experience. That counts for a lot with college admissions people. I mean, kids go to tremendous lengths in these essays to pretend they've had a character-building experience. She's really had one."

Both of them nod. This is not new information.

"We've told her that," says Gerry. "She says she doesn't want to write about it."

"Why not?"

"She doesn't see that having been sick means she's done anything special. Jared's the same way. He was working at a store at the time of the surgery. When he needed time off, he wouldn't even tell his boss what it was for."

"Boy" is all I can think of to respond, thinking of how incredibly rare and admirable that is, and also how alien.

"I know," says Gerry, seeming to read my thoughts. "We told her to think about it; maybe she'll change her mind."

"I don't think so," says Earl, with a mix of grandfatherly concern and pride, "not much chance of that."

I understand why he can say it with such certainty. These things may not be genetically encoded, but in certain families, for all the shifting mores in the outside world, they may as well be. It is only in the car, driving back to the Turners, that I recall it was Earl's grandfather—Lauren's great-great-grandfather—who for so many years refused to cash all those government checks for the simple, extraordinary reason that it just didn't feel right.

CHAPTER 23

Growing old is not for wimps.

—STUART WALZER

WALZER AND GRANDDAUGHTERS HANNAH,
EMMA, AND NAOMI.

"You still smoke cigars?" I ask Boyd Huff as we take our seats this afternoon at the table.

His birthday is coming up, and I'm thinking a top-notch stogie might make a nice surprise; he was once such an enthusiast it earned him the nickname Cigar.

"Sure. Great habit! One of the true pleasures of my youth."

"How old were you when you started?"

"Early teens. I'd swipe 'em from my father's stock. It gave me great prestige among the boys of the town."

"Wish I'd known you," says Harry, settling in across the table. "I was deprived as a kid—we smoked newspapers, despite all the lead in the newsprint."

"We smoked corn silks on the farm," says Earl.

"My God, the idiocy of youth!"

"Christ, Turner, what the hell's wrong with you? The *joys* of youth! You can't grow up without doing some stupid things."

"It depends *which* stupid things. That's the big dividing line right there about how someone's life'll turn out."

Thus, in this curious and inadvertent way, begins a conversation in which the Girl Watchers will end up on the question that has quietly loomed over these sessions from the start: the one about the large and enduring lessons they have picked up over the decades. With time starting to run out, what is the wisdom they want to pass on to their grandchildren?

"Anyway, we didn't think smoking was stupid," points out Walzer. "We thought it was *good* for you. In the ads Joe DiMaggio said cigarettes gave you extra energy; you opened up a magazine, and there'd be *doctors* pushing cigarettes."

"And when you went in the army, *they* gave you cigarettes—even in combat. That's when I started smoking." Harry laughs. "*Slow* death was the least of your worries."

But this is one subject about which Moe has absolutely no sense of humor. He has always been rabidly antismoking. My wife, not easily humiliated, recalls her father standing up in crowded movie theaters and shouting. 'You in the first row, this is a No Smoking Section!'; and well into her twenties, as a very occasional smoker, she used to sneak around like a thief to protect him from the sordid truth.

"People can pretend they didn't know, but in Arkansas even when we were kids we used to call 'em coffin nails." He turns to Earl. "Your brother was a smoker, wasn't he? And wasn't it emphysema that got him?"

Earl missed a couple of meetings when he went back East five or six months ago for the funeral. "Right. Then he got pneumonia, so they had to ventilate him and put in a trach."

"Man, that sounds bad."

"It *was* bad, Moe," notes Stuart, "it was fatal."

"And look at Cooper's brother. He was a big smoker, and now he's also on his last legs."

"That might not be the best advertisement for your position," Cooper amiably points out. "He's ninety-three."

"I'm just saying he was like all the rest, in complete denial."

"That's true. He was a big smoker even back when he was in medical college, and I remember he'd bring home lung tissue samples to study from heavy smokers. When you looked at these things with a microscope, it was impossible to miss all the tar."

"And all the time he's looking, he's smoking, I bet."

"Exactly. See, what he'd do is put these samples next to other samples of black lung disease from coal miners. In contrast, the smokers' slides looked pretty darn healthy."

Even Moe has to laugh.

"Still," observes Stuart, "we certainly didn't know a tenth of what we know today."

Moe's not buying. "Maybe not, but there's such a thing as common sense; you knew the first few times you smoked one, you started coughing like crazy. It's not mountain air you were sucking in. As for today, anyone that still smokes knowing all we do is too dumb to be walking the streets. Even hating smoking as much as I do, that's why no one that gets sick should be able to sue."

"I'll tell you something," murmurs Earl, "my brother would be the first to agree with that."

"Look," I cut in, "the fact that kids are bombarded with all these anti-smoking messages is one of the *reasons* so many of them smoke. It's a form of rebellion."

"Your kids don't smoke, do they?" demands their grandfather with sudden intense suspicion.

I shake my head no. "That's not why I'm saying it, Moe."

"Turner'd disown 'em; they wouldn't inherit a single one of his toaster ovens!"

"Look, Moe," says Stuart, playing devil's advocate, "isn't that exactly what the tobacco companies argue? That people know the risks and it's a matter of free will?"

"And they're right! Just because they're evil and greedy doesn't make them wrong on that!"

"What about the way they go after young people by advertising at sports events? Isn't that an attempt to indoctrinate people too young to accurately assess the risk?"

"Then it's the parents' responsibility," counters Earl. "I read the other day that in San Fernando they're outlawing smoking in public parks because they don't even want children to *see* people smoking from a distance. Whatever happened to the idea that mothers and fathers should be accountable for their children?"

"C'mon, Earl, what a strange, old-fashioned idea," says Harry, laughing.

"I just think it's a pretty strange time to be young," notes Stuart. "Kids today are a lot smarter than we were and a lot dumber at the same time. Even when they understand the danger, they can't bring themselves to believe it could actually touch them. And today's dangers are so much more *dangerous*. Forget cigarettes, look at how available drugs are."

"And at all the stuff on TV. My God, the average six-year-old out there knows more about sex than we did at eighteen."

"Speak for yourself, Turner, speak for yourself."

"The thing is, even under the best circumstances, maturity happens in such tiny, painful increments," concludes Stuart.

The silence that follows shows no one is about to disagree.

"I once drove about sixty miles an hour into a ditch," says Cooper.

"You did!" exclaims Moe.

I'm almost as surprised myself. It is nearly impossible to visualize Cooper ever behaving so recklessly.

Harry follows suit. "Once in the Philippines, after the war, I got drunk at a party and ended up in the ocean. I'd waded out up to my chest before I woke up. That's when I gave up Scotch. Switched to bourbon."

"It's really sort of a miracle that anybody manages to grow up without getting killed," observes Stuart.

"Still, part of growing up, maybe the main part, is learning to take responsibility when you do something stupid or wrong instead of looking for ways to blame it on someone else. All this cracking down on tobacco companies just sends the wrong message."

"Right, Earl," agrees Huff. "Kids aren't idiots."

Harry volunteers a clarification: "Well, at least not all of them. Let's not generalize."

"And we shouldn't confuse stupidity with ignorance, either. There are a lot of kids out there with perfectly functional brains that just don't know anything."

This sparks something in Moe. "I was talking to a neighbor girl on the street here," he says, nodding vaguely toward the window. "Seventeen years old, a very bright child, and she tells me she's never heard of Robert E. Lee. It's all those years in the California public schools, where all this touchy-feely stuff has taken over. They talk more about 'self-esteem' than history."

"C'mon, Turner, she was pulling your leg."

"I hope so, 'cause I was pretty shocked. At some point I also got the idea she thought Lincoln was our second president. At least she knew Washington was the first. I met another kid who told me there was no such person as Martin Luther. He said I must be thinking of Martin Luther King."

"Between schools that are dumbed down and the effects of popular culture, there's just a different definition of what it means to be educated," says Walzer. "I mean, it's sad to say, but this girl who'd never heard of Robert E. Lee probably has an encyclopedic knowledge of Britney Spears."

"But whose fault is *that*? The parents!"

The only one there who is the father of actual young people, I remain conspicuously silent. I certainly understand where Moe, in particular, is coming from. Growing up in his home, my wife was inundated with high culture. At one point, her father even set up a sound system so he could pump classical music into any room of the house at any time, meaning she was apt to get blasted by Mozart any time she flicked on the living room TV—that is, during the several years of her childhood the family actually *had* a TV. The end result was my wife is a voracious reader and a lover of great music.

Not so incidentally, under her tutelage, so is our daughter; this despite the fact that her father grew up, far more typically, plopping himself down before the TV every afternoon for *The Mickey Mouse Club*, and even now is far more conversant with the Beatles and the Stones than Beethoven and Strauss.

My daughter's relative sophistication was a source of enormous pride for me; it's easy to feel superior to parents of kids infatuated with the likes of Madonna when your child is doing time, as for a few years mine did, in the Metropolitan Opera's children's chorus.

But the smugness lasted exactly as long as it took us to realize our second child, three years younger than his sister, was far more my child; which is to say, both a wise guy and a popular culture sponge.

I vividly recall the July day in his tenth year when the two of us, in London on a father-son trip, boarded an early morning train at Paddington Station, heading for Bath. The weather was glorious, the passing countryside—*Persuasion* country—astonishingly lush, and alone with my little boy, I was at peace. Then, beside me, he began to softly sing:

Seven-Up, it's an up thing,
Seven-Up does it every time, Yeah,
Seven-Up, it's an up thing,
It's clear and it's wonderful and it's totally fine.

The truth is, while popular culture has always had tremendous appeal to the young, with the advent of cable, DVDs, and video games, never has it been so ubiquitous and insidious as it is today. With certain children, fighting it means virtually going to war, not only with the times but with the child himself, and with precious little tactical support. For the key difference between today and forty years ago is in the *adult* world. Where once by definition grown-ups regarded popular culture, if not with Moe's outright hostility, as an indulgence of the young which they would soon outgrow, today most of us embrace it as avidly as our children. In our tastes, many of us are still locked into the era from, say, 1965 to 1980. And how do you preach old-fashioned standards, or insist on the distinction between quality and crap, when even the prestigious *New York Times* characterizes (never mind the Beatles and Stones) almost *everything*, from comic books to graffiti to going onstage covered with chocolate, as art?

"Well," I say lamely, "that's one of the ways it's probably harder to be a parent than it used to be. At least my kids know their history."

"I should hope so!"

"I mean, a kid today says 'I'm a high school graduate,' and it's really hard to know what it signifies," says Walzer.

"Usually nothing!" says Moe decisively. "Not a damn thing! History is only part of it. Where they really do the dumbing down is in math and science."

"I had solid geometry, trigonometry, spherical trig, introduction to calculus in high school," muses Cooper.

"So did I," notes Huff, "not to mention four years of Latin."

"I didn't have any of that in high school!" exclaims Moe. "Down there in Arkansas we really *were* deprived."

"Get over it, Turner."

"But at least everyone had beautiful handwriting. I look through my old yearbook today, and I can hardly believe it! My God, my own children write something down, and I can hardly decipher it. And they can't spell worth a damn, either."

"They don't focus on that much anymore; everyone has a computer and spell-check."

"But I wouldn't go too far with this," says Cooper. "It seems to me there are still some awfully good public schools out there if you're lucky, including the one my grandson Augie goes to in San Francisco. I've helped him with his science and math, and I've been very much impressed by the curriculum."

Moe perks up. "Speaking of Augie, my daughter Sue's coming out soon with her family. Why don't we set up your grandson with my grand-daughter?"

"Which one?" wonders Harry. "Susan has two."

"Either one, doesn't matter. We can do it like the old days, Gene, let the grandparents decide."

"We'll have to see about that one, Moe." Cooper looks at him, not knowing if he's serious, though I don't doubt for a second he is. "Any-way, today's kids really do get some awfully mixed messages. They're supposed to excel without being superior, and have high self-esteem whether they achieve anything or not."

Earl nods. "As soon as anyone seriously talks about upholding stan-dards, he has to worry about being accused of snobbery."

"Elitism," corrects Huff, "that's the word they use. Christ almighty, I remember when being part of an 'elite' was a good thing!"

"This self-esteem stuff is just deadly. The only way to really feel good about yourself is to *earn* it. Otherwise it's just so much hot air."

However we've arrived at this point, the question seems obvious. "Is this something you've made a point of trying to pass on to your grand-children?"

"Speaking of hot air," mutters Moe.

"I know *you* haven't, Moe."

Though I intend it lightly, I can see that the remark wounds, and start to make amends.

"No, no," he cuts me off, "the best they can learn from me is *not* to follow my example. I'm always saying the key to everything is perseverance, yet I've had ideas my whole life and not done 'em; I just dream about them."

"Like what?"

"I had a million different ideas for inventions." He pauses. "Say, Gene, remember I was telling you about that idea to use a heating coil and a flywheel to add power to car batteries? If anyone wants to do something with it, go ahead—we'll split the profits."

"Not your best idea," observes Cooper dryly. "The fuel cell would have to weigh about seven hundred fifty pounds, and the car would only hold two people."

"Well, there are plenty more where that came from; I still get 'em all the time. Another thing I always wanted to do was write a book called *Quick and Dirty*—neat and easy ways to solve all kinds of scientific and mathematical problems."

"Why don't you write it now?"

He gives a curious half smile. "Like I say, it's too late to change my stripes."

"Turner, that's the stupidest piece of philosophy I ever heard! And I say that as a friend."

"Listen, Moe," consoles Stuart, "in my book what 'quick and dirty' means is forget about a problem and it'll solve itself. Because sooner or later everything does."

"Right, Stuart, there's one you can pass on to your grandchildren."

"All in all, I think I'm learning more from them than the other way around." He smiles. "I was talking to my four-year-old granddaughter not long ago, and she asked, 'Why are your eyes so strange underneath?' 'Well,' I told her, 'those are bags under my eyes.' 'What about your chin?' 'Those are called jowls; that's part of being old, too. You know, a lot of things change when you're older.' 'Do you like being old?' she asked, and I really had to think about it. I finally told her that, yes, it feels just right. And a big part of that is I now have some- one like her in my life. The two of us being there together, talking this way, her being four and me being seventy-eight, was exactly how things *should* be."

"A lot of people would disagree with you," remarks Harry.

"Well, you know, there's plenty to be said for accepting your age and not fighting it."

"A lot of plastic surgeons'll argue with that one."

"But a lot of regular surgeons will agree. I foolishly tried to climb a steep hill not long ago and took a tumble. I ended up with an infected leg and a huge hematoma all along my side. When I was younger, it never would have happened, but balance is one of the first things to go."

"Earl, how old were you when you quit flying?" asks Moe.

"Forty-nine. But I didn't fly off the ship after forty-two or -three."

"Think if you got in an airplane now, you'd still be able to fly it?"

"Oh, I think I could probably get it onto a good long runway. On the ground." He smiles. "Let's leave it at that."

"Let's face it," observes Stuart, "growing old is not for wimps."

"So what kinds of advice do you give your grandkids?" I ask him.

"I'm not so arrogant as to claim to have the answers. I'm still learn- ing how to live myself. Anyway, they can hear about your mistakes all day, and it won't sink in. In the end, they've got to make their own."

"That's the frustration, isn't it?" agrees Earl. "Because so many of yours were such doozies and you wish you could save them the trouble."

Moe, as I well know, has no such hesitation. He's as profligate with advice to his grandchildren as with everyone else, and doesn't much care who listens. "All I know is that if they buy into this perseverance thing, they're way ahead of the game. There's a tremendous amount of dirt work to getting ahead, and most people just don't want to do it. Back when I was a graduate student at Berkeley, there were a whole group of us that were very bright, and we felt pretty special. But some of the ones who weren't so bright were hardworking devils, and they ended up going the farthest."

"I think if we're talking about life lessons, we should touch on how afraid many people are of failing that they won't take any risks," says Harry. "The upshot is they never even find out what their capabilities are. The truth is, when put to the test, they'll probably perform better than they think."

"In that sense, the war forced a lot of people to find out what they were made of," says Stuart.

Harry nods. "A few bad things may happen along the way—in wartime that's a given—but you learn to just block them out and press on. And that's also true of all sorts of challenges in life. I mean, if women remembered childbirth, how many do you suppose would ever have a second child?"

"The other thing is to get a job you love," says Earl. "My older son's an airline pilot, and he still can't believe they pay him to do it."

As everyone at the table knows, that was once an ambition Godfrey had for himself until events—notably Vietnam—intervened.

"What about this business of regrets? Looking back over your lives, is there much you would have done differently?"

At this, Stuart has to laugh. "Listen, given the expectations I started out with, how can I have regrets? I used to tell my friends, 'Boy, if I could ever just make twelve thousand dollars a year, I could live like a king.' And I meant it, if I could've made that deal then, I'd have taken it in a second."

"Why not? Christ, you could buy a house for four or five thousand."

"If you go back far enough, it gets ridiculous," notes Cooper. "The first house Jody and I bought in Louisiana just before the war was twenty-seven hundred dollars, plus five hundred dollars for an extra lot. And we passed up a mansion with ten or twelve beautifully land-scaped acres that we could've had for about ten thousand. It would be worth millions today. Speaking of regrets." He chuckles, making it clear he doesn't really give a damn. "But it is a funny thing about the chances you have that you pass up. I had some talent in the direction of architecture, and for a while I was thinking about going into that field. But very early on at the university, I went by the School of Architecture and ran into one of the guys that taught there and this character absolutely turned me off. You know, you hear about these mentors who play an important role in a young person's life—this fellow was a sort of antimentor. I wouldn't call it a regret, but it's funny how things work out."

"I'll tell you one," says Stuart. "I don't know if it falls into the category of a regret, but it was certainly a great mistake. I made a bitter enemy of a judge."

"What'd you do?" asks Moe, delighted.

"I insulted this guy in front of a very large audience at a dinner, most of them lawyers," says Stuart. "It was madness, but I couldn't help myself; I was compelled to do it because this guy was such a jackass. He got up and started spouting off about something he knew nothing about, and about which I had written a book. I'd been drinking some wine, and when he was all done, I said loudly, 'Give me a drag off that thing before you throw it away.' He said, 'What did you say?' And I repeated it louder, and he stalked out of the room. A week later he saw me and demanded a public apology. I told him, 'You're not getting one.' And, boy, did he ever make me pay. Judges are like little old ladies; they hang out together and gossip, so pretty soon they were all ganging up on me. Fortunately, he died before he could do me ultimate damage."

"You were glad to see him die, were you?" asks Moe.

"Oh, very! But it was still an extremely foolish thing to have done."

"Bet it felt good at the time, though."

"Of course. But there's a certain type that tends to reach the top—and they *never* do things like that. They not only know what backs to scratch; they know how to do it deftly. It's a great talent. I don't have it."

"I don't have it either," admits Earl. "Never did."

"We are who we are, right? I mean, little streaks of temper can flare up in me where I say all the wrong things."

"Oh, me too," says Moe, in his case belaboring the obvious.

"Well, I was a military guy," says Godfrey, "and that's also a career where a talent for office politics is essential, at least once you've reached the senior ranks. Only I was terrible at it, absolutely unfit to function in a political environment. If I had something to say, I just came out and said it. That isn't supposed to be the way you operate."

"Earl, I think you'd've been a success in any field you went into," says Huff earnestly.

"I don't know about that. I don't know that I was successful even as a naval officer. I didn't make flight rank."

"You could've," says Moe.

"Maybe. If I'd been a different kind of person. But maybe that's the most foolish kind of regret you can possibly have."

He goes on to describe one episode where he spoke his mind that proved especially damaging to his career—but quickly tells me it is off the record; the only time I've heard those words since I've been around the guys.

"How come?" I ask, surprised. To my mind, the incident casts him in a highly favorable, even a heroic, light.

But it seems that is part of the problem; he regards it as unseemly. "I'm just giving you my point of view on the issue; others might disagree."

"There's no activity in human life, at least those played for high stakes, that doesn't involve making a good many enemies," offers Stuart.

"Absolutely so," agrees Harry.

"No question about it," says Boyd, with feeling, "most people in this world will go along to get along. That's a good part of the folly of the human condition. If we're talking about advice to kids, the place to start is with integrity and honor. Because in the end, nothing you possess is more valuable."

"But not just to make a show of those things," cautions Stuart. "Pick your spots—when it really means something."

Earl nods. "That's right. If it's necessary to be shot down for a principle, okay, go ahead and be shot down. Just be very, very sure you've done it for the right reason."

✦ CHAPTER 24 ✦

Ken was about seventeen when that photo was taken. Man,

he loved that BMW. I was a little concerned about it, but,

you know, you have to trust them; you can't keep them

little children.

—GENE COOPER

FATHER AND SON.

When it comes to Moe and Boyd and the Saturday morning garage sales, time is frozen. Though it's been a couple of months since my last visit to Monterey, sitting in the backseat of Huff's Daewoo, it might as well be ten years ago, or next week.

"Where to now?" demands Huff, a half hour into this morning's rounds.

Moe rechecks the paper. "Tenth and Lincoln in Carmel. 'Plants and tools,' it says."

"Christ, Turner!"

"You know I'm interested in tools. How long's it gonna take me to just take a look?!"

"That's what I'm worried about!"

Moe pauses a moment, then seeing his friend will make no further protest, adds, "We'll go down to Rio Road, the same way you get to Harry's house."

"Goddammit, just tell me when to turn."

There's a brief lull in the conversation, then Huff chuckles. "Did I tell you an old Alpha Delta Phi fraternity brother of mine sent me a photograph he ran across of a girl I used to take out? Highly attractive girl, had the most splendid legs."

"Really? I'd like a look at that."

"I tell you, Turner, she looked just wonderful!" He laughs. "For a woman of eighty-six!"

"Gawd, talk about making you feel old. She had her clothes on, I hope."

"Oh, yes, she kept her dignity." Ahead a light turns yellow, and Huff speeds up to beat it. "Didn't make me feel old, not at all."

Unfortunately, he's miscalculated, and the light turns red as we speed through the intersection.

"Watch where you're going!"

"Jesus Christ, don't know what I was thinking. About her, I guess."

"Was your buddy Don Lindsay in your same fraternity?" asks Moe.

The reference is to one of Huff's closest childhood friends, a Spokane businessman who died last summer.

"No, Don was a Sigma Nu."

"I thought you two were best friends."

"We were; we were bosom buddies—doesn't mean we have to agree on everything!" He pauses. "And now my other old boyhood friend Jack Hardy also died."

"He did? You're kidding."

"Christ, Turner, you're getting as bad as me. I told you about this!"

"I thought you said it, but I couldn't believe it."

"Well, Jesus, I could hardly believe it myself, because he called just a couple of days earlier and we had a long talk. He was as bright and cheery as ever. He was just out of the hospital for some damn procedure, but he was feeling great. Very chipper. Two days later his wife calls me up and he's dead!"

"Well, he didn't suffer, then."

Boyd snaps his fingers. "Just like that."

"That's the way to go. A good life ending in a good death. And he had all his wits about him till the end, didn't he?"

"Oh, yeah."

"That Cooper, I really don't know why he's bothering with all that chemo nonsense. If it was me, I'd just gorge on fattening foods. I'd rather die of a heart attack than cancer any day of the week."

"Do him a favor, Turner, keep that advice to yourself."

"Oh, yeah, even I know that."

Moe has been monitoring his friend's progress on a daily basis. Though Gene still makes it to the Girl Watchers' luncheons, lately he has been in sharp decline.

"Why don't we stop by and see him on our way out in Carmel Valley?" he suggests now.

"Yes. Good idea." Boyd drives for a moment in silence. "Am I heading the right way?"

"Keep going straight. I'll tell you where to turn."

Huff glances at me in the backseat. "Hardy was a physicist, played an important part working on the bomb at Los Alamos."

"Soon all those guys'll be gone," observes Moe. "That whole thing'll just fade into history."

"Afterward, he went to work for the company headed by the present secretary of defense—they're old friends," says Huff. "I grew up with Jack, met him in grade school. He used to ride up to our family home, and my mother would send him right back home. My father would say, 'What are you doing that for?' and she'd tell him, 'He's bad.' 'But he hasn't done anything.' Well, he's going to be bad; I can tell just from looking at him.' "

"The bad guy was her own son," offers Moe.

Huff laughs. "God, Jack was a horny bastard!"

"In grade school?"

"Christ, my whole fourth-grade class was horny—a whole bunch of horny little males. We had this young teacher, she was pretty green, and we had a practice of pretending we had hard-ons. We'd all lift our legs in the aisle at the same moment, and start pushing on them, 'Get down, get down.' " He laughs again at the memory. "This innocent young teacher would run into the principal's office crying. Christ, the principal, Miss Witt, used to paddle me and Jack all the time. When she'd walk into the class, every leg would sink."

"Boy, oh boy, how'd you even know about that sort of stuff?"

"Hell, we'd get all the forbidden books and read up on it. They had sexual manuals at that time—very explicit, too."

"More clinical than erotic."

"Plenty good enough for me. You might say we had premature puberty."

"Turn at this street here!" exclaims Moe suddenly.

Too late, we're already past it. "Why didn't you warn me? Christ, just let me know how you want me to go."

"I told you, Reo Road."

Boyd executes a nifty U-turn. "So now we turn here?"

"There, to the left!"

"Then why do you make the hand motions in the other direction?" Boyd makes the left turn.

A moment later Moe points at the "Sale Today" sign, before a yard ablaze with flowers. "Good, you made it. Park there."

"It's a driveway, goddamn it! I'll park here!"

The sale proves a bust. The tools in the ad turn out to be a random assortment of screwdrivers, hammers, and garden shears, surrounded by random bits of glassware and old stuffed toys. Heading immediately to the book table, Huff finds such titles as *Dance of Anger: A Woman's Guide to Changing the Patterns of Intimate Relationships* and *The Self-Esteem Companion.* "Jesus Christ," he stage-whispers, "we know all we need to about these people! Let's press on, Turner."

But even here Moe thinks there must be something he needs: he's staring fixedly at a half-filled bag of birdseed, with a two-dollar price tag stuck on the side. "Why don't you get this, Boyd? I'll get 'em down to a buck."

"No, thank you," says Boyd, already heading back to the car.

Reluctantly Moe follows. "Don't you want to attract songbirds into your yard?"

"Christ, no! There are enough problems with the cats as it is. We had a ruckus just this morning: Beverly got up and couldn't find our new cat, Bo, the one we got after poor Mack II was banished to a ranch. She's getting all excited, moaning about how he got out and the raccoons must've got him. Turns out he was locked in my closet the whole time. Fell asleep on my shoes."

"Mack II's gone?" I say, as we get back in the car. "When did this happen?"

"Didn't you know? Had to get rid of him after he killed her other cat, Rocky. Goddamn it, the story got around the neighborhood, and they sent a deputation of women over to tell me they didn't want him around killing their cats. Everything but pitchforks." He shakes his head, but he's smiling. "I don't know what the problem was—there were four cats; he only got one. Seems to me he's very tolerant. Anyway, we gave him to the Collie Rescue Service, and they found a female rancher in the valley to take him. She might've had her doubts, but, Christ, Mack went up to her and licked her and shook her hand. He's a great hand shaker, charmed her right off her feet." He laughs heartily. "He's gonna think a lamb is a cat, but, hell, it's her problem now. Where to now, Turner?"

Moe is studying the paper. Though the morning is still young, his customary zeal for the hunt already seems to be waning. "I don't know, Boyd. . . . There's the sale over at the Carmel Valley Community Center. It's probably not much, but we can go right from there to Cooper's."

"Good idea."

"Benny wrote Gene a nice poem for his birthday, you know. Right from the heart. Let him know how much he means to her."

"Like I say, Turner, the only reason she didn't leave you long ago is she's so damn moral."

"That's about the size of it, all right." He pauses. "You remember how to get to Cooper's, I hope. You only lived on that street a dozen years."

"Yes, Turner, I remember."

That settled, Moe flips open the paper and reads for a moment. "Here's a story for you: 'Elderly Woman Swindled.' 'A Monterey County senior citizen,' they call her. Some crook convinced her she won the German lottery. Could've been you, Boyd. It says she gave him thousands of dollars to 'cover the taxes.' "

Huff cracks up. "Christ, almighty!"

" 'Police said there was little chance of recovering the money,' " Moe reads. "Boy, the way they prey on the elderly!"

"Well, all in all, that's a very kindly scam. At least she had a little momentary excitement."

"They've put out another warning to us old folks about these guys who call out of the blue on the phone."

"They're right. Personally, I'm always too kind to these telemarketers because it's such a damn hard job. I'm especially a sucker for the high school girls who phone up with little wispy voices and call me 'Sir.' It's probably a sixty-year-old woman in fishnet stockings with a cigarette dangling from her lip."

"The ones that get me are those little alumni girls from the University of Arkansas who phone up with that Arkansas accent. I always give 'em a little bit of money; I've still got a soft spot for the University of

Arkansas. After all, they made me"—he catches himself and laughs—"whatever it is I am."

There are a few seconds of silence.

"You know, this thing with Hardy's dying has got Beverly even more upset than me. She wants to know 'How the hell am I gonna handle it when you go?' I have four plots down there in the local cemetery—Martha and Andy are down there—but I think I'm just gonna change my final instructions and have myself cremated."

"You should tell her, 'What are you talking about? You'll go before me!' "

"How often would you and Hardy get together?" I ask.

"Oh, several times a year. He had a place in southern California and another in Reno. We'd talk, dine out, drink. Matter of fact, he's the one I was supposed to see on nine-eleven when they hauled us off the plane."

"Which would you say was a better friend, him or Don Lindsay?"

"Oh, Christ, Turner, what a goddamn stupid thing to ask. I don't make choices that way!" He pauses. "I was fortunate to get up to Spokane a couple of weeks before Don died. I remember his wife, Patsy, beautiful girl, coming in and saying, 'Don't tire him out,' and Lindsay said, 'No, no, Ceegar's always good for me.' "

"He used to smoke those foul things with you, did he?"

"Absolutely. Loved every minute of it."

"You know, both Grant and Freud died of throat cancer."

"Well, those must've been some pretty rough cigars. We smoked my father's Daniel Websters; they tasted just wonderful."

"I've kept track of about three or four friends," offers Moe, "but not as long as you have."

"Well, they're great friendships; I make a point of maintaining them."

"You don't work very hard on your friendship with me, I'll tell you that."

"I certainly don't."

We're now in Carmel Valley, and Moe indicates an orchard off to the right. "See here? This is Leon Panetta's place, the guy that was Clinton's chief of staff. He grows pears and walnuts."

"The most honorable man in that whole goddamn administration."

"So," adds Moe, "I guess you only got one of your close friends from out there left . . ."

"Well, Russmore, and O'Reagan—"

"I've known you as long as Russmore."

"That's true. You're one of my oldest friends." Boyd pauses, adds with surprising warmth. "You'll have to bury me, Moe."

"You, too, Boyd. You're one of my oldest . . ."

Moments later, Huff, turns from heavily traveled Carmel Valley Road onto Cooper's quiet street. Easing the Daewoo past their friend's house, he stops two houses down—before the one he used to live in with his first wife and two sons. "Long as I'm here, I always like to have a look."

One story like all the homes around here, the house is a bright yellow and larger than most. A wagon wheel has been set out front, and an American flag flies over the front door.

"That's a pretty house, all right," says Moe. "They're keeping it up very well."

"They seem to be." Huff pauses. "The Coopers were great neighbors. Kenny and Jerry were best friends—they used to dig all kinds of holes back there, make underground caves." He stares a moment longer, then starts into a U-turn. "We had a wonderful life in that house. Each kid had his own bedroom, and I had a separate room to keep all my books."

We park on the street and walk down the Coopers' sloping driveway, past the two white Acura Legends under the carport and to the front door.

"Strange," remarks Huff, after pushing the doorbell, "not hearing those two little dogs yapping."

Both the Coopers' aged Malteses died within the past year.

Jody Cooper appears at the door, surprised but deeply pleased. "Oh, my goodness," she exclaims, "I must look awful; I haven't even washed my face yet."

"Oh, horrors," teases Moe, "that's terrible!"

Jody laughs.

"And how've you been, Jody?" asks Huff.

"Oh, you know, I have a pocketful of pills over there, but I'm all right. I just sort of live with my little health problems." She looks at the two of them warmly. "It's so good of you to come over and see Gene; he needs his friends to come over and talk."

As strong and self-reliant as her husband, within their circle Jody is known to be good at just about everything; a legendary cook, a wizard with needle and thread, a gifted artist and designer. Born two generations earlier, she would have been the very personification of the classic pioneer woman. But now it's impossible not to see the strain on her face.

Moe nods awkwardly. "I thought the poem Benny wrote for Gene was very good, didn't you?"

"It was. I wish he'd read it every time he's not happy about himself. Because it's getting so hard for him." Jody pauses, not bothering to hide her concern. "Does he look much different to you? He's lost all that weight."

"Oh, I think he looks all right," says Huff.

"Gene's a real nice looking guy," offers Moe. "My father was nice looking, but his son's not."

She manages a smile. "You should've see him when he was young."

She leads us into the house, tastefully furnished and immaculate, the walls hung with paintings and photos by friends and family.

"He's right out there," she offers, nodding through the windows of the sunroom toward the backyard, where Cooper can be seen, a tall, stooped figure holding a garden hose, watering his rosebushes, his clothes hanging loosely on his tall frame. The sight is reminiscent of the elderly Marlon Brando in his tomato patch in *The Godfather.*

"How's it going, Gene?" booms Huff in greeting.

"Not bad. Just doing a little watering."

This is not one of the better days. Cooper seems weary, and there is a distant look in his eyes. But his handshake is still firm.

"So how have you been feeling, Gene?" I ask, not having seen him in a while.

"Oh, you know, I take it day to day. Seems like we spend half our time going to doctors."

"Does it do any good? That's what I wonder," interjects Moe.

"Actually, I don't feel too bad, except that I'm weak and haven't got much of an appetite."

"Well, I don't take any chemotherapy, and I feel just like you do," says Moe, laughing. "No appetite and weak."

The view from here this glorious spring day is nothing short of spectacular. Though the Carmel Valley area has been massively developed in the fifty years the Coopers have lived here, beyond their backyard fence only heavily forested hills can be seen. To complete the picture, a hawk swoops directly above, like the one in the lyric from *Oklahoma!,* making lazy circles in the sky.

When I point it out, Cooper nods at a massive eucalyptus tree on the corner of his property. "We've got a pair of them nesting up there. I'm not sure what kind they are, 'cause they're bigger than most of the chicken hawks you see around here."

"Call 'em Cooper hawks," suggests Moe.

Cooper gives an appreciative chuckle. "They do seem to have an affinity for the place. Sometimes Jody'll throw out some meat, and those hawks'll swoop right down into the yard."

Huff indicates a tiny structure high atop the distant hillside. "Is that lookout station up there still manned?"

"No, they've abandoned it."

"I suppose now that they have planes dive-bomb fires with retardant, they don't have the problems putting 'em out they used to. Christ, when we first moved out here, everybody'd turn out to fight the fire. It was a community effort, a damn bucket brigade."

"My son Ken used to hike up to that fire station—must be three and a half miles, almost entirely uphill." Cooper smiles, seeming to literally bloom in his friends' presence. "Those were awfully good times, all right."

"So how's the garden coming along, Gene?" asks Moe.

"I'm not doing quite as much as I used to. I'll give you the grand tour, such as it is."

He leads us past a long row of his rosebushes to a plum tree, then a walnut, then a fig, offering avid commentary on the idiosyncrasies and growth cycles of each.

"Boy," offers Moe, nodding, as we head back to the house. "I see your tomatoes are really going this year, Gene."

Cooper acknowledges this with a nod. "Actually, I'm thinking of putting a few more down. Keeps me a little active, anyway."

As the others head into the house, Gene draws me aside; there's something he wants to clarify. "What I said the other time about Moe's invention . . ."

My look must be totally blank.

"The fuel cell that would make the car so heavy . . ."

"Oh. Right." The conversation was more than two months ago now.

"I didn't mean that the way it might've sounded. Moe's a very clever fellow; he has some awfully good ideas."

I look into his eyes and reassure him I understand it was meant in fun, and with affection.

"I just wouldn't want anyone to have the wrong idea . . ."

When we join the others inside, I ask Cooper about the series of black-and-white photos covering most of a wall in the dining room. They are professional quality and, aware of his prowess with a camera, I assume they are his work.

"Actually, some are mine, some Jody's." He points to a shot of a children's church choir, the white-robed kids at once angelic and mischievous. "She took that one, for instance, and this one here of our daughter Jeannie with the horse and the Australian sheepdog. Jeannie must've been around twenty-three there; she was going around collecting for the Red Cross on horseback. Notice the dog has a Red Cross flyer in its mouth?" He indicates another, a shot of a weather-beaten fishing boat approaching the Monterey docks that has all the grit and texture of a Dorothea Lange Depression-era photo. "That one's mine—from back in the days when the canneries were still open and they were still doing sardine fishing out in the harbor. I'd guess the very early fifties. That one, of the fog rolling in, won a prize about twenty years ago in some exhibit."

"Do you still do photography?"

"I stopped about five years ago." He points again. "That's what the midvalley looked like about forty years ago, if you can believe it. No more than ten minutes from here. Almost nothing there; today it's almost solid housing."

He indicates several more as he leads me around the corner, down a short corridor outside the master bedroom. This wall, too, is crowded with photos. He pauses before one of his son, as a teenager with a motorcycle, a bemused middle-aged Cooper watching and letting him figure it out for himself. "Ken was about seventeen when that photo was taken. Man, he loved that BMW. I was a little concerned about it, but, you know, you have to trust them; you can't keep them little children. But this here is what I really wanted to show you." He nods—this one is not a photo but a black-and-white sketch of a man at a piano keyboard. The details are sharp, and the perspective is unusual, since the figure is seen from above and to the side. "Kenneth was about nine years old when he did that."

"Nine?!"

"Pretty remarkable, don't you think?" he says, as we head back to the dining room. "The stuff he does now is pretty far out; in some ways I have trouble appreciating it. Very abstract. But it sells."

"Was your son down this week?" asks Huff, as he and Moe rejoin us. Ken has lately been making the trip from San Francisco regularly. (The Coopers' daughter Jeannie, the nurse, lives nearby and has been intimately involved in his care and treatment.)

"Just left yesterday, as a matter of fact. Kenneth has the talents of my wife, and of course his wife is also an artist. But Augie comes from me. A pure engineer."

"Amazing child," agrees Moe.

Cooper chuckles; there's nothing he enjoys talking about more. "I still remember him when he was this big"—he indicates with his hand—"just taking things apart and putting them back together, working on locks and all kinds of things. It's just so funny how things work out."

"How tall is Augie now?"

"About six-two, and he's only fifteen."

Overhearing as she approaches with mugs of tea and a platter of cookies, Jody laughs. "He likes basketball."

"I've been telling Gene I want him to meet my fourteen-year-old granddaughter."

Jody places the refreshments on the table. "Well, you know, Gene's always saying he reminds him of himself at that age. Doesn't work as hard as he might, but it doesn't seem to matter. They say he's in the ninety-ninth percentile for reading comprehension."

"And a couple of years ago he was hardly reading anything," notes Gene. "But you know how it is, boys take a while to develop."

"But when they do, my goodness," says Jody, as she retreats from the room, "there's no stopping them; they just rule the world."

It takes me just an instant to realize she is talking about not just her grandson but also the men in this room.

Cooper slowly takes a seat and picks up something from the table, an electronic device roughly the size of an harmonica. "Kenneth brought his guitar this time and look what he left behind. This thing has a little crystal inside, it reproduces notes very precisely, so you can tune up your instrument right on the button."

"An electronic tuner," marvels Moe. "What a neat idea, wish I'd thought of it!"

"If you had, it would've stayed an idea," says Huff.

"That's true, I'd've forgotten all about it ten minutes later. So he serenaded you, did he?"

"He brought down two volumes of stuff that Bach composed for the lute which have been transcribed for guitar—it was just wonderful. And the guitar he had—sorriest-looking thing you ever saw, but, man, the sound coming out of that thing. Few guitars have a really good tone over the whole range, but that thing was amazing. Said he picked it up from a master guitar maker in Spain."

"Remember that famous Spanish composer—what's his name?— that drowned when his ship got torpedoed in World War I?" asks Moe. "What a terrible waste. You guys think that terrorists might try to pull something on the high seas?"

"I'm sure that's a contingency that's being seriously considered," allows Huff. "It's certainly one we'd have dealt with in our day at the Navy School."

"Of course, the problem is that something like that is almost impossible to prevent," says Cooper. "All you'd have to do is pack enough ammonium nitrate on a ship and set it off. Like what happened by accident in Texas City in nineteen forty-six."

"Boy, Gene, they've had some pretty impressive disasters down in your part of the country, haven't they?" says Moe. "How about those hurricanes around where you grew up?"

"Texas-sized." Cooper smiles. "The big storm, the one they wrote about in the book, was in nineteen hundred. After that, a lot of people thought Galveston would disappear, but they got to it and rebuilt the whole town, raised the island, and built this huge sea wall; solid concrete, twelve feet high, twenty feet at the base, with immense granite boulders in front of it, just a tremendous job. Actually, the one in nineteen sixteen was bigger, but the sea wall saved the place."

"Were those hurricanes pretty scary to live through?" I ask.

"Well, of course, as a kid you don't look at it quite the same way. Whenever there was a big one on the way, my mother and I would drive out toward the beach on the Boulevard. I'd root for it to get worse, and she'd be rooting for it to get better."

His friends laugh, eighty years later still completely identifying.

"Your people were from the South from way back, weren't they?" asks Moe.

"Originally, they were from all over the place. Mother had relatives who fought on both sides of the Revolutionary War. But, yes, by the Civil War they were all Confederates. In our home, growing up, we had pictures of those soldiers hanging in the hallway. Didn't mean a thing to me."

"In Arkansas when I was young we still sang 'Dixie' in school and celebrated Robert E. Lee's birthday instead of Lincoln's. There were still women around who were alive during the Civil War, and man, *they* hadn't forgotten. They hated the Yankees a lot worse than any man."

"What's amazing is to think how recent all that was," says Cooper. "When we were young, the Civil War was the equivalent to what World War II is today—there were also still lots of veterans walking around—but to us it may as well have been ancient history."

"Exactly how we're perceived by the younger generation today," notes Huff. "But, Christ, in historical terms, this country is still an ongoing experiment! That's what's so remarkable when you hear people taking it for granted. If they don't care enough, or aren't conscientious enough about defending their liberties, the whole thing could still fall apart."

"Personally, I take a pretty dim view of Robert E. Lee," muses Moe. "He realized full well that slavery was wrong but fought for the South, anyway."

"But you can also argue that in the end he *saved* the union," points out Huff, "because if he'd given the word, a lot of those Confederate soldiers would've taken to the hills and fought a guerrilla war. I'll bet a lot of those goddamn fanatic women you grew up around were sorry they didn't."

"Well, thank goodness most people down there did eventually come to realize there were amends to be made," notes Cooper. "As much as anything, that's what motivated Lyndon Johnson to push through the civil rights bills—all the guilt the South still carried on its shoulders."

"I don't care. I still can't stand Johnson!"

"Listen, Moe, bad as he was in Vietnam, he actually did a lot of good things."

Moe isn't buying this; he has a whole different set of criteria. "He was a very unpleasant person. He treated people terribly."

"Christ, Turner, that's the most infantile piece of political analysis I ever heard!"

"You know what he said about Hubert Humphrey, don't you? 'I won't have any problems with him; I have his pecker in my pocket.' What a disgrace!"

"It was Humphrey's pecker, and *he* didn't appear to worry about it— it apparently fit very nicely."

Hearing the laughter as she returns to the room, Jody smiles. "Don't worry about me, I've heard all the jokes before. Also the stories."

"The folklore," corrects her husband.

"We like to hear the ones about you," says the gentlemanly Huff, "the Texas girl. Gene tells us you carried on quite an intense correspondence before you were married."

"You carted those letters around for a long time, didn't you?" asks Cooper.

"Not all of 'em, just the choice ones." Jody places a hand gently on her husband's shoulder. "I think I'd better destroy them before I go to heaven."

"I had a gal once—very ambitious, she knew exactly what she wanted, and it wasn't me," Moe tells us. "She said she wouldn't marry a guy that didn't make at least five thousand dollars a year, but that she'd save my letters. She liked them."

"We weren't talking about anything special," Cooper tells Jody. "Just doing a little reminiscing."

Boyd rises to his feet. "Actually, it's about time for us to be pushing off. Thanks so much, Jody."

She gives him a hug. "You recently celebrated a birthday, didn't you?"

"Not too long ago. My sweet eighty-seventh."

"That's a good number of years, Boyd, congratulations," offers Gene.

"Well, we'll see you," says Moe, avoiding the possibility of getting caught up in any overt display of sentiment. He starts toward the door, then stops. "You know, I'll tell you what turned me against that guy LBJ in the first place—hearing he had no good friends in college. I say any guy that can't even make friends in college, there *really* has to be something wrong with him."

✦ CHAPTER 25 ✦

*Cooper promised her the moon, then spent his whole
life delivering it.*

—MOE TURNER

GENE AND JODY COOPER, 1940.

"Paul Eugene Cooper, 86, a professor, died Saturday at his home in
Carmel Valley," begins the obituary that runs in the *Monterey Herald* on
February 13, 2003.

All in all, it was a good death, especially given the cruelty of the disease. Gene was at peace, ready to go. The care provided by his nurse-daughter spared him having to be removed to a hospital. He had time to say his good-byes and said them all.

In the days that follow, I find myself reading the *Herald*'s obits more carefully than I ever have, paying special attention to men of a certain age. There are usually at least a couple each day. Different as they may have been in every other respect—in background and social status, in the dreams with which they started out and the degree to which they achieved them, in the success or failure of their personal lives—they have that one, crucial, defining fact in common. There is Marion Lewis Jones, seventy-nine, "a retired correctional officer," who "served in the U.S. Army during World War II"; Kenneth V. Ramoni, "a skilled silversmith for more than 70 years, crafting custom buckles, bits and spurs," who "served with the U.S. Navy during World War II"; Robert J. "Bob" Blaisdell, seventy-six, "a former computer analyst," who "served in the U.S. Army, 124th Cavalry Regiment in Burma"; Robert Arthur Gingrich, eighty-five, "a Baptist minister," who "served in the U.S. Navy during World War II"; Alexander Herrera, seventy-seven, a salesman "called a 'workaholic' by his family," who "served in the U.S. Army from 1944–47"; John R. Weimer, eighty-four, "a retired railroad engineer," who "served in the U.S. Army during World War II with the 54th Signal Battalion"; William C. Miller, seventy-eight, "a retired Pacific Bell Co. employee," who "served in the U.S. Army during World War II and later in the U.S. Navy during the Korean War"; and on and on and on, all in this single, relatively sparsely populated (estimated population, 407,000) California county.

A generation is literally disappearing before our eyes.

Cooper's obit, which features a photo of Gene as a much younger man, is longer than most that appear in the paper and includes several things I had never known. For one, no one has even once within my hearing referred to Cooper as Paul; nor in any of our conversations did Cooper himself ever mention that he was on the board of Monterey

Peninsula College or that he served as president of the Carmel Valley Planning Commission. Then, again, some of the achievements that caused his peers to hold him in such high esteem get hardly a word at all.

It's no one's fault. How do you even begin to sum up so varied and full a life in five hundred words?

How do you describe the influence such a life has had on the lives of others?

"At the family's request," notes the obituary, "no services will be held." But when they get together the following day, Valentine's Day, for their regular weekly luncheon, the Girl Watchers give him a send-off of their own. We are gathered in the restaurant in the Travel Lodge on Freemont, an establishment with burgers and sand dabs on the menu and decor heavy on railroad material, including an elevated electric train that circles the place. As soon as the orders have been placed, Earl Godfrey raises his water glass.

"To Gene Cooper," he announces, "a wonderful guy and a gentleman in the truest sense of the word. We'll truly miss him."

Iced tea glasses, coffee cups, and water glasses clink around the table.

"Gene was full of wisdom," speaks up Moe. "Everyone knows that. But he was also one of the most moral people I ever met."

"Hear, hear," intones Harry.

"I don't know about that obituary, though," Moe adds. "With all Gene did, there's a whole lot more they could've said."

"They do have to leave room for other news, Moe," replies Stuart. "Put in a little something about Iraq."

"Well, anyway, all I'm gonna have them put there is my name, that I taught at the Navy School, and my wife, kids, and grandkids. That's it; the hell with the rest of it."

"Write it down now, Moe," cautions Earl. "You may have to send it in yourself so they'll know you're dead."

The guys laugh; already it has become a regular meeting.

"You going to have them play taps at your funeral?" Harry asks Boyd.

"Absolutely!" booms Huff. "All the ruffles and flourishes. Wouldn't miss it!"

Handler nods, considering. "But I think I'll dispense with an open casket. My grandmother used to go to funerals and wakes to keep busy, and this one time she went to the wake of some fellow she didn't know who'd died sitting up. Rigor mortis set in, so they tied him down with weights in the casket. Well, right in the middle of the wake the ropes broke, and he sat up. That was the last one she ever went to."

"I've never been to a wake," says Moe, "but I got a wake rhyme." He recites:

Here lies O'Malley,
  They buried him today.
He lived the life of Reilly
  While Riley was away.

"Have you heard 'The Senility Prayer'?" offers Harry in response. "The what?"

Harry pulls out the sheet of paper on which it's written—"I know you don't expect me to *memorize* it"—and reads:

Grant me the senility to forget the people I never liked anyway,
The good fortune to run into the ones I do
And the eyesight to tell the difference.

He looks up. "It's neck and neck which goes first, the eyesight or the memory, but I'd have to go with memory."

"The memory," concurs Boyd, "no question."

"As a matter of fact," adds Harry, "my wife gave me a note to make sure I followed through on an assignment she gave me—to pick up a half dozen sympathy cards."

"A half dozen?"

"I buy them in bulk these days. She told me to get something suitable. I think she's worried I might come home with something that says, 'I'm glad you're dead, you rascal; I'm dancing on your grave.' "

"Boy," says Moe, laughing with the rest, "pretty cheerful subject for a guy who's just been told he has cancer."

This last has come as a shock—though it probably shouldn't have. A couple of weeks back, forced by a bad case of shingles to take the extraordinary step of seeing a doctor, Moe was told he has growth in his prostate; and now, just days after his friend's death, tests have confirmed it's malignant. In a man his age, this isn't necessarily calamatous, since the disease progresses so slowly something else will probably kill him before it does. Still, the news is unsettling.

"Well, look at it this way," notes Harry, "at least you saved all that money on doctors' bills."

Moe laughs. "Actually, I'm starting to regret that one. The doctor I'm seeing turns out to be a real nice guy. I told him what they oughta do is give all us cancer people a lethal injection so we can just drift off to sleep."

An image leaps to mind of a doctor earnestly breaking the tough news, face-to-face with a patient unlike any in his experience. "What did he say?"

"He said he didn't think the damn lawyers would allow it."

Stuart leans my way across the table and stage-whispers, "A bit of advice—you better finish this book *fast*."

After lunch, I walk with Moe, Boyd, and Stuart out to the parking lot.

"I've got to go pick up a Valentine's Day gift for my wife," notes Walzer. "I'm thinking of getting her a gift certificate to a spa."

"You're a good man, Stuart," says Huff approvingly.

"I know what's good for me—it's not exactly the same thing. You getting something for your wife?"

"Oh, hell, I don't know what. Ordinarily I'd get some champagne, except he"—he jerks a thumb Moe's way—"went and told Beverly I drink too much. I haven't had a carefree moment since."

"This must be a hard day for Jody," says Moe, ignoring this. "What a great husband he was! Cooper promised her the moon, then spent his whole life delivering it." He pauses. "Is that movie *Chicago* still in town?"

"I think so," says Stuart, unfazed by the non sequitur.

"I was thinking I might take my wife."

Talk about a stunner. Moe almost never goes to movies to start with, and in all the years I've known him, he has never come close to seeing a *musical*.

"Well," he says, catching my look of surprise, "I gotta refurbish my image before I leave, don't I?"

"Christ, Turner, if you ever do get sick, you'll just be hell on Benny. You'll have that poor woman waiting on you hand and foot."

"I know. Makes me feel sorry for her just thinking about it."

Walzer laughs, "On that note . . ." Waving good-bye, he veers off toward his car, as Moe, Boyd, and I head for the Daewoo.

"Hey," calls back Stuart, "any idea where we're meeting next week?"

PHOTO CREDITS

Page xxii (*top*): Courtesy of the Turner family.

Page xxii (*bottom*): Harry Stein.

Page xxiii (*top*): Courtesy of the Handler family.

Page xxiii (*bottom*): Harry Stein.

Page xxiv (*top*): Courtesy of the Huff family.

Page xxiv (*bottom*): Harry Stein.

Page xxv (*top*): Courtesy of the Walzer family.

Page xxv (*bottom*): Harry Stein.

Page xxvi (*top*): Courtesy of the Godfrey family.

Page xxvi (*bottom*): Harry Stein.

Page xxvii (*top*): Courtesy of the Cooper family.

Page xxvii (*bottom*): Harry Stein.

Page 1: Susan Polhmann.

Page 10: Ewing Krainin/Time Life Pictures/Getty Images.

Page 30: U.S. Army.

Page 43: Courtesy of the Huff family.

Page 54: U.S. Marines.

Page 68: Courtesy of the Cooper family.

Page 82: U.S. Navy.

Page 92: Corbis Photos.

Page 106: Courtesy of the Huff family.

Page 119: Courtesy of the Turner family.

Page 130: Courtesy of the Turner family.

Page 145: Courtesy of the Huff family.

Page 145 (*inset*): Courtesy of the Huff family.

Page 159: David Rodgers.

Page 168: U.S. Navy.

Page 187: Courtesy of the Cooper family.

Page 196: Courtesy of the Turner family.

Page 208: Courtesy of George Hahn.

Page 220: Courtesy of the Turner family.

Page 235: Courtesy of the Huff family.

Page 248: Courtesy of the Walzer family.

Page 261: Courtesy of the Cooper family.

Page 267: Courtesy of the Godfrey family.

Page 275: Courtesy of the Walzer family.

Page 289: Jody Cooper

Page 306: Courtesy of the Cooper family.

Page 312: Steven Rothfeld

ACKNOWLEDGMENTS

First, above all, heartfelt thanks to the men I write about, who gave so unstintingly of their time during the more than two years this book was in the works; and to their wives and children, who also put up with me with grace and equanimity.

This was not an easy project to pull off. To the extent it succeeds, much credit (maybe even the lion's share) belongs to the editorial team at HarperCollins: David Hirshey, who is as smart and (not necessarily the same thing) perceptive an editor as any with whom I've ever worked, and whose wit eases the passage over even the roughest patches: Susan Weinberg, who has also believed in and supported this project from the outset; and Emily McDonald, David's assistant, who I expect will herself shortly achieve recognition as one of the top editors in the business.

My own little team is headed, as always, by agent extraordinaire Joy Harris and her terrific staff; and by my wife, Priscilla, who in this instance was as invaluable a source of information as of comfort. I appreciate her more than she'll ever know—since she never believes me when I tell her.